International Political Economy Series

Series Editor

Timothy M. Shaw
Visiting Professor
The University of Massachusetts
Boston, USA

Emeritus Professor
The University of London
UK

Aim of the Series

The global political economy is in flux as a series of cumulative crises impacts its organization and governance. The IPE series has tracked its development in both analysis and structure over the last three decades. It has always had a concentration on the global South. Now the South increasingly challenges the North as the centre of development, also reflected in a growing number of submissions and publications on indebted Eurozone economies in Southern Europe. An indispensable resource for scholars and researchers, the series examines a variety of capitalisms and connections by focusing on emerging economies, companies and sectors, debates and policies. It informs diverse policy communities as the established trans-Atlantic North declines and 'the rest', especially the BRICS, rise.

More information about this series at http://www.springer.com/series/13996

'Bringing together insights from international political economy, cultural studies and economic sociology, this book provides a thoughtful analysis of the potent role of the Disney company in global, national and everyday life.'

– Jacqueline Best, University of Ottawa, Canada

'Alexandre Bohas has given us an empirically rich account of the political economy of Hollywood in general and Disney in particular. A great read for those interested in either cultural political economy or the politics of the film industry.'

– Matthew Paterson, University of Ottawa, Canada.

Alexandre Bohas

The Political Economy of Disney

The Cultural Capitalism of Hollywood

Alexandre Bohas
Université Paris 1 Panthéon-Sorbonne
Paris, France

Partly translated from L'Harmattan publishing house

Internationa Political Economy Series
ISBN 978-1-137-56237-1 ISBN 978-1-137-56238-8 (eBook)
DOI 10.1057/978-1-137-56238-8

Library of Congress Control Number: 2016943521

Printed on acid-free paper

This Palgrave Macmillan imprint is published by Springer Nature
The registered company is Macmillan Publishers Ltd. London

To Claire, Colette and Georges

Acknowledgements

I would like to express very warmly my sense of gratitude to Professor Josepha Laroche, who supported me during my postgraduate years. Her advice and comments were crucial for my training.

I also express my thanks to Professors Philip Cerny, John Groom and Daniel Drache for their encouragement to follow through on this book. And I am also greatly indebted to Professor David Sheehan who agreed to help me edit this book. His insights, advice and interest in my research were truly beneficial to the book.

Contents

List of Abbreviations

ABC — America Broadcasting Company
AOL — America OnLine
CBS — Columbia Broadcasting System
CCTV — China Central Television
CD — Compact Disc
CPE — Cultural Political Economy
DVD — Digital Versatile Disc
EAO — European Audiovisual Observatory
EPCOT — Experimental Prototype Community of Tomorrow
ESPN — Entertainment Sport Programming Network
GATT — General Agreement on Tariffs and Trade
HD DVD — High-Density Digital Versatile Disc
IIPA — International Intellectual Property Alliance
IP — Intellectual Property
IPE — International Political Economy
LAEDC — Los Angeles County Economic Development Corporation
MGM — Metro-Goldwyn-Meyer
MPA — Motion Picture Association
MPAA — Motion Picture Association of America
MPPC — Motion Picture Patent Company
NBC — National Broadcasting Company
OECD — Organization for Economic Cooperation and Development
PG — Parental Guidance
RCA — Radio Corporation of America
RIAA — Recording Industry Association of America
RKO — Radio-Keith-Orpheum
SEC — Securities and Exchange Commission
TV — Television
UNESCO — United Nations Educational, Scientific and Cultural Organization
WTO — World Trade Organization

List of Graphs

CHAPTER 1

Introduction

The Need for a Cultural Political Economy of the Disney Company

A cultural political economy (CPE) of the Walt Disney Company[1] could appear to be redundant or pointless. Previous studies have castigated this transnational firm for its supposedly standardised content and entertainment, while others have already depicted the activities of Hollywood corporations organised in a studio system which has remained incredibly stable despite structural changes. In addition, the Frankfurt School has considered that such cultural industries destroy art.[2] However, there remain many unanswered questions, for which a CPE analysis of the Walt Disney Company is likely to provide answers.

The Disney firm has already been the subject of abundant literature which portrays it successively as conservative, sexist and mercantilist. Research hostile to its activities focuses on its consumeristic dimensions[3] but overlooks many other elements worth studying. Firstly, this kind of theoretical approach neglects its worldwide attraction. Such negative observations could explain a boycott of the company by consumers, which has not happened. In fact, researchers have produced subjective studies rather than employing audience data and feedback. In this respect, Thomas Doherty noted in his article entitled 'The Wonderful World of Disney Studies' that, 'unlike the company's consumer base, scholars have

A. Bohas, *The Political Economy of Disney*, International Political Economy Series, DOI 10.1057/978-1-137-56238-8_1

never much cuddled up to Walt and his friends, never wanted a souvenir photo with that guy in the Goofy outfit'.[4] Therefore they resort to oversimplifying schemes, such as propaganda and alienation, in order to explain this emotional attachment and devotion. Inspired by the methods used in cultural studies, the cultural perspective takes spectators' feelings, emotions and opinions towards Disney characters and narratives seriously by examining rather than dismissing them outright.

Secondly, another line of research is the study of the motion picture sector where interdependent major companies compete with one another in the box office market. Looking at these organisations from a business perspective, researchers have missed a crucial change in the current Hollywood environment which makes Disney an ideal type. Indeed, they regard studios as everlasting behemoths in the mostly stable milieu of the studio system, even if structural changes have occurred. The studios are viewed as central and united. They remain central to audio-visual spheres since they control the crucial steps of financing and distribution and they appear all the more unified when they interact with one another abroad. Nevertheless, ongoing Hollywood trends continue to take place in the way major studios are functioning.[5] Changes have indeed transformed classical studios that were traditionally centred on movie theatres into entertainment companies where films are only one activity among many. Besides, the description of Hollywood as a predominantly stable entity does not explain its continuous success while other national movie sectors have collapsed. In this respect Disney forms an ideal type of current Hollywood, since it has never owned theatres and has never produced only movies. Based on the accumulation of ideational and material capital, Disney takes commercial advantage of the creative imageries and narratives of the studio's output and the emotions that they cause among audiences.[6] The Disney Company has had long-lasting appeal among generations of audiences to which it has sold myriads of movies, products and activities. Thus, the result has been an exceptional concentration of resources which taken altogether comprises the basis for cultural capitalism.

Thirdly, studying the cultural dimensions of the Disney Company can appear nonsensical since the Frankfurt School regards this type of cultural industry as annihilating art. But the denial of an artistic dimension may also lead to one missing a reliance on creativity. Admittedly, this capitalist industry markets its goods on a massive scale, thus reducing their artistic aspect, but this in turn makes artistic renewal all the more necessary for the company to continue its expansion. The Frankfurt School also underlines the similarities existing between cultural industries and the rest of the economy, but these theorists take into account only hard-headed Hollywood business attitudes wherein films are produced only to entertain and to make money. Their analysis is limited to the standardisation of production, audience acquiescence and the corruption of art. In this study, these common beliefs about the motion picture industry will be questioned.

Approaches, Concepts and Methodologies

A CPE perspective implies the use of specific concepts and methodologies which provide a better grasp of cultural facets of the Disney phenomenon. We will refer to sociological concepts and cultural studies but also to world-economy theories which adopt a global focus on the Disney Company. All these approaches fit in an institutional analysis of the Disney phenomenon which considers the company as much as it does the consumers-spectators,[7] including their cultural, economic and social interrelationships and interdependences.

Such a study supposes that one considers the intersubjective dimensions of culture and their reproduction through peoples' behaviour: social practices always include culture even if the latter cannot be reduced to them.[8] Taking inspiration from the works of Jessop and Sum as well as Best and Paterson, we maintain that culture can be regarded, on the one hand, as an agglomeration of routines, living practices and rituals and, on the other hand, as ideational, that is a system of meanings and 'webs of significance'[9] in Geertz's words, and as defining identity/difference relations, rationality and ethics.[10] Bourdieu's sociology of habitus[11] and Giddens' structurationist concept of practical consciousness[12] will be instrumental in accounting for culture which exists as a social fact only through individuals' practices and discourses.

However, looking at the ideational sphere leads to specific methodological concerns. First, one should adopt an internal view on fundamentally social facts which are grounded in specific contexts, experiences and practices. Second, one should focus on people's everyday routines because these spaces turn out to be major ones. They are likely to reveal the most entrenched knowledge and practices of people. Third, Gramsci-inspired concepts, such as bloc, formation and material/semiotic co-evolution, lead to a neglect of the functioning proper to the ideational sphere and the possibility that it can lastingly diverge from material spheres. In fact, the assumption of a co-evolution underlies a submission of either the material or the ideational spheres. To the contrary, I will argue that if material and ideational spheres *co-construct* the world, they *evolve* differently.

Practices, narratives and imageries will be observed from a power perspective and their 'variation, selection and retention'[13] in combined material and ideational worlds will be identified. This book will follow Strange's knowledge structure, defined as 'what is believed (and the moral conclusions and principles derived from those beliefs); what is known and perceived as understood; and the channels by which beliefs, ideas and knowledge are communicated'.[14] Although reductive of the ontological importance of knowledge,[15] it places emphasis on the field of knowledge as an ever-evolving result of power arrangements and a contributor to structural power in an interwoven and interactive interplay with all non-knowledge structures. In addition, Strange's concept leads us to denaturalise culture by considering the means by which it is adopted and altered, to what extent it is shared and how it influences people's behaviour. This process indicates the ability to mould others' interests and preferences which ensure one's domination.[16] In other words, this should be viewed as 'meta-power'[17] or 'intransitive power'[18] which shapes not only people's identities but also the issues themselves in order to obtain the 'chance to be obeyed'.[19]

Since Disney narratives and imageries give firms a sociocultural competitive advantage which enables them to prevail in markets, sectors and social trends, Hollywood contribution to American power is regarded as structural through the formation of 'perceptions, cognitions and preferences in such a way that they [the people] accept their role in the existing order of things'.[20] This dimension refers to a set of practices and fields broader than politics strictly speaking, which tend to exert a structural power in favour of America.[21] Generally the cultural dimension remains neglected in International Political Economy even though numerous research studies in International Relations have dealt with the subject by using constructivism.[22] When it is approached, it is all too often either assimilated from the beginning with a form of imperialism or minimised as regards power. In this respect, Joseph Nye's soft power obscures this underlying stake.[23]

Besides, Braudel's world-economy,[24] which conceptualises a preponderance[25] of markets free of state control, gives theoretical insights for the study of the Disney Company at the global level.[26] This concept introduces a hierarchically organised world ordained around a central cluster, making it possible to think of the Disney force outside nationally-based and state-centred references.[27] Furthermore, all Hollywood films, attractions and merchandising form economies, mentalities and ways of life, underpinning a world civilisation of entertainment, all disseminated by Hollywood companies themselves which, on the one hand, socialise people to their symbolic systems and on the other hand, support particular practices through the type of media that they use. All too often forgotten, if not neglected, they influence considerably what determines socio-economic continuities of a civilisational order which 'dictates attitudes, directs choices and roots prejudice'.[28] In addition, major studios are involved in many social spheres which encompass the 'immense kingdom of the usual and the routine, this great absent from history' according to Braudel.[29] Their capacity is felt as much in the field of collective representations as in the field of material universes. They shape the daily lives of people.[30] This study of culture in global markets will thus examine the extent of Disney civilisation and how it structures consumers-spectators' everyday lives.[31]

In this research, cultural studies, especially reception analyses, will be pivotal in assessing the nature and the extent of power.[32] Individuals live on a daily basis among non-state actors' transnational flows that they construe, adopt and reject. This should be analysed at the micro-political level in the manner of the 'Everyday International Political Economy' to complement the 'Regulatory International Political Economy'.[33] To this end, one must also focus on those individuals involved in a plurality of roles and from now on in direct connection with colossal organisations which operate at the global level. If scholars acknowledge the rising role of non-states actors, the reconfiguration of political, economic and social spheres and the pluralisation of the world, they rarely indulge in research at the individual level. Global phenomena or world organisations are examined on the international scene but rarely with a sociological approach leading to the individual level. Yet, our study of Disney will observe real individuals' knowledge and behaviour—their 'structure of feelings'[34]—rather than assuming them. Indeed, the existence of Disney's power comes from the emotional, artistic and evocative dimensions of Disney productions, which make them central to the ideational sphere. This will provide the opportunity to appreciate the strengths and the weaknesses of multinational corporations such as Disney, and by doing this bring about a deeper understanding of their power.

As I follow March and Olsen's institutionalist perspective,[35] the Disney Company has disseminated a civilisation which is a 'collection of rules and organised practices, embedded in structures of meaning and resources' that are relatively 'invariant' and 'resilient' to individuals and circumstances[36] (Graph 1.1). We shall focus on the practices and the knowledge of agents, Disney employees and consumers-spectators, all of whom exert an influence on the Disney narratives and imageries. Based on interweaving material and ideational structures, these sets of narratives, contents and practices form resources and constraints for all the stakeholders in production, business, consumption and social domains. Disney executives, animation artists and employees initiate contents, practices and values as much as answer perceived demands and desires from the audiences. In turn, consumers-spectators variously adopt or reject these productions. We shall also ask how the Disney civilisation has adapted to rising competition, to changing times and to different foreign societies. How does it maintain and transmit its worldwide popularity? Our study will take into account the specific domain of entertainment to which the Disney Company belongs by asking how it has renewed itself and remained attractive through successive generations around the world. The power of Disney narratives and productions should be assessed globally as a whole phenomenon, which implies rejecting traditional modes of thinking and separation of disciplines coming from academia and common sense. The Disney Company must be analysed with its audiences who may be categorised as consumers, spectators and park visitors. The films themselves must be analysed with their by-products and the goods with their symbols. There is a close interdependence linking the company with

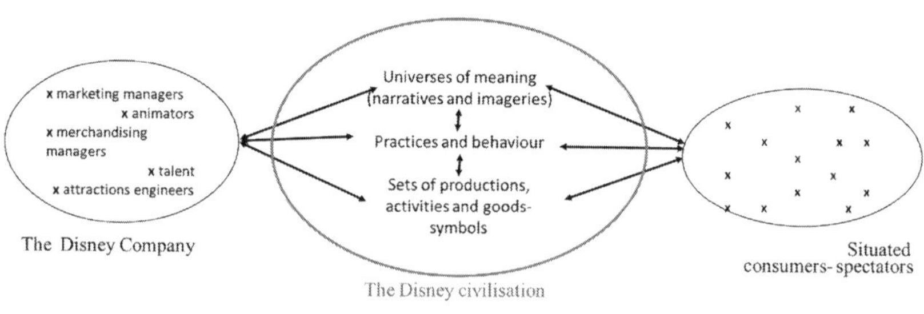

Graph 1.1 The institutional dimension of the Disney phenomenon

its consumers-spectators who enjoy, reproduce and transmit its narratives and goods-symbols. The Disney Company and its audiences interrelate in the market place, which leads the firm to adapt and to change accordingly. In the same way, spectators are shaped by their purchasing and interaction with the company.

Purpose of this Book

In this book, the relevance of the cultural approach in International Political Economy will be shown. It will ponder the specificity of Hollywood and the uneven globalised imagination revealed by the reception of its production content. In brief, this perspective will make it possible to identify the strengths and weaknesses of this industry. Consequently it will give a more accurate view of Hollywood's contribution to American power while supplementing international business theories.

I will address the reasons for Hollywood's worldwide success from a cultural point of view. Whereas many other Western cinema centres have failed to gain recognition and remain active, the Hollywood milieu consists of an unrivalled concentration of creative, financial, productive and distributive capitals. It favours increased rationalisation of the productive process. It achieves authentic cultural capitalism by minimising steadily the artistic dimension of its creations. Through investigations of executives in charge of production at Disney, I will assess the specificity of Hollywood and the reasons behind its privileged relations with the rest of the economy. Constituting a global business, it has undergone many changes since the classical era of the studio. This industry is positioned as the world centre of entertainment generally rather than only motion pictures.

Behind the seemingly unchanging situation of an everlasting studio system, I will also examine the extent to which this unstable sector is marked cyclically by creative destruction. In other words, the capacity to make imageries and narratives attractive remains a random and even mysterious work. In this respect, the Hollywood milieu is fully subject to uncertainty, although its distribution networks constitute durable organisations. Besides, these cultural capitalists rely heavily on creative imageries and narratives whose evocative power conditions the success and the profitability of all their productions. As cultural goods in general convey fantasy, illusion and pleasure, their artistic and emotional aspects prove to be central to the prosperity of an entertainment firm. In this respect Disney has been an ideal type, since from the very beginning its growth was determined by the copyright ownership of its production content without the support of theatrical networks and the funding of a parent company.

Moreover, it will be important to look at these Hollywood studio companies in the context of the uneven pluralisation of the global sphere.[37] Globalising processes deeply and discontinuously reconfigure social, cultural, economic and, as a consequence, political domains while global flows, stakes and actors disrupt the primacy and the exclusiveness of national identities.[38] Indeed, the latter interweave with many other identities and symbols emerging from below, across and above the national level.[39] Although they remain important, they are increasingly intertwined with symbols of various sources diffused by private operators. Thus they are filled with a wide range of values and references.

Besides, states appear less central than in the past when they used to hold a monopoly on the international arena, successively appearing as the intermediaries, the mediators and the representatives of their societies. A plurality of actors is from now on committed to world phenomena wherein the interstate and transnational spheres are linked.[40] All this leads, in the words of Jessop, to a 'reordering of economic, political and socio-cultural differences and complementarities across different scales, places and networks'.[41] This brings about anything but a uniform world. In this set, studios profit from world reorganisation at the same time as they constitute one of their matrices.

This uneven development will be scrutinised in our study by observing the Disney phenomenon through the collective knowledge and the consumer behaviour within one country, France. Furthermore, the power of major Hollywood studios such as Disney derives from a material and ideational preponderance in global markets through the transnational scope of product and symbolic universes. Consequently, markets should be analysed within a web of social, cultural and political dimensions which forms its embeddedness.[42] Consumer behaviour will be considered in interpersonal relations without a unique perspective of utility maximisation or self-expression of people.[43] These processes are also accompanied by a pluralisation of fields.[44] Consequently, we will be examining the global power of firms whose activity affects not only politics and the economy, but also cultural and social fields.

It is crucial to study the power dimension of Hollywood through the prism of Disney and its symbols, to show whether in 'directing'[45] rather than in 'dominating' the world sphere, its companies fully contribute to American supremacy based on their preponderance in economic-symbolic domains.[46] Instead of considering the United States' (US) governmental, diplomatic and military capacities, I would like to highlight the socio-cultural shaping by its companies, non-state actors and society. The latter is delivered at the individual level with a socialisation of people with whom an emotional and cultural proximity is maintained, conferring a fundamental advantage over their competitors. Also, it is essential to show the important role these vectors of soft power can play in America's domination. Cultural supremacy remains strongly interdependent with political, military and economic might.

Eventually, this interdisciplinary perspective on Disney will be designed also to supplement the predominant international business approach for professionals. At the sectoral level, I will examine the specificity of the Hollywood cluster compared to Porter's diamond model. In addition, I will look at how Hollywood's imageries and narratives confer supremacy and value to other companies on global markets, which results in competitive advantage and synergies. The analysis of Disney operations will lead us to ponder the globalisation of Hollywood and its international management—the marketing, advertising and customer experience management of such global companies will appear much more delicate and vulnerable than it does at first sight. The companies actually have to adapt to different audiences and to react quickly to disruptive socio-economic changes. In addition, the institutional approach of the Disney phenomenon will reveal the uneven extent and depth of the relations between companies and their customers, which highlight the limits of even the most effective and controlled customer experience management.

In the second chapter, I will show that the Walt Disney Company draws on the capitalism of entertainment which is common to all the major studios. A specific ethos has favoured the accumulation of capital in Hollywood, allowing the studios to expand globally and making Hollywood the world centre of the entertainment industry.

In the third chapter, I will argue that the Walt Disney Company represents a model for today's Hollywood since the firm has been developing creative productions and activities in extended spheres of entertainment from the very beginning. A multiple-level perspective will show the interweaving of cultural and economic domains at the worldwide, sectoral and individual levels.

In the fourth chapter, I will focus on the civilisational dimension of the Disney phenomenon resulting from the worldwide dissemination of imageries, narratives and productions across a myriad of domains. This results in challenges and constraints for the Disney Company, notably continuous renewal and constant adaptation.

Finally, a close examination of Disney customers' knowledge and consumption will provide the opportunity to assess the extent of Disney's impact in shaping the world. Despite global recognition, familiarity with and depth of knowledge relating to the Disney brand among consumers-spectators are mixed, affected by socio-economic factors. In addition, the reception of Disney narratives and symbols varies according to social and national contexts and individuals' strategies for dealing with the company.

Notes

1. For an overview and a timeline of the Walt Disney Company, see Appendices 1 and 2.
2. On the cultural industries and their destruction of art, see M. Horkheimer and T. W. Adorno (2002) *Dialectic of Enlightenment. Philosophical Fragments* (Stanford: Stanford University Press); for an early, opposing and convincing thesis on movies, see E. Panofsky (1966/1934) 'Style and Medium in the Motion Pictures' in D. Talbot (ed.) *Film: An Anthology* (Berkeley: University of California Press), pp. 15–32.
3. Since Dorfman and Mattelart's seminal book, many works have denounced the purported intrigues of the firm. See A. Dorfman and A. Mattelart (1976) *Donald l'imposteur ou l'impérialisme raconté aux enfants* (Paris, A. Moreau); E. Byrne (1999) *Deconstructing Disney* (London: Pluto Press); E. Bell, L. Hass, L. Sells (1995) (eds.) *From Mouse to Mermaid: The Politics of Films, Gender and Culture* (Bloomington/Indianapolis: Indiana University Press); E. Smoodin (1994) (ed.) *Disney Discourse: Producing the Magic Kingdom* (New York/London: Routledge); M. Budd and M. Kirsch (2005) (eds.) *Rethinking Disney: Private Control, Public Dimensions* (Middletown: Wesleyan University Press). On the mystification of Disney, see S. Harrington (2014) *The Disney Fetish* (New Barnet, UK: John Libbey).
4. T. Doherty (2006) 'The Wonderful World of Disney Studies', *Chronicle of Higher Education*, 19 July, B10–B11. For a work on Disney studies, cf. J. Wasko (2001) *Understanding Disney: the Manufacture of Fantasy* (Cambridge: Blackwell).
5. The major studios representing the largest motion-picture production companies based in Hollywood are: Paramount Pictures Corporation, Sony Pictures Entertainment (which brings together the Columbia Tristar and the Metro Goldwyn Meyer (MGM) studios), 20th Century Fox Film

Corporation, Universal Studios, Warner Bros. Entertainment and the Walt Disney Studios Motion Pictures.

6. For an approach of emotions in International Relations, cf. A. Ross (2006) 'Coming in from the Cold: Constructivism and Emotions', *European Journal of International Relations*, 12 (2), June, 197–222.
7. I will resort to compound words to deal with the Disney phenomenon in its entirety. The Disney success lies in the fact that its customers are both consumers of goods and spectators of art forms. Similarly for goods-symbols, branded products have at the same time symbolical attributes related to the universes of meaning. On the symbolic dimension of consumption, see W. Dolfsma (2007) (ed.) *Consuming Symbolic Goods: Identity and Commitment, Values and Economics* (London: Routledge).
8. B. Jessop (2004) 'Critical Semiotic Analysis and Cultural Political Economy', *Critical Discourse Studies*, 1 (2), 159–74; J. Best and M. Paterson (2010) (eds.) *Cultural Political Economy* (London: Routledge).
9. C. Geertz (1973) *The Interpretation of Cultures: Selected Essays* (New York: Basic Books), p. 5.
10. Best and Paterson, *Cultural Political Economy*, pp. 1–25.
11. Bourdieu's habitus is defined as 'a system of durable and transposable dispositions which integrating all past experiences, works each time as a matrix of perceptions, appreciations and actions and makes possible the achievement of infinitely differentiated tasks'. See P. Bourdieu (1972) *Esquisse d'une théorie de la pratique* (Paris and Genève: Droz), pp. 178–79. My translation.
12. Anthony Giddens describes the central concept of practical consciousness as 'all the things which actors know tacitly about how to "go on" in the contexts of social life without being able to give them direct discursive expression'. See A. Giddens (1984) *The Constitution of Society: Outline of the Theory of Structuration* (Cambridge: Polity Press) pp. xxiii and 41 *ff.*; Alexander Wendt (1987) 'The Agent–Structure Problem in International Relations Theory', *International Organization*, 41 (3), 335–70.
13. Concept coined by D. T. Campbell and used by B. Jessop. See D. T. Campbell (1969) 'Variation and Selective Retention in Socio-cultural Evolution', *General Systems*, (14), 69–86 and B. Jessop and N.-L. Sum (2006) 'Towards a Cultural International Political Economy: Poststructuralism and the Italian School', in M. De Goede (2006) (ed.) *International Political Economy and Poststructural Politics* (Basingstoke: Palgrave Macmillan), p. 158. See also N. L. Sum and B. Jessop (2013) *Towards a Cultural Political Economy. Putting Culture in Its Place in Political Economy* (Cheltenham: E. Elgar).
14. S. Strange (1994) *States and Markets* (London and New York: Continuum), p. 119.
15. P. Langley (2009) 'Power Knowledge Estranged: From Susan Strange to Poststructuralism in British IPE', in M. Blyth (ed.) *Routledge Handbook of*

International Political Economy (IPE). IPE as a Global Conversation (Abingdon and New York: Routledge), pp. 126–39.

16. S. Lukes (2005/1974) *Power: A Radical View* (London: Palgrave).
17. J. P. Singh (2010) (ed.) *International Cultural Policies and Power* (Basingstoke and New York: Palgrave Macmillan).
18. G. Goehler (2000) 'Constitution and Use of Power' in H. Goverde, P. G. Cerny, M. Haugaard and H. Lentner (eds.) *Power in Contemporary Politics. Theories, Practices, Globalizations* (London: Sage), pp. 41–59.
19. M. Weber (1995) *Économie et société* (Paris: Plon/Pocket), p. 95; Strange, *States and Markets*, pp. 24–5.
20. S. Lukes, *Power*, p. 11.
21. Strange, *States and Markets*, pp. 24–5.
22. Among many others, see N. Onuf (1989) *World of Our Making: Rules and Rule in Social Theory and International Relations* (Columbia: University of South Carolina Press); A. Wendt (1999) *Social Theory of International Politics* (Cambridge: Cambridge University Press); R. Abdelal, M. Blyth and C. Parsons (2010) (eds.) *Constructing the International Economy* (Ithaca, NY: Cornell University Press).
23. J. Nye (2004) *Soft Power. The Means to Success in World Politics* (New York: Public Affairs). For a critical reflexion, cf. A. Bohas (2006) 'The Paradox of Anti-Americanism: Reflection one the Shallow Concept of Soft Power', *Global Society*, 20 (4), October, 395–414.
24. F. Braudel (1985) *La Dynamique du capitalisme* (Paris: Arthaud-Flammarion), pp. 85–6; F. Braudel (1993) *Civilisation matérielle, économie et capitalisme XV–XVIIIème siècle, vol. 3. Le temps du monde* (Paris: Armand Colin); I. Wallerstein (1974) *The Modern World-System: Capitalist, Agriculture and the Origins of the European World-Economy in the Sixteenth Century* (New York: Academic Press).
25. On purpose, the term preponderance rather than predominance will be used in order to express deeply-grounded power in social, economic and cultural domains. I am definitely not referring here to the realist idea of a prevalence gained over others. The *Oxford English Dictionary* defines to 'preponder' as 'to attribute greater weight or importance to' and 'to outweigh in importance'. Accordingly, preponderance means 'the fact of exceeding in weight; greater heaviness' and 'the superiority or excess in moral weight, power, influence or importance'. As for the term predominance, it expresses the fact of 'having ascendancy, power, influence, or authority over others'. Consistently, the verb predominate generally signifies 'to have or exert controlling power, to lord it over; to surpass in authority or influence'. For a realist view in International Political Economy, see R. Gilpin (1981) *War and Change in World Politics* (Cambridge: Cambridge University Press).
26. On the world of cinema, cf. C.-A. Michalet (1987) *Le Drôle de drame du cinéma mondial: Une industrie culturelle menacée* (Paris: La Découverte/FEN); Braudel, *La Dynamique*.

27. I. Wallerstein (1999) *The End of the World as We Know It: Social Science for the Twenty-First Century* (Minneapolis: University of Minnesota Press); W. Robinson (2004) *A Theory of Global Capitalism: Production, Class and State in a Transnational World* (Baltimore, MD: Johns Hopkins University Press); R. Cox and T. Sinclair (1996) (eds.) *Approaches to World Order* (Cambridge: Cambridge University Press).
28. F. Braudel (1987) *Grammaire des civilisations* (Paris: Arthaud-Flammarion), p. 47.
29. Braudel, *La Dynamique*, p. 21. My translation.
30. Cf. S. Zukin and P. DiMaggio (1990) *Structures of Capital. The Social Organization of the Economy* (Cambridge: Cambridge University Press).
31. J. Hobson and L. Seabrook (2007) (eds.) *Everyday Politics of the World Economy* (Cambridge: Cambridge University Press). For a sociological and philosophical approach on daily life, see H. Lefebvre (1958) *Critique de la vie quotidienne* (Paris: Arche).
32. I undertook research to examine how products and narratives disseminated by the company entered the daily life of individuals. My intention was to highlight the reception and the appropriation processes of people who were in turn spectators, consumers and visitors. For more information, see Appendix 3. On the cultural studies, see R. Williams (1961) *The Long Revolution* (London: Chatto and Windus); R. Hoggart (1958) *The Uses of Literacy: Aspects of Working-Class Life* (London: Penguin); S. Hall, D. Hobson, A. Lowe and P. Willis (1980) (eds.) *Culture, Media, Language: Working Papers in Cultural Studies, 1972–79* (London: Hutchinson); J. Staiger (2005) *Media Research Studies* (New York: New York University Press); On the reception of Hollywood productions, see M. Stokes and R. Maltby (2005) *Hollywood Abroad: Audiences and Cultural Exchange* (London: BFI Publishing).
33. Hobson and Seabrook, *Everyday Politics of the World Economy.*
34. Williams, *The Long Revolution*, p. 48 *ff.* The 'structure of feeling' is defined as 'the culture of a period: it is the particular living result of all the elements in the general organization'.
35. J. G. March and J. P. Olsen (2005) 'Elaborating the 'New Institutionalism'', Arena: Centre for European studies, University of Oslo, Working paper no. 15, 4. See J. G. March and J. P. Olsen (1989), *Rediscovering Institutions* (New York: Free Press).
36. The structure shown in Graph 1.1 illustrates the way the Disney phenomenon is conceptualised in this book. It also shows how the Disney phenomenon can be distinguished from the Disney civilisation which cuts across material and ideational spheres. The civilisation concept is made up of three interrelated levels: universes of meaning which Disney narratives and imageries encapsulate; specific practices and behaviour inspired and encouraged by Disney; and all the goods-symbols and activities which include Disney.

37. P. G. Cerny (2010) *Rethinking World Politics. A Theory of Transnational Pluralism* (New York: Oxford University Press); D. Drache and M. D. Froese (2006) 'Globalisation, World Trade and the Cultural Commons: Identity, Citizenship and Pluralism', *New Political Economy*, 11 (3), 361–82.
38. J. N. Rosenau (1990) *Turbulence in World Politics: A Theory of Change and Continuity* (Princeton, NJ: Princeton University Press).
39. On the heterogeneity or the complexity of globalisation, see J. Tomlinson (1990) *Globalization and Culture* (Chicago: Chicago University Press); A. Appadurai (1996) *Modernity at Large: Cultural Dimensions of Globalization* (Minneapolis: University of Minnesota Press).
40. Cf. Rosenau (1990) *Turbulence in World Politics.*
41. B. Jessop (2013) 'Dynamics of Regionalism and Globalism: A Critical Political Economy Perspective', *Ritsumeikan Social Science Review*, 5, 3–24.
42. M. Granovetter (1985) 'Economic Action and Social Structure: The Problem of Embeddedness', *The American Journal of Sociology*, 91 (3), 481–510.
43. S. Zukin and P. DiMaggio (1990) *Structures of Capital*; V. Zelizer (2005) 'Culture and Consumption', in N. Smelser and R. Swedberg (eds.) *The Handbook of Economic Sociology* (Princeton, NJ: Princeton University Press), pp. 331–54.
44. P. G. Cerny (2006) 'Plurality, Pluralism, and Power: Elements of Pluralist Analysis in An Age of Globalization', in R. Eisfeld (ed.) *Pluralism: Developments in the Theory and Practice of Democracy* (Opladen & Farmington Hills: Barbara Budrich Publishers), pp. 81–111.
45. A. Gramsci (1996) *Cahiers de prison. 1* (Paris: Gallimard), pp. 40–54. The Italian scholar distinguishes dominating classes from directing ones. To come to power—and thus dominate—directing classes needs the achievement of a sort of cultural and social predominance. Cf. P. Musso and P. Durand (2005) (eds.) Special Issue: 'Gramsci, les médias et la culture', *Quaderni*, (57), (Spring), 51–115. For a Gramsci approach on International Relations, cf. R. W. Cox, 'Gramsci, Hegemony and International Relations: an Essay in Method', in R. W. Cox and T. J. Sinclair (1996) (eds.) *Approaches to World Order* (Cambridge: Cambridge University Press), pp. 124–43; S. Gill (1993) (ed.) *Gramsci, Historical Materialism and International Relations* (Cambridge: Cambridge University Press).
46. Bohas, 'The Paradox of Anti-Americanism'. On the cultural soft power of France, cf. J. DeJean (2006) *The Essence of Style. How the French Invented High Fashion*, Fine Food, *Smart Coffees, Style, Sophistication, and Glamour* (New York: Free Press).

CHAPTER 2

A Capitalism of World Entertainment

The Hollywood Ethos of Entertainment

The Incomplete Rationalisation of Movie Creation

Motion picture studios promote a particular ethos of creation which regards the motion picture as simple entertainment. Strictly controlling any form of creative imagination, they structure every step of production and distribution to take full advantage of films and, consequently, to accumulate cinema capital.

In his famous diamond model, Michael Porter makes the case that the competitive advantage of companies relies on clusters whose key attributes are first production factors, second demand conditions, third related and supporting industries, and fourth firm strategy, structure and rivalry. He adds government and chance as factors which can intervene positively and negatively on the degree of competitiveness of companies.[1] In his analysis, the national presence of intense competition among firms, challenging demand, special resources and strong supporting industries will be decisive in forming a successful cluster of companies which will compete at a world level. As analysed below, these elements are present to various degrees in Hollywood, which enables it to outperform rival production centres. Despite their many alliances and partnerships, US major studios compete fiercely with one another. They vie for supremacy in the world of entertainment where the domestic

A. Bohas, *The Political Economy of Disney*, International Political Economy Series, DOI 10.1057/978-1-137-56238-8_2

market still accounts for a large part of their turnover. Hollywood centralises the best pool of resources in terms of entertainment. But the cultural element appears to be decisive in the prevalence of Hollywood as a motion picture centre. Cultural capitalists have imposed a world economy of entertainment based on a specific ethos, which has led them to form powerful networks of distribution and global diplomacy.

If, during the classical era, major studios rigidly controlled every step of the movie sector, they nowadays focus on financing and distribution, leaving other activities to smaller entities. But Hollywood practices still favour the accumulation of productive capacities. A specific ethos of rationalising the creative process characterises the sector, positioning it in 'elective affinities' with capitalism. From the very beginning of the classical studio system in the 1920s, Hollywood creation has unfolded under a very strict mode of production. Artistic work takes place in a structured framework along the stages of pre-production, direction and post-production as David Bordwell et al. have clearly shown.[2] Practices and values, such as the search for a formula, the division of labour and a collective definition of work, shape the Hollywood production process through different forms of organisation and types of behaviour. They ordain daily work and give orientation to action, structuring the latter in a 'lifestyle', a 'lebensführung' in the words of Max Weber.[3] Today, this specific format remains the norm despite the fragmentation of production and the transformations in the sector.

Some repetitive practices and know-how indicate an organised and structured industry. Regarding plots, narratives consist of a clear causality, particular times and places while genres classify films in a uniform way. The same rationalisation is still at play, giving way to standardised forms, even if the functioning and the practices in the sector have changed. For example, the 'high concept' method rests on the principle of a plot formulated in a few words, referred to as 'the pitch'. These few words must convince the studio to finance the project and then the public to go to theatres to watch the film. In the same way, the rise of popular sequels also illustrates the reliance 'upon the replication and combination of previously successful narratives'.[4] The current reinforcement of the business aspect only strengthens these practices within the sector. Some have gone further, arguing that 'classical filmmaking constitutes not just one stylistic school [...] the classical tradition has become a default framework for international cinematic expression, a point of departure for nearly every filmmaker'.[5]

The entire film-making process is strictly ordained in a way to keep creative talent from having too great an influence on the decision-making process. Current practices keep creative talent in check by imposing a dominant conception of the film as a collective work. Hollywood productions rely on a pool of creativity rather than on the work of any one creative artist. This avoids personal idiosyncrasies. Thus, while the producer often remains at the origin of the project, he employs several teams to develop the script in order 'to eliminate personal characteristics'.[6] Furthermore, studios resent giving to one person a plurality of functions, whatever the function may be: producing, directing, acting or screenwriting. Major studios prefer to remain in control of the whole production process: they buy the scenarios (spec script), the film ideas (pitch) and the film copyrights of books even though most of what they purchase will never be turned into films.[7]

This way of rationalising artistic work is also common among studio moguls. They try to establish formulas that justify their artistic choices. With the same reasoning, as head of Paramount and then CEO of Disney, Michael Eisner 'preferred to develop ideas generated internally rather than high-priced agents and "packagers", a strategy aimed at hitting "singles and doubles", as he put it, rather than home runs'.[8] Through this analogy to baseball, Eisner expressed his preference for producing low-cost moderate successes, rather than risky blockbusters. In other words, he wanted to make movies without expensive actors, whose attraction is based on the originality of the subject. As a consequence, in economic terms, this lowers the break-even point of films, making it easier to reach profitability.

In fact, in the 1980s, Disney launched popular productions with moderate budgets that brought in considerable profits. Studio executives exerted strict control, which could be termed 'micromanagement'. Speaking about his work with Disney at the time, a screenwriter said that executives from the studio 'want to know every single detail; they want to take as much spontaneity out of the process as possible [...] they are obsessed with details that don't matter'.[9] They also indulged in cut-throat negotiations, as the agent for Nick Nolte and Richard Dreyfuss has affirmed. Having dealt with Disney for the film *Down and Out in Beverly Hills* (1986), he severely criticised the company by saying 'there is no way to overestimate their stinginess'.[10] This slightly changed, however, with Joe Roth and Nina Jacobson as heads of production who wanted to attract innovative artists by 'interfering as little as possible in the creative process'.[11] Even though Eisner has said the contrary, Disney went back and forth between favouring low-cost movies and producing blockbusters with stars, big production budgets and high distribution costs.[12]

In addition, lawyers, agents and studio executives introduce legal and economic constraints which continuously run parallel to creative relations within the industry. The twofold relation is of crucial importance in striking a deal. As a former lawyer said, 'decisions proceed from both levels at the same time'.[13] On the one hand, a team of advisers provides support to creative talent, each member of whom has his or her specialist field such as law and deal-making.[14] On the other hand, studios remain involved in cinema projects at every step of the process. Not only do they decide whether to finance the film through the process of 'green-lighting' but they also supervise production. For these reasons, they thoroughly analyse previous films with similar budgets. As an executive from Buena Vista has asserted, 'each division estimates future income, based on statistics, script and external studies'.[15] As a result of such studies, the studio can modify any element of the cast, the direction and the post-production. Hence they maintain rights on the final cut as well as on the sneak previews that the studio conducts before releasing the film. After establishing how he controlled creative work in his previous job at Disney, Adam Leipzig declared that he 'does not consider [himself] the filmmaker. The role of a vice president for production—functions which I occupied in the Disney firm—consists in offering a favourable environment so that they [artists] can succeed in their work [...] because ultimately it is their film'.[16] Moreover, creative artists have generally very little control over their work since the major studios become owners of the copyright.

In the production process, the producer is the project supervisor, the 'creative entrepreneur',[17] starting from the birth of the idea right up to the final release of the film. She initiates the project, makes the case for the film towards financiers and studios and establishes the relations between creative talents and studios. Then she controls the screenwriting team, selects the cast, supervises the direction and checks the cut. Lastly, she is involved in the commercial launching and distribution.[18] Thus, she is plainly regarded as much an artist as are the director and the actors.[19]

The collective definition of artistic work is in radical opposition to European cinema which highlights the individual personalities in the production process. In this configuration favourable to the author, the director overshadows, if not dominates, the producer.[20] The producer's function is to provide him with the necessary support to achieve his work.

The director is the author of the film. Consequently, this model opposes the limitations of the Hollywood system, which explains the difficulties French directors have in adapting to the US sector. In fact, the Hollywood system removes prerogatives from directors and largely limits their autonomy. This author film approach can be found elsewhere in the world. In Asia, similar concerns in respect of art films have arisen. Protests in Hong Kong have taken place against cuts and modifications arbitrarily operated by major studios on the film *Shaolin Soccer* (2001). On the very subject, 9,000 people even signed a petition on the Internet in 2002.[21] In another case, the famous Japanese animator, Hayao Miyazaki, was adamant about keeping final cut rights in a deal with Disney. He also refused to authorise any demands for cuts or to grant merchandising rights.[22]

Differing from the mindsets of other film-making centres, the ethos of Hollywood can be traced back to the conditions of its foundation. The geo-cultural factor, the atypical population and the concentration of entities gave birth on the west coast to this original ethos. Indeed, this world centre of cinema developed quite far away from traditional artistic centres. At the beginning of the twentieth century, workers set up studios in California away from any of the urban centres of the period. They wanted to escape from the control of the Motion Picture Patent Company (MPPC) trust. At the time, the MPPC, headed by Thomas Edison, imposed a monopoly on all aspects of film-making and consequently control over anyone who wanted to make films.[23] Then, as the milieu remained autonomous and self-regulated, it became subjected to major competition and concentration, which turned the sector into a studio system.[24] In the early twenty-first century, working values and practices still remain infused with the vertical structuring of the classical era.

Hollywood then attracted many migrants seeking to make money in show business.[25] Away from large cities, intellectuals and art centres, Hollywood avoided any artistic ideology. To the contrary, the economic aspect was systematically predominant in Los Angeles, hence the formula, 'It is all about the money'.[26] Even today, major differences exist between New York and Los Angeles which lie in 'the state of mind'[27] and 'the different attitudes'.[28] The milieu in New York appears as 'more artistically and less commercially-oriented' than the one in Los Angeles. New York producers 'see themselves more as artists than as businessmen'. James Stewart adds that 'a lot of artists and directors live in New York because they do not want to live in Los Angeles and because they think Los Angeles is crass and does not appeal as much to the intellect'.[29] On this subject, Adam Leipzig evokes a 'different vibe [vibration]', a different mindset. In New York, there is a higher 'level of excitement and energy that is unique' while in Los Angeles 'we are less intellectual, but we work harder and longer'.[30] If the Hollywood milieu works with seriousness and rigour, its managers express a disproportionate belief in the creative process. According to them, the rational division and the depersonalisation of creation would solve issues inherent in the creative arts. As a good observer of the Hollywood milieu, Jean-François Lepetit has referred to 'a mix of professionalism and naivety'.[31]

It is worth pointing out that the successful accumulation of cinema capital takes place materially and ideationally. The vast organisations of the major studios, their production and distribution capacities and their products and activities, all resulting in massive revenues, only show one side of this accumulation. Indeed, there is a corresponding but distorted cumulation of imageries and narratives in collective representations. This results from their successful dissemination by companies and their adoption by consumers-spectators. The *Star Wars* franchise, for example, is one of the most achieved contemporary cases of capital accumulation in entertainment. Since 1977, six movie episodes have been released and have spawned a vast set of by-products from clothes to toys. The *Star Wars* universe has appeared in Disney theme parks. Overall, sales revenues of consumer products have amounted to $32 billion. Released in December 2015, the seventh episode, *The Force Awakens*, has already been a big hit grossing $1.5 billion worldwide in 20 days. Turnover coming from merchandising is forecast to reach $5 billion in 2016.[32] The acquisition of this franchise in 2012 by Disney was in retrospect a very clever and logical move.

However, the rationalisation of creation leading to accumulation is incomplete. This process remains questioned by widespread friction arising between the studios and creative artists. Actually this tension already existed in the very early days of Disney between Walt and his companion, Ub Iwerks. In his daily work, Ub had a hard time following Walt's instructions and limiting himself to only one type of drawing. Moreover, he had difficulty accepting the arbitrariness and the control exercised by Walt on the composition and the layout of his drawings.[33] In addition, the prestige, recognition and fame of talent such as Steven Spielberg and George Lucas only weakened the preponderance of the major studio. In fact, famous stars have always tried to keep control over their films.[34] This is why they set up their own production companies to achieve autonomy and to raise money from entities other than the major studios.[35] In fact, despite studio control, budgets have increased partly due to actors' demands for higher wages as well as to substantial profit-sharing in total box-office sales. Average production and marketing costs reached respectively $70 million and $36 million in 2007 while in 1985 they amounted only to $17 million and $5 million.[36] Since 2007, production and distribution costs have not decreased at all. In the field of park attractions, another interviewee also complained about the lack of limits imposed on creative talent: 'we let them go too far in Disneyland Paris. This resulted in excessive production costs'.[37]

In addition, a difficulty arises from artistic creation which relates to the entire entertainment business: the conditions necessary to make a film attractive are random and, above all, continuously changing. Irreducible to a simple formula, they elude any clear rationale. Analysing the failure of the Disney movie, *Atlantis* (2001), the producer Igor Khait observed in retrospect that

> the Disney studio lost its ability to create compelling stories that would resonate with the audience [...] all of a sudden, what you found interesting the audience didn't. They liked what John Lasseter was doing [at Pixar]. They found it fun and exciting [...] Disney kept a more traditional form of story. Disney people tried to be edgy and they seemed kind of dull, old-fashioned and not very fun compared to studios like DreamWorks.[38]

In 1984 as in 2005, top executives at Disney failed to maintain the studio at the forefront of film creation and innovation, while remaining reluctant to leave their positions despite failures. In the 1980s, the company returned to success thanks mainly to the arrival of a new management team headed by Michael Eisner, Frank Wells and Jeffrey Katzenberg. The new leaders renewed production and changed the scope of the studio, turning it into a real global corporation.[39]

The structured but simplified and reductive approach to motion pictures places the Hollywood industry in 'elective affinities'[40] with capitalist thinking because it denies the artistic aspect of films. Like capitalism, this way of considering movies encourages a certain accumulation of capital. Indeed, there is an osmosis between these two processes, which 'are adapted and assimilated reciprocally until finally the development of a close and unshakeable unity takes place'.[41] Eventually, they form a 'cultural symbiosis' and mutually reinforce one another.[42] In other words, a more or less narrow congruence exists between the phenomena of a different nature, not a simple causal link. The ethos of Hollywood induces behavioural patterns similar to those required in the economic structure, which implies an anti-artistic attitude. In his time, Walt Disney declared that he simply wished 'to entertain people [...] in bringing pleasure, particularly laughter, to others, rather than being concerned with "expressing" myself or with obscure creative impressions'.[43] Obviously, this profile fits an anti-intellectual approach. For instance, when the short film *Three Little Pigs* (1933) was released and provoked controversy on its values, Walt Disney explained:

> I don't know [...] I'd like to find out myself just why people liked this film [...] It was just another story to us [...] and we were in there gagging it just like any other picture. After we heard all the shouting, we sat back and tried to analyse what made it so good.[44]

There is no doubt that Walt Disney—better than anyone else—wanted to embody the traditional ideals of 'middle America'.

The movie industry denies, if not hides, the artistic dimension of its films. Systematically, words are substituted and used to understate the artistic aspect of motion pictures; for example, 'artistic' is designated as 'creative', 'artists' as 'storytellers' and 'art' as 'entertainment'. A common saying in Hollywood has it that 'Europeans make show art, whereas we make show business.' Leading figures such as Steven Spielberg or Jeffrey Katzenberg have always claimed that they are storytellers and all film projects start with a good story. Moreover, the financial aspect of production is always underlined through 'bottom line mentality' formulas such as 'you are worth what your last films have earned'. Only 'bankable'[45] producers are on the short list for future films while the box office, not the number of cinema admissions, measures the success of a film's release. The Frankfurt School did not call into question this denial of making art. According to them, 'films and radio no longer need to present themselves as art. The truth that they are nothing but business is used as an ideology to legitimise the trash they intentionally produce'.[46] Academics have taken this denial for granted too readily.[47]

However, as we shall see below, the objectives of Hollywood's creative artists go beyond the notion of greed. Walt Disney underwent many humiliations before achieving success. He also put at risk, several times, his personal fortune to carry out innovative projects such as his first cartoon film,

Snow White (1937). Likewise for the theme park Disneyland in Anaheim. Moreover, his focus on innovation, his perfectionism and his quest for the recognition of cartoons as a real genre form goals having little to do with mercantilism.

In Hollywood, the spirit behind artistic creation is replaced by the work ethic. In the image of Disney, an ideology of great professionalism characterises the Hollywood industry. All the people I interviewed have pointed this out. Igor Khait, for example, states that Americans differ from the French or the Canadians by this moral principle 'which often turns into an obsession here in Hollywood'.[48] A former manager in animation declared that

> I have never worked for Disney, but there have always been stories. A common theme is that the Company presumes its employees work all the time. Some time ago, there was a funny story about Katzenberg who supposedly sent around a memo and instead of 'if you don't come in on Saturday, don't bother coming in on Monday', it said, 'if you don't come in on Saturday, don't bother coming in on Sunday'.[49]

Referring to their jobs at Disney, all the interviewees mentioned 'the intelligence of the team, the level of its excellence [...] its members were very effective in problem-solving and very focussed'.[50]

The anti-artistic posture of Hollywood encourages a true accumulation of cinematographic capital since it allows control over production and a strict division of creative work. It reinforces the establishment of hierarchical and durable structures, so much so that some spoke about 'the engineering of enchantment'.[51] In this respect, the Disney Company appears as a model. The production of animation demands discipline and rigour from the workforce. Even as a precarious independent in the 1920s, the Disney studio formed a considerable bureaucracy. While it did not exceed several dozen employees in the beginning, it reached 200 a decade later and 1,200 people in 1940, 60 of whom were dedicated only to special effects. In other words, as Watts explains, 'the achievements of Disney, we must remember, were not the achievements of one man alone, no matter how brilliant or forceful, but of a complex organisation enlisting dozens, eventually thousands of extremely talented people'.[52] A strict separation of functions and a systematic hierarchy were necessary to coordinate effectively such a great number of employees. For example, in cartoons, animators were divided between those dealing with heroes and actions and those colouring the background animated picture. Then, these two divisions were organised with the masters, the assistants, the simple drawers dealing with minor celluloses and finally clean-up artists. Behind the ideal image of the 'easy-going Disneyan democracy',[53] the firm, in its quest for quality and discipline, went through an ongoing process of bureaucratisation.

Its founder, Walt Disney, is often described as a brilliant artist whereas he actually quit drawing in 1924. Instead, he devoted his time to management, operations and promotion, appearing truly brilliant as 'a conductor'.[54] He would choose stories, work with screenwriters, select team members, stimulate them and supervise their creation. Consequently, like Zanuck, Thalberg and Zukor, Walt Disney came to fame by managing innovative cartoonists. In this respect, he thus followed the line of the most emblematic figures in Hollywood. David Bordwell et al. have expressed this with a certain contempt by writing that 'Walt Disney built his career upon transposing the narrative and stylistic principles of classical cinema into animated film'.[55] During his stint at the head of Disney, Michael Eisner maintained strict order. His studio was described as 'a very professional organisation, very structured and very corporate'.[56] Another manager adds that during the Eisner years, the studio was described as 'highly disciplined and very controlling. They were one of the first studios to put in key card access to individual floors. It was said that it was not to control access but to track where their employees were and how long they stayed on any floor'.[57]

Production executives, creative executives or development girls in studios play a key role. They embody the artistic constraints that the studio imposes in return for its investment. Their rationalising of the filmmaking process accompanies and even facilitates capital accumulation. They select and supervise the projects of producers that Vice Presidents and Presidents of the studio have decided to finance. As Adam Leipzig explains, 'we were very involved with every stage of the productive process which we direct thoroughly'.[58] These studio executives are concerned with the success of a production from a box office perspective. Moreover, they form the centre around which converge marketing and distribution branches. So they put limits on the activities of artists.

The same phenomenon occurs in the domains of animation where, according to Igor Khait,

> 'management does offer a lot of support to the staff. You take care of your artists and ensure that they are as productive and creative as possible. But there is also a flip side. Everybody is watched all the time. Everything they do is tightly scheduled: how many drawings they make and how much time they spend on each drawing are carefully planned'.[59]

Although smaller companies do not have such a large structure, they nonetheless carefully supervise their employees. Thus, the spirit of keeping tight control over employees, time and activities has allowed companies to set up and maintain such elaborate controlling infrastructures, all of which has led to the fast emergence of mini-major studios. This ethos is commonplace in most Hollywood studios.

In contrast, in Europe and particularly in France, film industry employees have fought hard for the artistic recognition of cinema, as did many writers of the nineteenth century for appreciation of their work.[60] They have tried to make the movie sector stand out from the business sector, a sector wherein 'a disinterested play in sensitiveness' and 'the pure exercise of the faculty to feel' prevail.[61] This claim flourished with the directors of the *Nouvelle Vague* (French New Wave) in the late 1950s.[62] They criticised the 'craftsman' conception defended by the previous generation. In addition, following the examples of Baudelaire or Valéry, artists proclaimed that their work had nothing to do with hard labour and technical expertise. They considered creation spontaneous and detached from any kind of know-how.[63] Consequently, such a position stands in direct opposition to the dominant ideology prevalent in the Hollywood sector, which has never sought such autonomy from business, claiming to belong to entertainment.

The artistic perspective on cinema has prevented large-scale organisations from being set up in Europe. Indeed, Steve Hulett stressed that as regards animation, 'In Europe, there are a lot of little studios with three to four people. And if one studio goes bankrupt; you simply move on to another little studio. There are no large facilities [...] no large studios which are international in scope'.[64] It is important to recognise the lack of hierarchical structuring in Europe. Moreover, by limiting the concentration of in-house production, public regulations favour sectoral fragmentation. Consequently, it seems appropriate to differentiate between European craftsmanship and an American industrial ethos, as French director Jean Renoir did when he stated, 'my difficulties in Hollywood come from the fact that the work I try to produce has nothing to do with the film industry. I have never been able to see cinema from an industry standpoint'.[65] In addition, ideological cleavage between independent entities and the larger groups further weakens the French sector, which prevents 'dialectical exchanges, cross-transfers and cross-fertilisation between the two worlds'.[66] As a result, economic reasons and divergent conceptions account for significant differences between European and Hollywood cinemas. Arguably the existence of these two radically different perspectives explains the audio-visual trade conflict which occurred between France and the United States during the Uruguay Round and the World Trade Organization (WTO) negotiations in the 1990s.[67]

The Hollywood Constitution of an Organic Solidarity

The Hollywood cluster is traditionally regarded as the studio system of the classical era. Yet, an unstable and fractured configuration replaced the rigidly hierarchical model of the 1930s which represents quite a unique moment in the history of American cinema. We are going to examine successively the classical studio system and the mid-twentieth-century structural changes in the light of the rise of the Disney Company. The industry was indeed radically transformed, passing from a sector structured by vertically-integrated studios to one united by the interdependence and specialisation of tasks, or a collective 'organic solidarity'.[68] The latter notion takes on the kind of relations that exist inside a cluster for a sustainable competitive advantage to emerge, as Porter has stressed. Indeed, if a lack of competition can cause the decline of such a cluster, intense competition can prove to be just as destructive. Beyond rivalry, this organic solidarity allows emulation, imitation and the sharing of talent in a competitive context.

The studio system of the classical era formed an oligopoly which accounted for 90 % of US box office receipts by producing three quarters of the full-length films. This dominant sector consisted of rival companies which maintained interdependent economic-cultural relations with their own label, imageries, stars, technique and style. The rigidity of the creative process was reflected in the relationship between these symbols and their organisations. Indeed, the industry was built around vast companies which owned all the assets of production, distribution and movie theatres within a vertical monopoly. Moreover, employees, including actors, were almost permanently tied to companies through the establishment of long-term contracts. The number of productions was decided in New York by the heads of studio, who determined motion picture activity. The industry also agreed to a form of self-regulation in the form of the Hays Code which prohibited films from contravening moral values.[69]

As for dissemination, there was a similar hierarchy of entities at national and international levels. The distribution networks of major studios successfully imposed their desired working strategies through the use of block-booking and blind-selling practices by which major studios forced independent theatrical networks to buy movies without being able to watch them beforehand.[70] Concerning cinemas, a system of differentiated prices and progressive releases structured the activity of cinema theatres and, consequently, reduced competition just as much within the sector. These mechanisms ensured low costs and minimum income for each release. As early as the 1920s, Americans established offices in all key European cities. Companies specialised more or less explicitly in precise genres, 'each studio having a globally recognisable style, a family likeness'.[71] The employment of the same film stars and technical crews within the studios directly explained the phenomenon. In addition, this specialisation resulted from a strategy of development based on consumer loyalty with clearly identified logos and familiar heroes which were associated with particular films. The studios endeavoured to build a 'brand image'.[72] For example, MGM represented the studios of famous actors—such as Joan Crawford, John Barrymore, Greta Garbo and Jean Harlow—allowing for the possibility of romantic scenes played by professional performers. This rigid structuring suited societies where cinemas were a social institution, offering the only audio-visual media.[73]

Outside the major studios system, small entities survived precariously. In this respect, many independent artists such as Disney underwent many setbacks and company failures so often faced by small businesses. In the wake of his layoff from Pesmen-Rubin Commercial Art Studio, Walt Disney launched successively several studios which quickly went bankrupt in 1920, Iwerks-Disney Commercial Artists and Laugh-O-Gram Films.[74] Ruined, he then decided to migrate to California in the summer of 1923. In Los Angeles, Walt Disney signed a distribution contract in the same year with Margaret Winkler and Charles Mintz for *Alice Comedies*, then in 1927 with Universal for *Oswald the Lucky Rabbit*. However, he found out in 1928 that he did not hold the copyright for any of the 26 episodes of *Oswald*. Then, the majority of his employees left him to join Mintz. The same year, he concluded an agreement with Patrick Powers. In spite of the success of *Steamboat Willie* in 1928 and *Silly Symphonies* in 1929, a conflict arose over the latter on profit-sharing of box-office sales.[75] In addition, his close companion, Ub Iwerks, joined this distributor. However, with the growing notoriety of his short films, Disney succeeded in staying afloat thanks to successive agreements signed in 1930 with Columbia Pictures and then, two years later, with United Artists and Bank of America, even if he still refused to sell the copyright of any of his work. Producing the first animated full-length film in 1937, he found the necessary financing from RKO which saved him from bankruptcy.[76] Despite the triumph of *Snow White and the Seven Dwarfs*, Odlum, head of RKO, exerted financial pressure on Walt Disney, forcing him to decrease the wages of his staff. According to Douglas Gomery, this decision contributed to triggering the great strike of 1941.[77] In fact, the studio only became continuously profitable when Buena Vista, a distribution division, was set up in 1953, enabling the company to benefit fully from the success of its releases. While the profits of the Disney Company amounted to $500,000 in 1952, they exceeded $3.4 million in 1959 and $11 million in 1965.[78]

The Disney Company did not form a major studio in the classical sense of the term. It never became an entity integrated vertically from preproduction to the movie theatres. It remained independent only thanks to the copyright ownership of its popular cartoons and by-products. In adopting this form of business structure, Walt Disney heralded the emergence of the current period in which the film industry's major companies earn income from both multimedia distribution and sales of a huge range of ancillary products.

After the Second World War, a few key events threatened the rigid organisation of the motion picture sector, provoking radical changes inside the Hollywood milieu. They led to an organic solidarity binding producers, artists and distributors-financiers. While distributors form lasting organisations, production entities change periodically. During the post-war period, considerable changes affected the industry, so much so that the classical studio system would finally collapse: actors, producers and directors then launched their own production companies, putting an end to the seven-year-long contract system previously in place. The power of unions would limit profit, which had already decreased due to the Great Depression and the Second World War. Externally, in 1938, the Roosevelt administration launched antitrust action which led to the break-up of links between movie theatre networks and the rest of the industry. The arrival of television also upset the socio-economic behaviour of audiences, reducing box-office sales. The importance of movie theatres declined from the 1940s onwards eventually becoming a loss-making activity in the early twenty-first century. Thus, cinematic industry experienced profound turmoil.[79]

Studios gradually withdrew from production, preferring to concentrate on multidimensional distribution and finance. By this withdrawal, they were attempting not only to control costs, but also to adopt an organisational structure that allowed for more flexibility in research and development through the recruitment of new talent and taking on new projects. Major studios competed strongly against one another, in particular to obtain talent or the rights to scripts, to the extent that their individual identities, their specific cultures, their actors and their divergent manner of producing films grew blurred. Providing financing as well as distribution and marketing infrastructure, they remained central to the industry. For example, although Bill Mechanic, head of Pandemonium, benefited from external financing, he underlined his dependency on major studios in these terms:

> All I can do is get the script ready and bring together the director and maybe the principal cast. I can't do anything else until somebody comes up with the funding for the picture. In my case I buy the rights, hire the writers, hire the director and at that stage the studio brings marketing, distribution and financing [...] This way, it gives me much more control.[80]

The productive fragmentation of the Hollywood milieu implies a less rigid and less stable field. Major studios sign deals with many small production entities, called 'shingles'. The latter are constantly questioned according to the results of film releases. Deal-making often gives rise to multiple negotiations and even fierce bidding between studio competitors. From 1996 to 2006, the Walt Disney Company signed 90 deals with production companies on motion picture and television activities.[81] Overall, 45 % of these shingles originated from producers, 18 % from directors and 16 % from actors. They were mainly first-look deals lasting on average three years.

In the 1980s, the Disney firm quickly integrated with the Hollywood milieu. Consequently, it underwent the same problems faced by other studios. Coming from Paramount, the new team led by Michael Eisner implemented an ambitious development policy in order to make Disney one of the largest studios. He undertook to produce 20 full-length films a year through Touchstone Pictures and then Hollywood Pictures. The central objective was to build up 'a large live-action non-Disney library to make Disney a more competitive major studio'.[82] Walt Disney himself launched the production of live-action films, such as *Treasure Island* (1950).[83] However, this never amounted to more than a minor share of his activity. Under the recently-created label, Touchstone Pictures, Michael Eisner recruited Jeffrey Katzenberg along with one hundred people from Paramount. This production entity acquired autonomy with regard to Walt Disney Pictures.

This strategy was widely successful since this additional production team provided content for the development of Disney in home video, international distribution and entertainment domains. Disney became a full-fledged major studio. It produced small-budget popular films, such as *Cocktail* (1988), *Honey, I Shrunk the Kids* (1989) and *Dead Poets Society* (1989); 27 out of the first 33 films were profitable, which is quite exceptional in Hollywood.[84] In 1990, *Pretty Woman*, produced with a budget of $14 million, exceeded $463 million in box-office sales. These impressive results generated an increase in releases so that, in the 1990s, studios were launching more than 40 full-length films per year. In addition, Disney launched the Hollywood Pictures label on 1 February 1989 in order to widen the range of its film production. The creativity of the studios started losing steam, however. In 1993, only one of the 40 live-action films appeared successful: *The Nightmare Before Christmas*. Furthermore, the Hollywood Pictures unit never found a profitable creative segment.[85] After the arrival of Robert Iger as CEO of Disney, the company refocused on the Walt Disney label, decreasing the activities of Touchstone Pictures.

Today, the canonical dichotomy between studios and independent producers deserves to be called into question since it is based on an obsolete difference from an economic, aesthetic and sectoral standpoint. Unsurprisingly Allen Scott defines Hollywood as 'a dense constellation of many interdependent firms and workers, functioning together in a project-oriented work environment along with a variety of institutional arrangements providing different sorts of coordinating services'.[86] This kind of agglomeration favours economies of scale and competitive advantage. Analysis of the sector takes into account its relative fluidity as well as its structure. But maintaining the category of independent producer underestimates the permanent complex interconnections among the various sectors of the film industry.

After the death of its founder, the Disney Company remained distinct from this milieu by its singular culture and a declining film slate. As Producer Robert Cort recalls, 'Prior to Eisner, Wells and Katzenberg coming to Disney in 1984, the studio made very few movies and it had very little creative currency in Hollywood [...] It was living on its past roots. Executives were no longer committed to animation, fearing it was dead'.[87] Actually, as of its creations, as James Stewart wrote, Disney 'had always held itself aloof from Hollywood—its glamour and hedonism, its star system and cutthroat deal making'.[88] This distinction certainly resulted from a strategy, but also from the background and childhood of Walt Disney, resolutely different from other creators. The company thus maintained an old-fashioned label which changed with the arrival of the new team. It led notably to an undeniable standardisation due to its integration within the Hollywood industry. Its structural change also implied a cultural change: 'Until 1984, the culture of Disney was much more WASP [White Anglo-Saxon Protestant] and conservative. It was a very formal and old-line company, very much dominated by the history of Walt Disney.' It has completely shifted, since 'they [its new leaders, among whom were Michael Eisner, Jeffrey Katzenberg and Frank Wells] completely changed it in less than a decade. Their successors have made even more profound changes'.[89]

It is also necessary to consider the new cohesion at the centre of the world-cinema. The rigidity of the classical studio system was connected with what Durkheim defined as a set of 'beliefs and feelings common to the average members of a society, [...] a collective consciousness'[90] which gave rise to a specific genre. The division of labour proceeded only inside each one of the five major studios which were capable of organising production. A mechanical solidarity firmly linked the professionals within each one of the major studios; seven-year-long contracts tied artists to one studio and prevented them from signing contracts with another. But the fragmentation of productive structures and the spin-off of movie theatres put an end to this configuration.

Nowadays, many companies come together just for the time it takes to make a film, each one fulfilling a particular function, such as financing, special effects, casting or insurance. Overall unity is ensured by the complementarity amongst all these functions. Whereas divisions between major/independent studios and among major studios prevailed beforehand due to the strong attachment of individuals to one company, nowadays, on the contrary actors and technical teams alike take part indiscriminately in blockbusters as well as in more ambitious movies created for more limited audiences. In addition, the different entities work together on distribution and production. A certain organic solidarity prevails today wherein the diversity of activities and values encourages an individual consciousness. It is worth pointing out that major studios no longer hesitate to invest in productions outside Hollywood. From this perspective, outsourcing results from a change in the configuration of the centre of the world-economy. In this process, the most vulnerable people are the groups which can be replaced by cheap foreign labour.[91] Conversely, irreplaceable famous actors benefit handsomely from these arrangements.

However, Steve Hulett is very well aware of Hollywood's precariousness and analyses it in these terms:

> the American animation industry will be in trouble when the studios make a film in India, China or Taiwan that brings in $300 million in box office returns inside the United States. Then the studios will leave for these countries because it is cheaper. And it will be a problem. [...] It doesn't make any sense for a studio director to make a film for half price in India if it doesn't make any money. There were four films that came out this year in CGI [computer-generated imagery]: *The Wild* did no business. It was made in Toronto, *Cars* [produced in the United States] hit, *Ice Age 2* [produced in the United States] hit, *Over the Hedge* [produced in the United States] hit.[92]

Companies compete against one another on all types of films. They vie for talent and scripts. The homogenisation of practices also leads to the generalisation of blockbusters designed for the whole family. In June 2015, the top 20 all-time worldwide grossing movies were all PG or PG-13 rated productions distributed by the major studios; eight by the Walt Disney Studios. 17 of them belonged to adventure, science-fiction and/or action genres, while 14 of them were sequels. All of them, except *Titanic* (1997), dealt with the adventures of heroes in fictional worlds, such as Batman, Captain Jack Sparrow and Harry Potter.[93]

One can also observe similarities in what may inspire the creation of new films. Jeff Holder remembers that when he worked at Hanna-Barbera an animated feature very similar to *The Lion King* (1994) was being developed. He also recalls that once, when developing a new series for Cartoon Network, he received three pitches in one week that were very similar: 'three people came and pitched a cartoon series all starring a super cow, a cow with a cape, who flies. Three independent companies working completely separately ended up working on similar subjects'.[94] In other words, Hollywood remains a very integrated cluster despite the fragmentation of its productive structures. A strong common ethos and a permanent circulation of new ideas and projects from within maintain a cohesion marked by mimetism and interdependence.

The Expansion Strategies of World Cinema

The Collaboration of Studios in a Globalised World

Hollywood wields its power on global markets thanks to the deployment of political and socio-economic strategies. Hollywood preponderance is transnationally grounded. On the one hand, the Motion Picture Association (MPA) acts on behalf of the studios in politico-legal domains; on the other hand, the Hollywood stranglehold on distribution networks ensures a decisive socio-economic advantage within foreign industries.

With its creation in 1922, the Motion Picture Association of America (MPAA), which was named at the time the Motion Picture Producers and Distributors of America, did not aim to play a major role in foreign politics. Directed by William H. Hays, it wanted to defend American cinema against criticism which portrayed it as breaching good morals. It notably instituted a strict code of self-censorship. But its lobbying rapidly took on an international scale with the success of Hollywood productions and the attendant foreign protectionism, particularly in Europe. This growing international involvement appeared blatant when the Motion Picture Export Association of America was set up in 1945. It was re-named the Motion Picture Association in 1994. Although formally separated, the MPAA and the MPA are in fact closely entangled, the one exerting constant pressure on the US government, the other coordinating a global policy in no less than 150 countries.

Nowadays, this two-pronged association coordinates the diplomacy of the major studios. It is involved in the politics of the US motion picture and television industries, which account for annual sales of $130 billion.[95] The MPA's main objective is to expand Hollywood world cinema by establishing free trade and respect for intellectual property rights.[96]

Hollywood nurtures a special relationship with Washington. The MPA lobby results in strong political support from US authorities both domestically and abroad. Throughout the twentieth century, the United States has promoted international development of its motion picture industry. During the 1920s and 1940s, it especially endeavoured to open new markets for its domestic industry.[97] Illustratively, at the end of the Second World War, the Blum-Byrnes commercial agreements planned to substantially reduce the French film support system, in exchange for loan and debt forgiveness.[98] More recently, US representatives largely fought for the removal of national film support schemes during the trade negotiations of the Uruguay Round in the 1980–90s, for the Multilateral Agreement on Investment at the OECD in the 1990s and against the Cultural Diversity Treaty at UNESCO (United Nations Educational, Scientific, Educational and Cultural Organization) in 2005. On the individual level, close relations reinforce US support for Hollywood. Actually, all the executives of the MPA are selected on the basis of their relations with the federal body. For example, before joining the association, all previous Chief Executive Officers (CEOs) as well as current CEOs William Hays, Jack Valenti, Dan Glickman and Chris Dodd worked in governmental institutions.[99] Through the MPA, the studios are associated with the decision-making process in trade matters.

Concerning intellectual property, the central position of the MPA in the US law-making process comes from its membership of the International Intellectual Property Alliance (IIPA). This representative of US copyright-based industries has defended the interests of the music, film, software and publishing sectors since 1984. In particular, the organisation has convinced public authorities to include copyright protection in its mandate.[100] However, behind the apparent symbiosis existing between the US government and the IIPA, they diverge on policy. Indeed, the privileged position in Washington DC of the IIPA and especially of the MPA/MPAA, should not keep us from overlooking the equally favourable position of other powerful lobbies. In other words, the power of creative industries depends on the balance between their lobbying strategy and their political capital, on the one hand, and the power of other actors' coalitions, on the other. As a consequence, the IIPA has sometimes run up against refusals from the federal authorities. For example, during the trade negotiations of the Uruguay Round from 1986 to 1994, France and Canada strongly opposed free trade in audio-visual matters. President Bill Clinton decided to exclude these domains from the agreement, which caused an outcry from the Hollywood industry.[101]

The studios are also very active in the fields of broadcasting, new technologies and telecommunications. They maintain complex interaction between companies and governments. The global reach of inter-firm policy corresponds to the reconfiguration of socio-economic and cultural issues in which interstate diplomacy has lost its pre-eminence. Over the last few decades, global operators have emerged owing to technological transformations, economic deregulation and space-time changes. In the context of interconnected spheres, they nurture consensual, friendly or conflictual relations, whose stakes consist of influencing national legislation, inter-sectoral practices and consumer behaviour. Thus, they are committed to contentious politics whose intention is to institute global governance in their respective sectors.

In addition, the MPA has joined forces with the music industry in their legal prosecutions at the international level.[102] Since copyright infringement affected the music sector before the broadcasting and film industries, representatives from the music sector have been taking legal action since the Napster website case in 2000. These lawsuits have had intense media coverage; their goals are just as repressive as they are dissuasive. They have taken on a global dimension because they are dealing with practices which unfold transnationally through networks of anonymous individuals. Indeed, according to Dara MacGreevy—regional director of the MPA for Europe, the Middle East and Africa—illegal downloads in these areas have exceeded in number those which have occurred within the United States since 2003.[103]

Also, technological innovations in the copyright domain have led the MPA and the Recording Industry Association of America (RIAA) to exert pressure on the highly interdependent industries of telecommunications and information technology. Their relations are conflictual because copyright industries would like to limit the possibility of intellectual property (IP) violations by computer users starting at the point of hardware manufacture. Even though both parties condemn illegal activities, they diverge on how to fight such practices.[104]

The MPA has lately changed its relations with national governments. While it has often maintained a hostile stance against them, the MPA is increasingly cooperating and forming alliances with administrations. The acceleration of globalisation, the individualisation of consumer behaviour and the limits of the state against powerful non-state actors have called for a common response from both government authorities and the MPA. Indeed, networks of illegal recording, reproduction and distribution have become a real threat to the expansion of the studios. The networks' transnational dimension and their links with criminal organisations make any control difficult and direct involvement of the MPA all the more necessary. The late Jack Valenti, at the time head of the MPA, highlighted the conditions of successful action: 'only when governments around the world effectively bring to bear the full powers of the state against these criminals can we expect to make progress. Only when industry and government join forces to fight these organized groups will we succeed in protecting America's greatest trade asset'.[105] Whereas the Hollywood association opposes state protectionism, it presently collaborates with foreign governments, benefiting directly from the prevalent position of its member-studios in audio-visual spheres in many countries. For instance, in July 2005, the MPA negotiated with China—with the Ministry for Culture and Administration of the Radio, Film and Television—for the reinforcement of co-operation between both countries in order to protect intellectual property.[106]

In this respect, national production centres have backed up the global policies of the MPA since they suffer the most from domestic copyright infringements. They constitute an inside lobby which contributes to the implementation of international and national law. Indeed, this sort of transnational partnership intensifies pressures exerted on public authorities. Presenting itself as the defender of copyright, the MPA also rallies many representatives in audio-visual sectors where illegal counterfeiting is particularly widespread. It claims a network of alliances in 30 countries which covers the main markets, including Western and emerging countries.[107] In China, the Hollywood association teamed up with the China Film Copyright Protection Association regarding lobbying and information exchanges.[108] In addition, the MPA can count on the socio-economic relations that its member-studios nurture with national cinema industries through co-productions. Networks of private actors play a crucial role in the fight against piracy. For example, the MPA and its Australian counterparts launched a joint venture called the Australian Federation Against Copyright Theft.[109]

Hollywood pressure exerted on political authorities appears decisive in the investigations of illegal organisations. Agencies from the MPA are involved in police operations which have been organised abroad with local police forces and domestically in New York, once called the 'capital of piracy'.[110] The MPA plays as well a strategic and complementary role in police activity. For instance, it analyses the fingerprints of seized compact discs (CD) in order to pinpoint the multinational chains of production and distribution.[111] Copyright infringement investigations have concentrated especially in Asia where illegal copies have resulted in the loss of $1.2 billion in annual earnings, according to the Singapore MPA agency.[112] On that continent, from May to mid-July 2005, 1,900 investigations in 12 countries, including 405 in China, took place in Operation Red Card. The anti-piracy initiative led to the seizure of six million discs, the confiscation of 1,480 CD burners and the arrest of 915 individuals.[113] The transnational coordination of these anti-piracy interventions forms the most appropriate response to the illegal groups operating globally and on the Internet. However, even considering the long list of actions which the MPA has initiated, this response remains inadequate. Technological innovations and transnational aspects of illegal organisations are continually calling into question the effectiveness of MPA actions. According to an MPA study, illegal copies of *Star Wars: Episode 1—The Phantom Menace* (1999) were on sale in Asia one week after the film's release in the United States.[114]

The state–Hollywood entanglement at a worldwide level reveals the success of the representatives of cinema companies because, as Fernand Braudel affirmed, 'capitalism triumphs only when it identifies with the State, when it is the State'.[115] These hybrid combinations largely exceed simple joint public-private partnerships and acts of 'state-firm diplomacy'.[116] They take on configurations wherein the MPA is at the centre of international coordination in assuming key functions of the state. Its lobbying, its intelligence-gathering and its capacity for pressure make it an inescapable force in the network of industry, government and film sectors. This confers authority to the MPA in the governance of the audio-visual industry. Its contribution to the deployment of the Hollywood world-economy lies in the imposition of the legal, political and economic conditions for free trade and for the respect of copyright. The MPA admittedly nurtures a kind of 'constitutionalism' project, contributing sustainable accumulation of audio-visual capital at the global level.[117]

In emerging economies, the Hollywood association appears to be crucial in expanding its markets, an essential condition for its member-studios' success. Thanks to its presence in Washington DC, it uses the US government to exert pressure on foreign governments just like an advocacy network.[118] As a result, public authorities vote and implement laws in favour of copyright and free trade. Its force lies in this constant lobbying within each national government. Thus, for example, it regularly employs the threat of negative reports to the US Congress and also files lawsuits in national jurisdictions.

In addition to the juridical and political action taken by the MPA, the capitalists of culture, the major studios, possess large distribution networks which work as 'matrices of world capitalism'.[119] They form the socio-economic bases for major studios' preponderance. Their world-wide box office revenue has kept on growing since the 1980s. In 2014, 20th Century Fox reached $5.5 billion, whereas Disney passed the $4 billion mark for the second time.[120] In this context, international business amounted to more than 71 % of the major studio revenues in 2014 compared to only 67 % in 2010.[121]

If producers have experienced splits diversification or even bankruptcy since the 1930s, many of the same distribution networks have continuously dominated the domestic and foreign sectors while diversifying their sources of income over the same period. Illustratively, they accounted for 67 % of European box office returns in 2011.[122] If notable differences can be observed among them from one year to the next, depending on how successful their films have been, their global weight on every market remains high over time. Subsidiaries of the studios retain year after year the majority of market share. For example, in Germany, major Hollywood studios have always occupied first place in the yearly distribution rankings.[123] Ahead of internal national content, the market share of their programmes in Europe reaches 58 % in TV broadcast, whatever the content may be: feature films, TV films or series and soaps.[124] Also, their presence is even more prominent in ancillary markets. In France, their 2014 market share was 65 % for digital versatile discs (DVDs) and 73 % for Blu-ray discs.[125] In the same year, the American market share in cinemas was only 45 %. Concerning prime-time television broadcasting, new American films are neck and neck with French national films, each with a 40 % market share, leaving less than 20 % for other foreign films.[126] Estimates on the breakdown of the worldwide audio-visual market give a similar picture with US companies earning 60 % of turnover.[127]

Presently, major studios are concentrating on emerging countries, especially China and India, whose development and demographic importance make them the growth engines of world cinema. In national box-office revenues, China already comes in second just behind North America with receipts of $4.8 billion in 2014, a figure displaying an impressive growth rate.[128] Although censorship, strict annual quotas of new foreign films and the growth of a home-grown film industry have impeded penetration of the Chinese market by US major studios, they have still managed to make above 40 % of box office over the past few years.[129] Franchises in particular, such as *Transformers: Age of Extinction* (2014) and *Iron Man 3* (2013) fared high in Chinese cinema. *Transformers* even made first place in the 2014 annual Chinese box-office ranking. India forms another challenge owing to its prosperous domestic industry. Its movie sector is first in terms of film production (1,500 per year) and admission tickets (2.6 billion per year), although total box-office receipts remain rather limited at $1.6 billion.[130] Confronted with radically different culture and living standards, major studios only represent 10 % of Indian box-office returns.[131]

Distribution networks ensure a socio-economic and cultural integration for American major studios at the global level, but the process can be extremely tricky and involves the subtle introduction of symbols into national cultures. To familiarise an audience with new films involves the adoption of an appealing commercial angle to transmit the message of the film. In this respect, Bill Mechanic explains that

> you have to have the feel of what these different pictures are and how to market them. You are not going to change the content but you are going to change the approach to selling them. This was exactly the case for *Good Morning Vietnam* (1987) which was played here as a comedy and overseas as a drama.[132]

For cartoons, companies use national leading figures. Walter Veltroni, at the time the mayor of Rome, provided the dubbing in Italian for the character Mayor Turkey Lurkey in Disney's movie, *Chicken Little* (2005).[133] The Disney Company dubbed *Frozen* (2013) into 41 different languages in order to penetrate local markets more easily and deeply.[134] Support from a studio confers strategic continuity to the commercial launching of a film, maximising global box-office returns while limiting losses for disappointing movies. As Steve Hulett from the Animation Guild states, while 'most European studios only supply domestic markets [...] today international conglomerates have a big edge because they are worldwide. They have a lot of reach. They can market across borders'.[135] In connection with animated films, Hulett adds that

> even Japanese cartoons do not travel well outside Japan [...] There are a number of people here who love Japanese animation. But it does not get a broad release [...] it does no business [...] Box office returns rise at most to $10 million even when foreign animation does fairly well [...] But if you look at Blue Sky's *Ice Age*: *The Meltdown* [2006], it reached $200 million in this country [the United States], it did over $100 million in Europe. Worldwide it made over $600 million [without counting the profits coming from ancillary markets which can generate revenues up to five times higher] it was a worldwide hit.[136]

Many interrelations among major studios reinforce their supremacy abroad, resulting from their sectoral, social and geographical proximity. These relational clusters are irreducible to a simple confrontation among rivals or an agreement among partners. In this respect, studios can be at odds with the rules of free competition in such a concentrated market. The European Union regularly conducts investigations on antitrust practices; in May 2006 a Spanish judge actually ordered major studios to pay $2.2 million for anti-competitive practices.[137] According to Douglas Gomery's studio system, only moderate competition exists between Hollywood distribution networks.[138] It is worth remembering that the Webb-Pomerene Act (1918) exempted certain companies operating abroad from antitrust laws.

Admittedly, major studios avoid competing directly with one another. For example, when new films come onto the market, the studios try to avoid releasing movies which address the same audiences, delaying or advancing the date of release. Trade newspapers continuously report these changes in the timing of movie and home video releases.[139] Indeed, Hollywood studios make their strategic decisions by taking into account other companies and their tactics. Also, in the distribution process, it often happens that a studio releases a movie for the home market while delegating foreign distribution to another studio—such was the case for *Titanic* (1997). In their strategy of expansion, studios invest together in foreign markets since they can pool financing, technological advances and productions. For instance, since the 1970s, two major studios, Paramount and Universal, have operated a joint venture for international distribution, first called Cinema International Corporation and later United International Pictures.[140] This joint venture changed over time—MGM became a partner and left while DreamWorks joined for several years. In addition, major studios formed alliances within the foreign branches of Home Box Office (HBO), the global pay TV leader.[141]

But major studio partnerships have remained flexible. When they enter oligopolistic market configurations, they form limited alliances with national companies with a view to taking advantage of their know-how, networks and reputation. Between 1993 and 2004, Buena Vista International thus chose to establish a partnership for distribution in France with Gaumont. At the European level, American firms ensure wider distribution than national entities, which Fabrizio Montanari observed in these terms: 'European films which are the most successful are co-productions involving American studios, wherein a major studio distributes the film and English is the language of production'.[142]

Major studios can be involved in disseminating and financing foreign productions, even forming joint ventures. They take part in the success of national productions, engaging in 'glocal' (global meets local) programmes. In this respect, a senior executive from Buena Vista International stated that he could decide to distribute national production provided that they enter the creative line of the distribution network.[143] Indeed, major studios want to gain ground on a sociocultural level. Admittedly, it is a matter of prestige and above all integration. On this subject, Bill Mechanic, founder of the international Disney network, made sure 'not to sell only *X-Men* [Hollywood films] but also to sell Almodovar's in Spain and Besson's in France. Selling Almodovar in Spain is a big deal [...] you become very important on the market place'.[144] Studios acquire a privileged status which helps them to disseminate their own productions. American companies seek to be involved in national films that show a profit. This approach is connected with the strategy of 'glocalisation' which does not mean a globalisation of the film activity. On the contrary, in addition to producing global blockbusters, Hollywood distributors also search to reinforce local production which they do in Latin America, in Germany and in the United Kingdom, supplementing their releases with national productions not destined for export.[145]

Major studios rarely decide to distribute foreign films at the international level. Indeed, global screening of European movies remains in fact quite exceptional. Hollywood studios prefer to promote their own productions. So, the sooner the major studio gets involved in producing a film, the greater its interest in promoting the widest distribution possible. In the case of Buena Vista, films of the Japanese artist Miyazaki have benefited from this type of agreement. Buena Vista International signed an agreement in 1996 to acquire the global video rights for eight previously produced animated movies, including *Porco Rosso* (1992) along with the world distribution rights of the feature film, *Princess Mononoke* (1997).

Disney became a nationwide distributor in the 1950s, acquiring domestic autonomy. In contrast, it depended on other companies for international distribution. On the initiative of Bill Mechanic, Disney set up its own international distribution system in the 1990s. Buena Vista International is the only network to have successfully arisen in the second half of the twentieth century. After several years, it even became the number one network owing primarily to its ambitious development strategy and its popular productions.[146] In this respect, the specificity of its animated films, including the Disney classics, gave the network an edge over its competitors. The Disney signature has always ensured a minimum box office and these films are usually released and re-released several times. In home entertainment, Disney acquired a leading position because its animated films became the latest craze for children. Under the new Eisner administration, annual home video revenues went from less than $100 million in 1984 to $3 billion in 1995. The latter sum accounted for 26 % of turnover and half of the company's operating income.[147] By the end of the 1990s, box-office returns of the major studio regularly exceeded $1 billion. In 2004, Buena Vista reached this threshold for the tenth time in a row.[148] A new phase in the expansion of distribution had begun with each hit attaining a worldwide box office of $1 billion. *Pirates of the Caribbean: Dead Man's Chest* (2006) was the first Disney movie to reach this mark. Box-office receipts of the Disney blockbuster *Marvel's The Avengers* (2012) made $1.5 billion. In 2014, as previously discussed, the studio went beyond the $4 billion threshold in worldwide gross returns for the second time. In 2015, it almost reached $6 billion, benefiting from the success of *Star Wars*.[149]

Hollywood, the Centre of World Entertainment

In addition to dominating foreign film sectors, Hollywood is the leading centre of transnational entertainment. Its major studios prevail in the field of entertainment by producing films enjoyed worldwide and by instigating events on a global scale. Major studios form a world-economy in themselves by setting up 'an economy on one portion of the planet [...] where it forms an economic whole'. Its preponderance distinguishes between the economy of the world and a world-economy, 'a "Weltwirtschaft" [...] a world on its own'.[150] Covering many societies and economies, the world-economy is ordained hierarchically with a centre and a periphery. The centre determines international exchanges, profiting from de facto or legal monopolies. It has supremacy in 'a given geographical area' which 'is divided into successive zones [...] the heart, the surrounding region [...] followed by the intermediary zones, around the central pivot. Lastly, and very broadly, the margins [...] are more subordinate and dependent than participative'.[151] While globalisation has partially decreased the concentration of production in Hollywood, it has reinforced the phenomenon of 'localized agglomeration' driven by a 'cumulative development process'.[152] At the Hollywood centre, world-economy theories and cluster analyses appear complementary to one another. The former, concepts in terms of world-economy, focus on the centralisation and domination of this centre over a transnational area. The latter have established analytical frameworks for understanding the economic concentration of interrelated companies in a given sector.[153] They identify key criteria which explain the maintenance of such centres.

Los Angeles is the centre of global entertainment. This metropolis attracts most of the social, economic and cultural capital in these matters. As producer Michael Taylor has said, 'Los Angeles, what we call Hollywood, is still the centre of film-making, the heart of the movie business. If you want to be a film-maker, it is important to be based here'.[154] Following the same logic, Jeff Holder explains that considering a move elsewhere is out of the question for him! He 'remains in Los Angeles because outside the city you miss trends and developments. You are out of the loop of what's happening before it actually happens'.[155] Admittedly, New York remains the artistic, literary and financial centre of the United States but Los Angeles is the global leading centre for motion pictures and entertainment. In this respect, Jason Squire goes even further by saying 'Los Angeles is considered the creative hub of global entertainment, attracting students and professionals from all over the world. For me, "Hollywood" is not only a section of Los Angeles, but is also located anywhere in the world where movies are being made to compete in the global arena'.[156]

The leadership of Hollywood is fourfold. It is based firstly on the concentration of productive capacity; secondly on financial capital; thirdly on human capital; and finally on cultural preponderance, which results in global polarisation around Hollywood with regard to entertainment.

First, the metropolis on the west coast polarises the productive entities in the field of leisure by the mere presence of the major studios. Indeed, world cinema is located in a part of the globe where cultural capitalists are continuously negotiating and deciding over the production and screening of movies. Their considerable video library, enormous budgets and colossal box office establish immense barriers to the entry of rival companies into the markets. Although there is no legal obstacle to the arrival of new competitors, dominant companies have been pre-eminent since the 1920s, for close to a hundred years! So, one may wonder about the 'real contestability'[157] of their position, that is their ability to prevent other competitors and film-makers from competing at the world level.

Hollywood blockbusters form the main transnational productions. They make lasting profits in the spheres of films and their by-products, establishing their imageries and narratives as global franchises. Major studios maintain a stronghold on these markets, which requires a massive distribution infrastructure just to pass the break-even point and to cover colossal production and distribution costs. In the same vein, Fernand Braudel has written about medieval merchants from Venice and Amsterdam: 'by the huge sums of capital they possess, capitalists were able to preserve their privileges and to control the great international businesses of their times'.[158] As observed in Europe, Hollywood films do not replace national productions. Instead, they pre-empt the international market. In fact, market share of films from the rest of the world, not including the United States, remains marginal at less than 5 % in Europe.[159] Even, the presence of European non-domestic films has decreased on the old continent, despite European Union regulations to favour the circulation of these films. For example, the market share of French films decreased in Germany, from 12 % of the admission tickets in 1975, to 8 % in 1985, 0.7 % in 1998 and 3 % in 2013. Outside France, French films have represented on average less than 5 % of those shown in main European markets since 2005.[160] As a result, deprived of outlets other than their own national markets, other motion-picture sectors can only finance small projects with limited returns. This appears all the more fundamental as cinema mobilises considerable funds.

Second, the Hollywood motion picture industry attracts investment since it is regarded as a profitable sector. A US producer, just as any other entrepreneur, can develop projects with the financial support of banks. She or he benefits from the backing of banks which may grant her or him enormous resources.[161] As René Bonnell asserted in 2006: 'The French Bank, Banque Paribas, which will never put one euro in the French cinema, is well-established in Hollywood and regularly lends money to young producers.' He justifies this practice inasmuch as 'Hollywood producing for a world market reaches considerable profitability. Thus, it is infinitely less risky to produce there than in France'.[162] Furthermore, confronted with a strong audio-visual demand, financial investors turn first to Hollywood because a deep trust has been established resulting from the particular ethos of Hollywood which I have already discussed above. Trust, as much as profitability, serves as the basis of exchange in the modern economy and explains the close connections between the two sectors.

In addition to banks, Hollywood attracts all the major investment companies which are willing to pay for popular programmes. In addition to European TV operators, companies from emerging countries have become increasingly involved with the American movie industry. Traditionally, European and Japanese companies have invested heavily in Hollywood with multiple-year deals. They have also partnered with less well-known companies that have appeared with overseas finance. Many such ventures ended up going bankrupt after a string of money-losing movies. In the 1990s, Carolco Pictures made big-budget films in partnership with the French Le Studio Canal+, the Japanese Pioneer Electric Corporation and the Italian Rizzoli Corriere della Sera Mediagroup, whilst under a domestic distribution deal with MGM.[163] In the 2000s, Spyglass Entertainment made the headlines when it was financially backed by the German Kirch Group and the Italian Mediaset—it was also under a distribution deal with Disney.[164] Recently, independent production studios have received funds from emerging countries in Asia through the usual schemes of multi-year production and distribution deals. If Chinese investment in Hollywood has grown to $5 billion, it is likely to increase even further as major media and online firms, such as Baidu, Alibaba and Tencent Holdings, are setting up in Hollywood.[165] For instance, in 2015, the 'mini-major' Lionsgate Entertainment concluded an agreement with the second Chinese TV network, Hunan TV.[166] The latter agreed to co-finance all the qualifying Lionsgate films over the next three years. Amounting to $375 million in film financing, the deal would account for 25 % of Lionsgate's film production costs of $1.5 billion. It also includes co-production and distribution of Chinese films outside China.

But the most dramatic Hollywood partnership with the emerging world has been the partnership of Spielberg's DreamWorks studio with the Indian media giant, Reliance Entertainment, which agreed to sign a $1.5 billion deal to produce movies in 2009.[167] Reliance first invested in Hollywood in 2006 through a multi-picture five-year deal with producer Ashok Amritraj's Hyde Park Entertainment. A year afterwards, it signed a deal with MTV Network regarding youth programmes.[168] Despite the financial crisis with decreased financing coming from banks, Hollywood is still central in movie deal-making.

Third, the Hollywood sector is based on well-trained and innovative human capital. According to studies, the US motion picture industry employs more than 200,000 people, 52 % of whom work in California.[169] In addition, a study on the creative economy counted 1.5 million direct, indirect and induced jobs for California. Of this total, direct creative sectors produced 695,000 jobs, 58 % of which were located in the counties of Los Angeles and Orange.[170] The median wage across all creative occupations was around $38,000 while median wages for producers, directors, animators, writers and multimedia artists were well above $80,000.[171] In particular, all the famous actors were included in the figures—modern moguls and artists belong to some of the wealthiest groups of people in the world.[172] Thus, understandably, the centre of the American cinema attracts foreign talent already renowned in their home countries. This trend is not new since many Europeans migrated to Los Angeles during the first half of the twentieth century. In the 2000s, 40 % of directors still came from the old continent.[173] In the domain of animation, 30 % of creative talent within DreamWorks were European because many came at the initiative of Steven Spielberg when he closed the London studio, Amblimation.[174] All these factors correspond to Braudel's description of the 'heart'[175] of the world-economy which brings together 'the splendour, the wealth and the happiness of life'.[176]

Fourth, many companies invest in the Hollywood sector to benefit from its preponderance in cultural fields, specifically in the knowledge domain. Indeed, the structural capacity of major studios gives them 'the power to shape and determine the structures of the global political economy within which other states, their political institutions, their economic enterprises and (not least) their scientists and other professional people have to operate'. The author, Susan Strange, adds that this structural capacity confers 'the power to decide how things shall be done, the power to shape frameworks within which states relate to each other, relate to people, or relate to corporate enterprises'.[177] Major studios are prime movers in the development of audio-visual sectors. They initiated pay TV in the seventies. More recently, they have engaged in mobile online content.[178] By being among the first in technical advances and innovation, major studios can develop these new fields along with their already-established sectors, maintaining their preponderance in a fast-changing world. Illustratively, the appearance of high-definition technology brought about conflict relating to the type of system to adopt. On the one hand, Columbia Tristar, MGM, 20th Century Fox and Disney favoured the Blu-ray model developed by Sony—with Sony owning the two first studios. On the other hand, Universal, Paramount and Warner preferred Toshiba's High-Density DVD. This competition on technological standards intensified rivalry amongst the giant organisations with adoption of the future system of high-definition technology at stake. Considering the economic and political influence potentially wielded by major studios, owning one would seem to be of key importance. A former executive at the French pay TV channel, Studio Canal+, considered that 'It is in the best long-term interest of the large groups to own one of the studios […] This gives them the possibility of positioning themselves at the forefront of innovation'.[179]

Hollywood appears central in the vast economic area in which its goods and its imageries are dispersed. This polarisation is based on the economic-cultural dimensions of its productions which attract audiences worldwide. In other words, its identity results not only from the artistic specificity of its films, but also from the strategies of its major studios. Hollywood cinema maintains its attractiveness through contracting world-famous stars, telling compelling narratives and producing powerful imageries. By doing this, it exports the American way of life. It develops loyalty with its audiences by commissioning sequels, all the while listening and responding to its audiences' preferences.

In this context, Disney, a firm based only on content, appears as the epitome of Hollywood's cultural predominance by maintaining its label, imageries and narratives across many generations and across many countries. With the aim of promoting and preserving the Disney brand, the organisation has created a structure overseeing all Disney activities on a worldwide scale—Walt Disney International. Set up in 1999, it established its headquarters in London, Tokyo and Buenos Aires. Its objectives are to maintain coherence and to spawn synergies. Bringing together senior executives in charge of maintaining the value of the brand, the organisation's aim is to combine global logic with the knowledge of 'local', national cultures.[180] Disney wants to capture 'opportunities for significant growth in international revenues over the long term'.[181] Under the leadership of Robert Iger, the Company has successfully refocused on its brand and its core competence, family entertainment, extending the logic of a content-based major studio. As a result, it reduced the movie productions of Touchstone Pictures while at the same time re-energising the animation studio in 2006 with the acquisition of Pixar for $7.4 billion.[182] Iger then successively bought out renowned imageries and narratives such as Marvel's heroes in 2009 and Lucasfilm's *Star Wars* franchise in 2012 for $4 billion each.[183] He has recently bought up the marketing and distribution rights for future episodes of *Indiana Jones*. The Disney Company revives, maintains, enriches and deepens all these narratives and imageries through highly profitable globally-diffused content, attractions and merchandising, giving company supremacy in cultural spheres.

Producing in the spheres of media and leisure, cultural capitalists compete permanently to retain the interest of consumers spectators. This question of attention span is crucial throughout the lives of narratives. Transnational companies wish to cause media events, 'monopolistic […] interruptions of routine' which 'cancel all other programs, bring television's clock to a stop […] their performance belongs to "sacred time", bringing all social activity to a standstill. For a while, the 'event' occupies society's "centre"'.[184] Multinational corporations want to bring a halt to the routine of everyday life so that the audience may share the same collective experience. In other words, although they do not propose live events, they attempt to impose a monopolistic attention and a common temporality over vast transnational spaces. This encourages the audience to visit such and such a park, for example, or to go and watch the latest *Star Wars* movie, *The Force Awakens*, released in December 2015. Twenty days after its release, the film had grossed $1.5 billion at the worldwide box office.[185] Studios seek to break the routine by using advertising, special effects, world-renowned actors and attractive storytelling for the whole family.[186]

As for by-products and film sequels, studios also take advantage of former successes. As soon as a project is given the green light, executives start to work on promotion of the future movie. Media coverage is organised in a period when the attention span of audiences is more and more fragmented, and greater financing is required to maintain public interest. In the same way, the launching of a new theme park attraction and the appearance of famous actors to promote it fall under the same marketing logic.

This intense promotion is also made necessary by the 'completely elastic demand'[187] which the Hollywood sector undergoes. While major studios can easily cope with one another and with rivals in the motion picture sector, they find external competition coming from the diversity of the leisure business more threatening. For example, sporting events represent major competitors at the world level. Thus, every four years during the summer, the football World Cup generates a significant shortfall in box-office returns for Hollywood, especially in Europe where this sport is very popular.[188] Although films have never been the only leisure activity, movie theatres once played a central role. Before the arrival of television, they could even be described as a social institution. Today, the increasing number of media channels makes promotion increasingly necessary, forcing major studios to invest massively in advertising.

The famous buzz sought by advertising executives which results from a successful launch of a film implies in turn considerable investment in many ancillary markets. In this context, the simultaneous release of movies at the global level aims at attracting media attention while taking advantage of the money spent in the United States.[189] On average, promotion costs for medium-size films amount to $40 million in North America, but the international prints and advertising expenses of blockbusters would reportedly cost $100 million domestically and an additional $100 million internationally.[190] Abroad, Hollywood creations also profit from considerable investments compared to foreign films. In 2014, in France each one of the 140 new releases from Hollywood benefited from an advertising budget of $1.1 million on average compared to funding of less than half of that amount for each of the 240 domestic movies produced.[191] The availability of American and French films in cinemas demonstrates a further inequality. For example, in 2014, in the first week after release, French films were shown in 119 theatres while American films were scheduled in 258 theatres.[192] DVD and Blu-ray formats represent the opportunity for Hollywood to gain predominance with a high market share of 65 % (compared to its market share in French cinemas).[193] The preponderance of American movies is reproduced in the rising sector of electronic home video.[194]

Disney's theme parks have adopted the same approach to attract the public's attention. The creation of events is the common way to bolster attendance. In 1992, Disney invested a lot of money for the inauguration of Disneyland Paris, at the time named EuroDisney. The Disney Company wanted to raise interest on the whole continent. Estimates of promotion costs ranged between FF200 and FF300 million, which was a huge budget at the time. The inauguration ceremony was broadcast by 11 channels to the entire world.[195] Since then, each year new media campaigns have been launched to attract visitors continuously. After the 25th anniversary of the park in Florida and the centennial of the birth of Walt Disney, the 50th anniversary of the Californian site saw nearly 18 months of celebrations take place in 2005. Admission tickets rose by 18 % and brought about a 10 % increase in income. In 2015, the 60th anniversary of Disneyland Anaheim gave way to large advertising campaigns during the year-long celebration.

Although Porter's diamond model stresses the interweaving combination of key elements,[196] it misses critical points which this chapter has underscored. First, the cultural dimension of the cluster is central to achieving competitive advantage. What I call the ethos of Hollywood allows the formation of cultural capitalism. Second, the relations among companies inside the cluster are irreducible to rivalry. Indeed, co-operation and common strategy are included. Third, Porter's theory remains nation-centred. Although major Hollywood studios are interconnected with other American transnational companies and the US government, they are autonomous, not bound by or dependent upon American interests. They can resort to using and working with non-US supporting industries, talent and governments. They rely on foreign production centres and on international demand to achieve supremacy in entertainment domains. They exert a transnational polarisation on the entertainment sector, which the next chapter covers more thoroughly.

Notes

1. M. Porter (1998) *The Competitive Advantage of Nations* (Basingstoke: Macmillan), p. 63 *ff.*
2. See D. Bordwell, J. Staiger and K. Thompson (1988) *The Classical Hollywood Cinema. Film, Style and Mode of Production to 1960*, 2nd edn. (London: Routledge).
3. M. Weber (1967/1905) *L'Éthique protestante et l'esprit du capitalisme* (Paris: Plon).
4. J. Wyatt (1994) *High Concept. Movies and Marketing in Hollywood* (Austin: University of Texas Press), p. 374.
5. D. Bordwell (2006) *The Way Hollywood Tells it: Story and Style in Modern Movies* (Berkeley: University of California Press), p. 14.
6. A. Sarris (2004) 'Toward a Theory of Film History' in T. Schatz (ed.) *Hollywood. Critical Concepts in Media and Cultural Studies*, vol. 2 (London: Routledge), p. 12.
7. For example, Buena Vista acquired 45 scripts and pitches between 2004 and 2005. See 'A Compilation of Script, Book and Pitch Sales for Film and TV Development for 2004', *The Hollywood Reporter*, 23 December 2004, 9. On this theme, see M. Heidenry (2013) 'When the spec script was king', *Vanity Fair*, March.
8. J. Stewart (2005) *Disney War* (New York: Simon & Schuster), p. 31.
9. Quotes from J. Kasindorf (1991) 'Mickey Mouse Time at Disney', *New York Magazine*, 7 October, 36.
10. Quotes from R. Grover (1991) *The Disney Touch: Disney, ABC & The Quest for the World's Greatest Media Empire* (Chicago: Irwin Professional Pub.), p. 90.
11. Interview with J. Stewart, famous journalist and author of the best-seller *Disney War*, 28 August 2006. For more information, see Appendix 5.
12. P. Bart (2002) '60 Candles for the Mouse King', *Variety*, 386 (2), 25 February, 2 (5).
13. Interview with a senior lawyer in entertainment, 27 July 2006.
14. Harold Vogel wrote in his reference book on the entertainment industry: 'No major actor, director, writer, or other participant in an entertainment project makes a deal without receiving some kind of high-powered help beforehand, be it from an agent, personal manager, lawyer, accountant, or tax expert. In some cases, platoons of advisors are consulted.' See H. Vogel (2011) *Entertainment Industry Economics: A Guide for Financial Analysis* (Cambridge: Cambridge University Press), p. 178.
15. Interview with D. Kornblum, at the time Vice President Distribution at Buena Vista International, 24 August 2006. For more information, see Appendix 5.

16. Interview with A. Leipzig, Vice President Production at Disney studios from 1987 to 1993, 19 September 2006. For more information, see Appendix 5.
17. J. Hazelton (2005) 'The Creative Life of Producers', *Screen International*, 4 March, 10–11.
18. Producers, such as Jerry Bruckheimer, have a crucial role in dealing with studios and talent: working on the projects, convincing actors and negotiating contracts.
19. On this point a producer answered 'absolutely'. Interview with a producer who used to work at Disney, 15 January 2007.
20. F. Casetti (2003) *Les Théories du cinéma depuis 1945* (Paris: Nathan), p. 85 *ff.*
21. W. Kan (2002) 'Fans Launch Protest Against Disney's Editing of Asian Films', *Variety*, 388 (13), 11 November, 14 (1).
22. B. Xan (2005) 'A God Among Animators', *The Guardian*, 14 September.
23. A. Scott (2005) *On Hollywood: the Place, the Industry* (Princeton: Princeton University Press).
24. D. Gomery (1986) *The Hollywood Studio System* (New York: St. Martin's Press).
25. N. Gabler (1989) *An Empire of their Own. How the Jews Invented Hollywood* (New York: 1st Anchor Book Edition).
26. J. E. Squire (2004) 'Introduction' in J. E. Squire (ed.) *The Movie Business Book* (New York: Fireside), p. 4.
27. Interview with J. E. Squire, a specialist of the Hollywood industry, editor of *The Movie Business Book* and Professor at the University of Southern California, School of Cinematic Arts, 19 July 2006. For more information, see Appendix 5.
28. Interview with J. Stewart.
29. Interview with J. Stewart.
30. Interview with A. Leipzig.
31. Interview with J.-F. Lepetit, French producer having worked with Disney, 1 June 2006. For more information, see Appendix 5.
32. 'Star Wars, Disney and myth-making', *The Economist*, 19 December 2015; 'The Force is strong in this firm', *The Economist*, 19 December 2015; P. McClintock (2016) 'Star Wars: Force Awakens' Tops 'Avatar' to Become No. 1 Film of All Time in North America', *The Hollywood Reporter*, 6 January.
33. S. Watts (1997) *The Magic Kingdom: Walt Disney and the American Way of Life* (Boston: Houghton Mifflin), pp. 52–5.
34. N. Garey, 'The Entertainment Lawyer' in Squire (ed.) *The Movie Business Book*, p. 188. This leverage of talents on the studios is at stake in the negotiations preceding the making of a film.

35. Tom Cruise has the Cruise/Wagner Productions company which co-produces films in which he stars; the same applies for Ben Affleck and Matt Damon with the LivePlanet production company.
36. J. Wasko (2003) *How Hollywood Works* (London: Sage), p. 30; MPAA (2008) *2007 Theatrical Market Statistics*, available at http://www.mpaa.com. Since 2008, the Motion Picture Association of America has given up publishing estimates on production and marketing costs.
37. Interview with a senior manager at Disney's Imagineering department in France, 10 June 2006.
38. Interview with I. Khait, former producer and production manager at the Walt Disney Studios, 6 September 2006. For more information, see Appendix 5.
39. See Appendix 4, Graph 3 on the year-to-year growth of each business division revenues. The growth of studio entertainment revenues was dramatic and was followed by considerable development in Consumer Products and Parks and Resorts divisions.
40. Weber, *L'Éthique protestante.*
41. Quotes from M. Löwy (2004) 'Le concept d'affinité élective chez Max Weber', *Archives des sciences sociales des religions*, (127), July–September, 99.
42. Löwy, 'Le concept d'affinité élective', 101.
43. Watts, *The Magic Kingdom*, p. 59.
44. Watts, *The Magic Kingdom*, p. 81.
45. Jean-François Lepetit, a French producer who worked with Disney, declared during the interview on 1 June 2006 that 'during years, I received invitations to exclusive previews and private parties in Long Beach and in Hollywood because I was listed among the "bankable"'. For information on J.-F. Lepetit, see Appendix 5.
46. M. Horkheimer and T. W. Adorno (2002) *Dialectic of Enlightenment. Philosophical Fragments* (Stanford: Stanford University Press), p. 95.
47. Quote from T. Guback cited by Janet Wasko. See J. Wasko (2004) 'Show Me the Money. Challenging Hollywood Economics' in A. Calabrese and C. Sparks (eds.) *Toward a Political Economy of Culture: Capitalism and Communication in the Twenty-First Century* (Lanham/Oxford: Rowman & Littlefield), pp. 131–51.
48. Interview with I. Khait.
49. Interview with J. Holder, animator and former executive at Hanna Barbera, 8 August 2006 (for more information, see Appendix 5). Opinion confirmed by James Stewart. See Stewart, *Disney War*, pp. 71–2.
50. Interview with a former Senior Vice President at Disney studios who has since become a producer, 5 January 2007.
51. Watts, *The Magic Kingdom*, p. 183.
52. Watts, *The Magic Kingdom*, p. xxi.

53. Watts, *The Magic Kingdom*, p. 166 *ff.*
54. Interview with B. Girveau, General Commissary of the 2007 Parisian exhibition on Disney's art, in B. Génin (2006) (ed.) *Disney au Grand Palais. Les influences européennes*, *Télérama Hors-Série*, September, pp. 22–7, p. 23; J. Wasko (2001) *Understanding Disney: the Manufacture of Fantasy* (Cambridge: Blackwell), p. 13; See also J. M. Barrier (2007) *The Animated Man: a Life of Walt Disney* (Berkeley: University of California Press).
55. Bordwell, Staiger and Thompson, *The Classical Hollywood Cinema*, p. 379.
56. Interview with I. Khait.
57. Interview with J. Holder.
58. Interview with A. Leipzig.
59. Interview with I. Khait.
60. See P. Bourdieu (1992) *Les Règles de l'art. Genèse et structure du champ littéraire* (Paris: Seuil), p. 395.
61. Bourdieu, *Les Règles de l'art*, pp. 397, 432. My translation.
62. Casetti, *Théories*, p. 85.
63. Y. Darré (2003) 'Le cinéma, l'art contre le travail', *Mouvements*, (27/28), May–August, 120–5.
64. Interview with S. Hulett, former animator and Business Representative at the Animation Guild, 1 July 2006. For more information, see Appendix 5.
65. Quote from E. Waintrop (1992) 'L'empreinte du Vieux Monde. L'Europe à Hollywood' in M. Boujut (ed.) *Europe-Hollywood et retour. Cinémas sous influences* (Paris: Autrement), p. 38. My translation.
66. L. Créton (1998) *Cinéma et (in)dépendance: Une économie politique* (Paris: Presses de la Sorbonne Nouvelle), p. 16. My translation.
67. On this point, see J. Laroche and A. Bohas (2008) *Canal+ et les majors américaines. Une vision désenchantée du cinéma-monde* (Paris: L'Harmattan), pp. 124–40.
68. On the dichotomy between organic solidarity and mechanical solidarity, see E. Durkheim (1998/1893) *De la Division du travail social* (Paris: PUF).
69. The Hays Code which organised the censorship of movie production was applied from 1930 to 1966. Confronted with puritan criticism, the Motion Picture Producers and Distributors of America, the representatives of Hollywood studios, implemented rules for the producers of its member-companies to respect moral values.
70. A. Hanssen (2000) 'The Block Booking of Films Reexamined', *Journal of Law and Economics*, 43 (2), October, 395–426.
71. J.-L. Bourget (1998) *Hollywood. La norme et la marge* (Paris: Armand Colin), p. 92. My translation.
72. Bourget, *Hollywood*, p. 94.

73. D. Gomery (2005) *The Hollywood Studio System: a History* (London: British Film Institute), pp. 23–5.
74. Stewart, *Disney War*, p. 22. On the early period of Walt Disney's life, see T. S. Susanin (2011) *Walt Before Mickey: Disney's Early Years, 1919–1928* (Jackson: University Press of Mississippi).
75. A. Bryman (1995) *Disney and his Worlds* (London: Routledge), p. 7.
76. Watts, *The Magic Kingdom*, pp. 29–31.
77. Gomery, *The Hollywood Studio System: a History*, p. 153.
78. A. Bryman, *Disney*, pp. 12–13.
79. M. Conant (2004) 'The Paramount Decrees Reconsidered' in Schatz (ed.) *Hollywood*, pp. 279–311.
80. Interview with B. Mechanic, former leading executive at Buena Vista and then at Fox, 4 August 2006. For more information, see Appendix 5.
81. All the business relations that the Walt Disney Studios constituted with other television and motion picture producing companies from summer 1996 to summer 2006 were studied. See Appendix 3. For a presentation of Hollywood deals, see H. Vogel (2014) *Entertainment Industry Economics*, pp. 189–91.
82. Interview with H. Richardson, senior executive for distribution at Disney studios, DreamWorks and then Paramount, 11 August 2006. For more information, see Appendix 5.
83. D. Smith (1998) *Disney A to Z. The Updated Official Encyclopedia* (New York: Hyperion), p. 332.
84. C. de Maussion (1992) 'L'autre Disney: le studio de production de Hollywood', *Communication & Langages*, (92), 49–61.
85. Interview with a former Senior Vice President at Disney studios who has since become a producer, 5 January 2007. See also Stewart, *Disney War*, p. 119, 142.
86. A. Scott (2004) 'Hollywood and the World: the Geography of Motion-Picture Distribution and Marketing', *Review of International Political Economy*, 11 (1), February, 38.
87. Interview with R. Cort, producer having worked with the Disney Company, 10 August 2006. For more information, see Appendix 5.
88. Stewart, *Disney War*, p. 22.
89. Interview with R. Cort.
90. E. Durkheim (1998/1893) *De la division du travail social* (Paris: PUF), p. 46.
91. Disney has tried to produce animated films outside the Walt Disney Studios since the 2000s, but has not been successful. Vanguard Animation's *Valiant* (2005) was created in the United Kingdom, while C.O.R.E. Feature Animation's *The Wild* (2006) was created in Toronto.
92. Interview with S. Hulett.

93. The ranking of the top 20 all-time worldwide grossing movies can be found at http://www.boxofficemojo.com.
94. Interview with J. Holder.
95. MPAA (2015) 'The Economic Contribution of the Motion Picture & Television Industry to the United States', accessed at http://mpaa.org.
96. T. Miller, N. Govil, J. McMurrin, R. Maxwell and T. Wang (2005) *Global Hollywood 2* (London: British Film Institute), pp. 50, 213.
97. N. Vulser (2005) 'L'alliance de l'économie et de la diplomatie américaines en Europe', *Le Monde*, 27 July, 25; J. Ulff-Moller (2001) *Hollywood's Film Wars With France: Film-Trade Diplomacy and the Emergence of the French Film Quota Policy* (Rochester: University of Rochester Press).
98. The Blum-Byrnes agreements were signed on 28 May 1946 between the US Secretary of State, James Byrnes, and the President of the French government, Léon Blum. They paved the way for the increased screening of American movies in French cinemas in exchange for US subsidies and support. See Laroche and Bohas, *Canal+*, p. 42.
99. B. McConnell (2004) 'Glickman Seizes MPAA Spotlight', *Broadcasting & Cable*, 20 December, 23; 'Glickman Replaces MPAA's Valenti' *Film Journal International*, 15 August 2004.
100. P. McClintock (2001) 'Copyright Campaign', *Variety*, 30 October.
101. P. Behr (1993) 'U.S., Europe Reach Trade Agreement', *Washington Post*, 15 December, A1.
102. D. Groves (2004) 'MPA Sues China Pirates', *Variety*, 15 February.
103. K. Bulkley (2004) 'MPA Strengthens Int'l Front in Its Fight Against Pirates', *The Hollywood Reporter*, 4 March, 6 (17).
104. A. Bohas (2015) 'Neopluralism and Globalization: the Plural Politics of the Motion Picture Association', *Review of International Political Economy*, 22 (6), 1199.
105. 'MPA Says Pirates Harder to Catch', *The Hollywood Reporter*, 22–8 July 2003, 69.
106. C. Coonan (2006) 'D.C.'s Piracy Barbs Find Mark in China', *Variety*, 15 February.
107. Cf., see the website of the MPA at http://www.mpaa.org.
108. J. Landreth (2006) 'Chinese Knock Anti-Piracy Effort', *The Hollywood Reporter*, 20 June, 6 (81).
109. B. Murdoch (2001) 'Aussie Group Targeting Piracy', *The Hollywood Reporter*, 13–9 April, 10.
110. E. Fitzpatrick (1997) 'MPAA Cracks Down on Piracy', *Billboard*, 109 (52), 27 December, 71.
111. B. Fritz ((2005) 'Studios Unite For a Piracy Fight', *Variety*, 19 September.
112. MPA (2008) 'Anti-Piracy Fact Sheet. Asia-Pacific Region', accessed on the website of the MPAA at http://mpaa.org, 1.
113. P. Frater (2006) 'MPA's Asia Antipiracy Drive Score', *Variety*, 25 July.

114. S. Wang (2003) *Framing Piracy: Globalization and Film Distribution in Greater China* (London: Rowman & Littlefield Publishers), p. 8.
115. F. Braudel (1985) *La Dynamique du capitalisme* (Paris: Champs/ Flammarion), p. 68.
116. See S. Strange and J. Stopford (1991) *Rival States, Rival Firms: Competition for World Market Shares* (Cambridge: Cambridge University Press).
117. S. Gill and A. C. Cutler (2014) *New Constitutionalism and World Order* (Cambridge: Cambridge University Press).
118. M. Keck and K. Sikkink (1998) *Activists Beyond Borders: Advocacy Networks in International Politics* (Ithaca: Cornell University Press).
119. Braudel, *La Dynamique du capitalisme*, pp. 84–9.
120. B. Lang (2014) 'Disney Hits $4 Billion at Global Box Office Thanks to "Maleficent", Marvel', *Variety*, 16 November; P. McClintock (2015) 'Fox Breaks Industry Record for Global Box Office', *The Hollywood Reporter*, 1st May. MPA-reported global box office revenues totalled $36.4 billion. According to early reports, Universal reached $6.9 billion and Disney 5.9 in a 2015 global box office of $38 billion. See D. McNary (2016) 'Universal, Disney Finish 2015 With Record Worldwide Grosses', *Variety*, 4 January.
121. CNC (2015) *Bilan 2014, Les dossiers du CNC*, May, 332, available at http://www.cnc.fr, p. 173.
122. P. Hoad (2013) 'Hollywood's hold over global box office—63% and falling', *The Guardian*, 2 April. The share of the US market around the world was estimated at 64 % in 2009, 67.4 % in 2010, 67 % in 2011 and 63 % in 2012. For the market share of US films in Europe, see European Audiovisual Observatory (EAO) (2012) *Yearbook 2012. Television, Cinema, Video and On-demand Audiovisual Services in Europe*, vol. 2 (Strasbourg: Council of Europe), p. 235.
123. EAO (2014) *Yearbook. Television, Cinema, Video and On-demand Audiovisual Services in Europe*, vol. 1 (Strasbourg: Council of Europe), p. 80. EAO (2007) *Yearbook. Film, Television, Video and New Medias in Europe*, vol. 3 (Strasbourg: Council of Europe), p. 30.
124. EAO, *Yearbook 2012*, p. 124.
125. CNC, *Bilan 2014*, p. 131.
126. CNC (2014), 'Films à télévision' in CNC, *Bilan 2014*, available at http://www.cnc.fr.
127. EAO, *Yearbook 2012*, p. 18.
128. MPA, *Theatrical Market*, p. 5.
129. W. Ma and L. Burkitt (2013) 'American Movies Lose Market Share in China', *The Wall Street Journal*, 23 October.

130. N. McCarthy (2014) 'Bollywood: India's Film Industry By the Numbers', Forbes, 9 March; MPAA (2015) *2014 Theatrical Market Statistics*, available on the MPAA website.
131. CNC (2014) *Bilan 2013*, *Les dossiers du CNC*, (330), May, 179.
132. Interview with B. Mechanic. Most revealing is also the dubbing of films. The Japanese version of the film Pearl Harbor (2001) was adapted for the audience. While the sentence 'a few less dirty Japs' has been replaced in Japan by 'a few less Japs', Alec Baldwin's reply 'I would kill as many of those bastards as possible' was suppressed. See C. Lyons (2001) 'Building a Safer 'Harbor'', *Variety*, 383 (2), 28 May, 2.
133. N. Vivarelli (2005) 'Pol Plucks Up Voice for Toon', *Variety*, 401 (3), 5 December, 9 (1).
134. R. Keegan (2014) ''Frozen': Finding a Diva in 41 languages', *Los Angeles Times*, 24 January.
135. Interview with S. Hulett.
136. Interview with S. Hulett.
137. By contractually limiting the distribution windows for theatres, and methods and costs of film transport, major studios were judged guilty of 'according their commercial policies with respect to the exhibitors and divvying up consequently a substantial part of the cinematographic distribution market'. See 'Spain Stuns Majors on Antitrust', *The Hollywood Reporter*, 16–22 May 2006, 51; A. Baker (2013) 'EU Probes Hollywood Film Licensing Deals with Pay-TV Groups', *Financial Times*, 22 November; A. Barker (2015) 'Brussels in Antitrust Case Against Sky and Six Hollywood Studios', *Financial Times*, 23 July.
138. Gomery, *The Hollywood Studio System: a History*.
139. For example, see 'Pixar Shifts Gears with 'Cars'', *Variety*, 397 (4), 13 December 2004, 1 (5). The article reports postponed theatre and video releases such as *Cars* from November 2005 to June 2006. Disney's film *Chicken Little* and Sony's sequel *The Legend of Zorro* took the slot left by *Cars* whereas DreamWorks shifted *Shrek the Third*'s release from fall 2006 to summer 2007.
140. See the website of United International Pictures, http://www.uip.com/about.php.
141. HBO settled as early as 1991 in central Europe, and in 1992 in Asia and Latin America where it has provided cinema channels. It belongs to the three major studios, Time Warner, Disney and Sony.
142. F. Montarini (2002) 'La distribution des films européens sur le marché américain' in T. Paris (ed.) *Special Issue*: *Quelle diversité face à Hollywood?*, *Cinémaction*, (92), March. My translation.
143. Interview with D. Kornblum.
144. Interview with B. Mechanic.

145. J. Hiestand (2002) 'Dis, Telefonica in Film Venture', *The Hollywood Reporter*, 4 (34), 24 January.
146. 'Mouse House Displays Foreign Prowess', *Variety*, 396 (3), 6 September 2004, 1 (2).
147. R. Smith (1999), 'Disney Story Old News to Wall St', *Variety*, 377 (1), 15 November, 5. The stated ratio does not take into account the activity of the ABC network in 1995.
148. Mouse House, *Variety*.
149. D. McNary (2016) 'Universal, Disney Finish 2015 With Record Worldwide Grosses', *Variety*, 4 January.
150. Braudel, *La Dynamique*, pp. 85–6.
151. Braudel, *La Dynamique*.
152. P. Dicken (2003) *Global Shift: Transforming the World Economy* (London: Sage), pp. 22–4.
153. On cluster analyses, see the reference book, M. Porter, *The Competitive Advantage of Nations*.
154. Interview with M. Taylor, independent producer, 3 August 2006. For more information, see Appendix 5.
155. Interview with J. Holder.
156. Interview with J. Squire.
157. W. Baumol, J. Panzar and R. D. Willig (1982) *Contestable Markets and the Theory of Industry Structure* (New York: Harcourt Brace Jovanovich).
158. Braudel, *La Dynamique*, p. 61.
159. EAO, *Yearbook 2012*, p. 236.
160. CNC (2015) *Bilan 2014*, May, (332), accessed at http://www.cnc.fr, p. 166 *ff.* See also C. Forest (2001) *Économie contemporaine du cinéma en Europe. L'improbable industrie* (Paris: CNRS Éditions), p. 223.
161. P. Parisi (2006) 'The Sky's the Limit', *Hollywood Reporter Independent Producers & Distributors*, 1 August, 98–9, 106; R. Keegan (2008) 'Financial Crisis Puts Squeeze on Hollywood', *Time*, 18 September; P. McClintock (2008) 'Industry Feels Wrath of Economy', *Variety*, 7 November.
162. Interview with R. Bonnell, former President Cinema at the Canal+ Group, 8 June 2006. For more information, see Appendix 5.
163. J. Bates (1992) 'Back in the Limelight: Carolco Pictures to Receive a $120-Million Bailout From Investors', *Los Angeles Times*, 25 December, http://articles.latimes.com/1992/dec/25.
164. M. Matzer (1998) 'European Firms to Invest in Spyglass', *Los Angeles Times*, 29 October; M. Goodridge (2003) 'Spyglass: the True Independent', *Screen International*, 12 December.
165. P. Frater (2015) 'China Rising: How Four Giants Are Revolutionizing the Film Industry', *Variety*, 3 February.
166. C. Coonan (2015) 'Lionsgate Unveils Film Financing Deal With China's Hunan TV', *The Hollywood Reporter*, 17 March.

167. P. McClintock (2009) 'Studio Gets $825 Million in Financing', *Variety*, 17 August.
168. P. Frater (2014) 'India's Reliance: Still a DreamWorks Backer, But Hollywood Sojourn Has Cost a Fortune', *Variety*, 14 May.
169. M. Taylor (2014) *Film and Television Production: Overview of Motion Picture Industry and State Tax Credits*, Legislative Analyst's Office, 30 April, available at http://www.lao.ca.gov, p. 10.
170. Los Angeles County Economic Development Corporation (LAEDC) (2015) *Otis Report on the Creative Economy of California*, April, available at http://www.otis.edu, p. 19; Los Angeles County Economic Development Corporation (2015) *Otis Report on the Creative Economy of the Los Angeles Region*, March, available at http://www.otis.edu, p. 20.
171. Los Angeles County Economic Development Corporation, *Otis Report*, Los Angeles Region, pp. 34–6.
172. For example, Michael Eisner, former CEO of Disney, earned a salary of $737 million between 1995 and 2000. See B. Schiffman (2001) 'Michael Eisner: Mouse in a Gilded Mansion', *Forbes*, 26 April.
173. M. Dale (1997) *The Movie Game. The Film Business in Britain, Europe and America* (London: Cassell).
174. Interview with S. Hulett.
175. Braudel, *La Dynamique*, p. 94.
176. Braudel, *La Dynamique*.
177. S. Strange (1994) *States and Markets*, 2nd edn. (London: Pinter), pp. 24–5.
178. M. Lev-Ram (2014) 'Disney CEO Bob Iger's Empire of Tech', *Fortune*, 29 December.
179. Interview with a former President of cinema in the Studio Canal+ group, 4 May 2006.
180. Working at the firm for 14 years, Etienne de Villiers, President of Walt Disney International Europe, comes from South Africa. As for Michael Johnson, after a stint of 13 years in the home video division, he is in charge of the Asian branch. See E. Guider (1999) 'House of Mouse Expands', *Variety*, 375 (7), 28 June, 27.
181. Walt Disney Company (2000) *1999 Annual report* (Burbank: Walt Disney Company), p. 13.
182. M. Marr and N. Wingfield (2006) 'Disney Sets $7.4 Billion Pixar Deal', *The Wall Street Journal*, 25 January.
183. B. Lang (2015) 'Disney Set to Dominate as it Unleashes Full Power of Pixar, Marvel and "Star Wars"', *Variety*, 22 April.
184. D. Dayan and E. Katz (1992) *Media Events. The Live Broadcasting of History* (Cambridge, MA: Harvard University Press), p. 5, 89. On the subject of media events, see N. Couldry, A. Hepp and F. Krotz (2010) (eds.) *Media Events in a Global Age* (Abingdon: Routledge).

185. 'Star Wars, Disney and myth-making', *The Economist*, 19 December 2015; P. McClintock (2016) 'Star Wars: Force Awakens'.
186. T. Sotinel (2007) 'Des mondes imaginaires pour bons et méchants', *Le Monde*, 28 March, 29.
187. R. Bonnell (2001) *La Vingt-cinquième image. Une économie de l'audiovisuel* (Paris: Gallimard), p. 14.
188. I. Mohr (2006) 'Summer Shakedown', *Variety*, 3–7 August; D. McNary (2006) 'O'seas B.O. Bounces', *Variety*, 29 December, 1 (2).
189. On these subjects, see C. Weinberg (2005) 'Profits Out of the Picture' in C. Moul (2005) (ed.) *A Concise Handbook of Movie Industry Economics* (Cambridge: Cambridge University Press), pp. 170–2; J. Arquembourg, G. Lochard and A. Mercier (2007) (eds.) *Événements mondiaux, regards nationaux*, *Hermès*, (46), spring, pp. 13–21.
190. P. McClintock (2014) '$200 Million and Rising: Hollywood Struggles with Soaring Marketing costs', *The Hollywood Reporter*, 31 July.
191. See CNC (2015) *Bilan 2014*, *Les dossiers du CNC*, (332), May, 112.
192. CNC, *Bilan 2014*, 101.
193. CNC, *Bilan 2014*, 131.
194. CNC, *Bilan 2014*, 136.
195. A. Feitz (1992) 'Euro Disney: Dissection d'un lancement', *Médias*, (327), April, 24–33.
196. Porter, *The Competitive Advantage of Nations.*

CHAPTER 3

The Rise of Entertainment Economy: A Disneyisation of Hollywood

The Integration of Hollywood in Global Strategies

The Organisational Transformation of Studios

Major studios have entered into much larger media strategies of giant conglomerates over the last few decades, playing a key economic role and forming an entertainment centre for the world-economy. Conglomerate logics have permeated the entire Hollywood sector, resulting in two major consequences. Firstly, conglomerates have acquired studios to ensure that they conform to and enhance their own entertainment business strategies. Secondly, Hollywood has become the centre of a globally organised audio-visual industry, in which motion picture production is no longer regarded as an essential activity—multimedia integration has deprived cinema of its unique status as an entertainment hub. It now represents only one vehicle for entertainment dissemination.

Following the evolution of their sectors, major studios are focusing on two major trends. Firstly, from a sectoral perspective, television programmes still represent considerable activity for major studios while the digital format is the fastest growing segment. From 2014 to 2019, global media and entertainment economies are expected to increase from $1.7 trillion to $2.2 trillion, growing at an annual pace of 5 %. Over the same period,

A. Bohas, *The Political Economy of Disney*, International Political Economy Series, DOI 10.1057/978-1-137-56238-8_3

global digital advertising is expected to grow by 12 %, and global electronic home video, including video on demand and over-the-top video/streaming, by 19 %. Notably, electronic home video revenue is predicted to overtake earnings from physical home video, including the purchase of DVD.[1]

Secondly, geographically, the Asia Pacific region holds most of the potential for growth in entertainment and media. In the next five years, growth in China is forecast to rise at an average annual rate of 14.5 % in film entertainment. It is poised to become the second largest entertainment and media market by 2018, just behind the United States.[2] From 2013 to 2018, India and China are expected to gain 750 million mobile internet subscribers compared with 94 million in the United States. This signals how growth in the entire sector is based primarily in these regions.[3] Although these forecasts always remain uncertain and controversial, they nevertheless underline that a global perspective in the media and entertainment sectors is essential for the study of Hollywood firms since they seek to invest in the most dynamic sectors.

In this context, the Disney Company represents the contemporary model of a major studio, disseminating commercial narratives outside motion picture sectors. Disney has been connected to the rest of the economy from the very beginning. Indeed, deprived of a network of cinema theatres, the company relied on non-audio-visual activities and consumer products to be profitable. Its expansion took place not only in the audiovisual domains but also in the entertainment industry generally.

In the history of Hollywood, and before the two sectors merged, the reluctance of the motion picture industry to produce for television is often discussed. However, the Disney studio began to work for television very early on. At the time, its leader, Walt Disney, wanted to develop a theme park in Anaheim, California. As this project required huge financial investment, Walt approached American TV networks offering a partnership. After the refusal of David Sarnoff and William S. Paley, respectively heads of NBC and CBS, he contacted Leonard Goldenson, Chairman of ABC, in 1953. They quickly signed a deal in which ABC agreed to finance the construction of Disneyland, taking a 35 % share in the park in exchange for the participation of Walt Disney on a weekly broadcast programme. A ten-year concession on the restaurants in the park was also included in the deal. In October 1954, the TV programme rapidly became popular, even appearing at the top of audience ratings.[4]

Although the company was already successful through animated films and their by-products, its television programmes reinforced familiarity with Disney symbolic imagery, while introducing TV viewers to the attractions of the theme park. The *Disneyland* programme was broadcast on ABC from 27 October 1954 until 3 September 1958. The show drew attention to the various 'lands' of the Disney Park which opened in July 1955. As Douglas Gomery wrote: 'The fundamental nature of the studio system changed on that hot July day [17 July 1955] as Disney and ABC linked film-making, television production and the amusement park business'.[5] In addition, the television film *Davy Crockett: King of the Wild Frontier* (1955) was also broadcast during the programme. It immediately reached record audiences, which led Walt Disney to turn it into a feature film. The latter became a hit. In addition to box office revenues, the original soundtrack remained at the top of US charts for 16 weeks and the sales of its by-products grossed more than $300 million. Capitalising on this notoriety, theme parks included activities using this narrative, such as the Davy Crockett's Explorer Canoes ride in Florida. The year 1955 was a momentous year for entertainment companies, with park and television combinations and the Davy Crockett phenomenon—the first fully fledged franchise.

Walt Disney used many forms of business synergies. Commonly, the term synergy refers to the opportunity for organisations to generate greater value. Five types of synergies can be identified that emphasise the benefits of companies working together: sharing know-how or tangible resources; pooling negotiating power; co-ordinating strategies; integrating vertically; and combining business creation. All of these can lead to more effective production and a better competitive advantage.[6] They explain the increasingly close integration of audio-visual sectors. Disney employed these techniques when, for example, it launched its distribution network in the 1950s and bought the ABC network in 1996. In particular, it was in the firm's best interest to acquire production and distribution capacities, which enabled it to cash in on the profits generated by its creations, stemming from the opportunities generated by new technologies and the expansion of transnational firms. For the past several decades, the notion of synergy has justified many mergers and acquisitions, whose potential benefits have sometimes turned out to be overestimated.[7]

Still, one crucial aspect of Disney imageries is missing in this analysis—its cultural dimension. The familiar Disney brand name coupled with well-loved and instantly recognisable story lines, content and characters, easily accessible in many forms—retail outlets, television, cinema, books, music and much more—represents what accountants refer to as an 'intangible asset', often a source of considerable profit in itself. The commercial preponderance of Hollywood studios can be measured in two ways. Firstly, they are major global audio-visual distribution companies from a economic standpoint. Secondly, they benefit from the attraction of familiar and compelling symbols and narratives. Their products have a transnational appeal which enables them to avoid sociocultural obstacles that they could encounter outside their home market, something Wasko refers to as 'cultural discount'.[8] This one specific type of synergy—the direct use or licensing of an intangible asset on a global basis—has accounted for a large proportion of studios' revenues.

Moreover, synergetic practices have intensified for several decades with the combining of motion picture studios and television companies. Audio-visual productions, like theme parks and by-products, increase the notoriety of narratives. In the routines of daily life, television contributes to instilling practices and to reinforcing recognition of symbols. The presence of Walt Disney in every home played a major role in the construction of the character 'Uncle Walt' in collective imaginaries, but also in the attachment to the Disney label. According to Steven Watts, Uncle Walt accompanied the American population throughout the twentieth century.[9] He appeared for years in US television programmes, embodying the values of middle-America, and audiences felt close to him. This dimension of producer-presenter was missing abroad, which deprived the company of an emotional dimension. In a questionnaire conducted among the French population, when the name 'Walt Disney' was evoked, only 1 % immediately referred to the historical founder of the firm, often in relation to an exhibition of his art which was taking place at the same time in the Grand Palais in Paris. In fact, as we will see later, national contexts—in this case 'structures of feeling'—intervene in the adoption of interwoven and dense global flows.[10]

The firm also became involved in children's TV programmes. As early as 3 October 1955, Disney produced a TV series dedicated to youngsters, *The Mickey Mouse Club*, which broadcast on a daily basis cartoons, documentaries, songs, dances and series, such as *The Adventures of Spin and Marty* (1955), *Border Collie* (1955–6) and *The Secret of Mystery Lake* (1956–7). Two adults, Jimmie Dodd and Roy Williams presented the show around a group of children, called the Mouseketeers, who wore Mickey's famous ears. In addition, this programme was an audio-visual adaptation of the real Mickey Mouse Club. Created in 1929, the club had more than one million members in 1932.[11] In this case, the 'spin-off' activity preceded the audio-visual content, so the TV content was the by-product. As I will point out later, contents have complex relations with their supposed by-products and spin-off activities.

In the United States, motion picture and televisual fields have merged. The integration of these two spheres has led to similar practices. Many actors, such as George Clooney or Johnny Depp, and many executives, such as Robert Iger and Michael Eisner, respectively CEO and former CEO of the Disney Company, began their careers on television. This interpenetration brought about the emergence of television stardom, which in turn resulted in considerable sales of goods. Successful series gave rise to franchises such as *Hannah Montana* (2006–11) and *High School Musical* (2006–8).[12] Hilary Duff became famous thanks to the series *Lizzie McGuire* broadcast on the Disney Channel from 2001 to 2004 and *The Lizzie McGuire Movie* (2003) released under the Walt Disney Pictures label. More recently in 2012, the TV series *Violetta*, a co-production of Argentine and European Disney divisions, has appeared in 140 countries and 15 languages. Entirely produced and programmed outside the United States, this franchise has generated many consumer product lines, music albums and concert tours in South America and Europe.[13]

Following the acquisition of the ABC group, the Disney firm became a colossal business entity whose media networks formed the main division. They have accounted for more than 40 % of net sales and more than 50 % of operating income in the last ten years.[14] They include the American ABC network and a number of thematic channels like ESPN and the Disney Channel. They also include the production and distribution activities regarding television. Over the last few decades, television activity has boomed abroad with the Disney Channel and the ABC-Disney Television Group. Launched on 18 April 1983, the Disney channel rapidly expanded at the global level. The Disney Channel Worldwide is a portfolio of 107 channels available in 163 countries and 431 million households and watched by more than 600 million viewers.[15] This has led analysts to conclude that television has replaced cinema as the key 'brand ambassador'.[16] As Charlie Nelson, former Vice President for marketing at Disney, asserted, 'the one luxury that Disney has over literally everybody else is the Disney Channel, watched by 80 million households [in the United States], 24 hours a day. All you see is Disney, Disney, Disney, Disney … That is a huge luxury'.[17] Disney Media Distribution is responsible for the diffusion of all 30,000 hours of programmes from the Walt Disney Company with 1,300 partners in 240 territories.[18] While the Walt Disney Studios, formerly Buena Vista, distribute movies, the Disney-ABC Television Group disseminates television programmes.

The transnational expansion of Disney content, narratives and symbols has seen vast platforms of merchandising become increasingly widespread globally. Its diverse programmes promote the rest of the firm's divisions, including its films, theme parks and by-products. This movement of concentration and integration is a general trend among media and telecommunications companies.[19] Many mergers and acquisitions have led to the formation of conglomerates acquiring activities often having nothing to do with motion pictures.[20] The compression of sectors notably results in media companies buying out strategic providers for their content. For instance, 20th Century Fox, the new company spin-off of News Corporation, and Time-Warner acquired complementary activities to content production, such as satellite and cable distribution firms. The acquisition of cross-sector businesses increases operational opportunities. Major providers are also seeking to acquire production capacities. When Comcast tried to purchase Disney for $66 billion in February 2004, its aim was to obtain considerable assets in audio-visual production, seeking to form an entire media group.[21] It would have brought Disney in line with the rest of the sector. Indeed, this company based all of its development on the ownership of content imagery, taking control of the ABC network and the independent production company, Miramax. Other major studios have fitted into giant conglomerates, such as Columbia-Tristar which is owned by Sony. However, Comcast failed to acquire Disney and eventually bought out NBCUniversal in 2013. In this context of sectoral mergers and acquisitions, Disney became a vast entity with economic and political power. Based on production content it remains the only stand-alone major studio.

The integration of major studios into the commercial strategies of conglomerates has changed considerably over the past century. Firstly, for much of the twentieth century, the practice seemed to be to the advantage of the major studios. Although the media sector was originally much more fragmented with businesses separated depending upon their technological base, strict regulations and individual practices,[22] the movie industry formed a rigid and stable bloc with five or six major studios securing most of the revenue. They were the spearhead of entertainment, dominating other sectors such as music and live comedy. With the boom in multimedia diffusion, the rise of television along with changes in sociocultural behaviour, these organisations were transformed and the stakes became very high with the onset of the globalisation of culture. In fact, global convergence appeared possible in a transnational and multi-format way. Similar to the advent of sound in films, this change in the scope of the movie industry resulted in winners and losers: the former profiting from a world market and colossal budgets; the latter marginalised owing to declining profits and foreign competition.

Secondly, where the studio system of the classical era was based on movie theatres, studios are now absorbed within larger companies which expand value chains.[23] According to estimates, revenues coming from global film entertainment will amount to $105 billion in 2019, representing 5 % of the $2.2 trillion leisure and media economy.[24] In addition and strictly speaking, movie operations, including development, production and distribution have turned out to be less profitable, even loss-makers at times.[25] This data must be compared with the two-digit operating incomes in the media and television sectors.[26]

Thirdly, major studios are now integrated in the expansion strategies of vast companies. During the interwar period, they maintained continuous relations with financing partners due to the large budgets required for production. The separation between movie theatrical networks and the rest of the studios made them even more reliant on external partners and financial sources. At the time, conglomerates owned major studios in order to diversify their business with countercyclical activities. In this context, the operations of major studios basically remained unchanged because they were acquired precisely for their economic specificity. Since the 1980s, major studios have faced a different kind of motivation for acquisitions. Large media companies bought out major studios to integrate them in their development strategy. An interviewee characterises such organisational changes in these terms: ‘beforehand, buying a studio came down to going to Hollywood. Today new owners use the studio according to their strategy’.[27] Indeed, mergers occurred between companies specialising in the information and audio-visual sectors. For instance, in 1986, the News Corporation purchased 20th Century Fox and, in 1989, Sony acquired Columbia Tristar which previously belonged to the Coca-Cola Company.

As Michael Nathanson, a sector analyst, has shown, the major studios have increased their profits between 2007 and 2012 by slashing producers’ housekeeping deals and overheads, decreasing the movie slate by 34 % and focusing on franchises and big films, the so-called ‘tent-poles’, driving revenues of the whole conglomerate to the detriment of middle-of-the-range movies.[28] Overall, these changes led to a reduction in operating costs and film revenues but an increase in profits and return on invested capital. At Disney, the change has been all the more sweeping and complete with Robert Iger as CEO because, since the 1980s, Disney has notably become a fully fledged company by developing movies outside the Disney label, notably with Touchstone Pictures, Hollywood Pictures and Miramax. Robert Iger refocused the company around entertainment based on franchises. Motion picture production drastically decreased from 28 movies in 2006 to 11 in 2015 while new movies concentrated on big-budget Walt Disney Pictures blockbusters leading to lasting franchises. The success of the media company now hinges on three or four successful franchises per year from which stem consumer product lines, television programmes, sequels, live-action sequels, theatrical shows and Disney attraction makeovers. In this light, Disney's acquisition of Pixar, Marvel, and Lucasfilm's *Star Wars* along with the securing of rights for future *Indiana Jones* films appear as part of the company redeployments around existing and new global franchises.[29] Since this reshuffling, the Disney Company's shares and profits have outperformed its competing major studios.[30]

Now creative artists find themselves more constrained by the financial objectives imposed by shareholders of the conglomerates. Although such a control has always existed, the business goal has changed these days. The choice of production slate is based on the return on investment of films not only in the movie sector but also outside it, in the entertainment business. So their creative role is redirected outside their primary sector, leading to a harshly-perceived financial restriction for medium-budget films. Many producers that were interviewed and who preferred to remain anonymous regretted that 'studios were more interested in making *Spiderman*, and *X-Men*, and *Superman* [...] If I want to make a small independent film, that's not a film that any studio is going to make'.[31] Even Bill Mechanic, who encouraged movies with a global audience, reproached top management from media companies for their lack of interest in cinema.[32] He headed the 20th Century Fox studio from 1993 to 2000, contributing to its expansion through major hits such as the *X-Men* series (2000, 2003 and 2006) and *Titanic* (1997). His outright opposition to Rupert Murdoch, News Corporation's CEO, clearly shows the friction existing between studios looking for profitable motion pictures on the one hand, and bigger conglomerates targeting entertainment strategies to create greater value for their shareholders on the other.

The Global Reordering of Production Processes

In the cultural domain, major studios relocate certain production phases outside Hollywood and the United States. This results in sectoral specialisation of national centres depending on the decisions made in Hollywood. Indeed, close but asymmetrical interdependence unites the centre to the periphery in world cinema. To a certain extent, the transnational division of cultural labour into productive spheres with the production of specific phases abroad can be observed.[33] As a result, major studios redeploy their activity outside Hollywood whose main role lies in making decisions rather than in actually producing films. The more the world-economy expands, the more the centre proves to be a global hub rather than a production centre.

The denationalising effect of globalisation has afforded many opportunities to produce movies at lower costs outside California, by using cheaper foreign infrastructures.[34] This phenomenon, along with increasing reliance on outsourcing, started to occur at the end of the classical era of the major studios. The studio no longer carried out every stage of production internally. The fragmentation of productive structures made foreign subcontracting possible because it decreased the 'mechanical solidarity'[35] and the loyalty of major studios to a particular staff. The generalisation of an 'organic solidarity' contributed to this international outsourcing. Consequently, delocalisations were part of the reordering of the studio system. Indeed, the interconnectedness of national creation centres has grown, forming a 'dense dynamic'[36] at the transnational level. On this subject, producer Michael Taylor explains that outsourcing

> happens all the time. It is a very old practice [...] Originally all films were made in Hollywood [...] All of a sudden that changed around the mid-fifties [...] That has been an issue for many years in this town [Hollywood]. I have made movies in Romania, Hungary, Canada and elsewhere such as Jamaica. None of those films were meant to take place in the country that they were shot in.[37]

In Asia, outsourcing appeared very advantageous for studios. When Disney increased its production in animation (feature films and TV films) in 1984, it settled in Japan. In April 1989, Walt Disney Animation Japan brought together its subcontractors. Then, Disney Japan went to China and South Korea because of a workforce shortage in Japan. At the time, producing an animated film would require up to 1,000 people.[38] As an example of the workforce diversity, Pacific Rim Productions in Beijing painted the bubbles of *The Little Mermaid* (1989).[39] More recently, the filming of traditional cartoons has been outsourced to Asia. These relocations have proved to be positive insofar as firms profited from the pre-existing industrial network. As they had already worked with Western television, they had developed know-how corresponding to Hollywood standards.[40]

Outsourcing certain phases of production nevertheless implies additional expenditure, even when considering films made in Canada. These require the insertion of US symbols and signs before the global launching of the film. In fact, it is mainly a question of replacing flags, license plates, police cars and mailboxes. For instance, in the *X-Files* series, the 'Americanisation' of the episodes consisted of shooting the FBI building in Washington DC.[41] In this respect, specialists in world cinema observed that 'runaway productions have been viewed as distinct cultural productions in need of intense international pre- and post-production editing, or cleansing'.[42] In addition, when the Disney firm has integrated local works into its programming, it needed close partnerships to develop specific types of content.[43]

These decisions depend on financial calculations about the production cost and savings that such relocation may bring about. In this respect, the huge salaries of film actors, growing distribution costs and escalating production budgets tend to reinforce the search for cheap labour and infrastructure. As world-renowned artists remain irreplaceable and expensive owing to their fame, studios make savings on the rest of the production process. Additional reasons for outsourcing are the differences in legal and socio-cultural contexts from one country to another. Companies take full advantage of heterogeneous sectors at the international level. For example, the remake of *Three Men and a Baby* (1987) was mainly shot in Toronto, except for one week in New York City, owing to favourable legislation on child labour laws.[44] In Paris, French animators working for Disney were appreciated for 'their more classical training [in painting and drawing] that the people in the States don't have'.[45] In this respect, Steve Hulett remembers a similar structuration in animation: 'The Disney studio in Paris was the only foreign site to deal with animated feature film. Other foreign studios, such as those of Toronto, Vancouver and Sydney were in charge of direct-to-video films'.[46] Moreover, the involvement of major studios depends on the local socio-economic network as well as existing assets. In this respect, digitalisation and world interconnectedness have made data transfer inexpensive and instantaneous, which has led studio executives to work with very remote creation centres. On all these subjects, globalisation has reinforced transnational industrial relationships. At the heart of this process, economic and cultural dynamics prevail over national criteria.

Successive studies have shown that this trend of runaway production is structural. The loss of activity in the Los Angeles area was estimated at $2.8 billion in 1998 compared to $500 million in 1990. These relocations have since only intensified, amounting to losses of more than $23 billion and 47,000 full-time jobs between 1998 and 2005.[47] A 2005 analysis conducted by the Los Angeles County Economic Development Corporation (LAEDC) estimated that 48 % of independent films were shot in the United States, outside California. As for films of the major studios, 45 % of the shootings took place outside the United States.[48] More recently, according to a FilmL.A. research study on 2014 Hollywood films, 69 of the 106 movies surveyed for the study were primarily produced in the United States and 22 in California, 4 of which were animated films.[49] Between 1997 and 2014, California's share of the top 25 movies at the worldwide box office fell from 68 % to 28 %. Outside California, almost all of them were produced in Canada, the United Kingdom, New York or Louisiana.[50]

In this respect, almost no developing countries appear as primary production locations, with the exception of Morocco and India in the 2014 rankings. In the pecking order for countries chosen for outsourcing, the most innovative tasks are performed in developed countries, while manufacturing is on the contrary primarily undertaken in the developing countries. A study on the origin of Disney goods has shown that 92 % of audio-visual relocations took place in industrialised zones. The manufacturing of toys, jewellery and ceramics amounted to 20 % from these countries. Thus, the productive redeployment of major studios follows pre-existing configurations which give rise to unequal exchanges between Hollywood and the rest of the sector.[51] In this respect, one can identify the three-tier 'world-economy' described by Fernand Braudel, referred to in the previous chapter. Outside the centre, his theory distinguishes the periphery from the semi-periphery. The semi-periphery has productive links and conducts trade with the world centre and yet is not totally dependent on it.

In addition, the power of each major studio is greater in foreign sectors than in Los Angeles where the presence of many production companies creates more favourable situations for talent and technical crews. Consequently, foreign centres remain dependent on the goodwill of Los Angeles production companies. As an example, Canada suffered from the reduction in the number of US film productions. While it attracted 80 % of outsourcings at the beginning of the 2000s, this share was gradually reduced, notably with the rise of filming in the United Kingdom.[52] Cyclically, during periods of low exchange rates of the US dollar, Canadians were competing not only with London, Prague and Sydney but also with the US domestic states which developed tax credit policies in favour of film productions. Nowadays, after a period when production started returning to the United States, outsourcing is once again on the rise.[53] Moreover, Hollywood companies resorted to using 'location blackmailing'. Thus, several times in the 1990s and 2000s, and under pressure from the major studios, Canadian workers accepted a reduction in, or maintenance at a low level of, their welfare benefits, preferring to work with reduced social benefit protection rather than seeing employment opportunities disappear.[54] This competition among national centres has led to a reduction in salaries and less social protection.[55] In other words, room for manoeuvring remains very limited for foreign sectors because they cannot consider outsourcing a long-term activity.

In such a context of transnational rivalry, public authorities are reinforcing the competitiveness of their creation centres at every level. One can observe a surge of subsidies, tax cuts and public investments at local, regional and national levels, designed to bolster the attractiveness of the industry. With this goal, they make the sector more attractive by training cheap labour, building infrastructure and implementing tax loopholes. They want to encourage foreign investors and to attract production.[56] These efforts reveal not only the interest that institutions have for films, but also their wish to preserve or revitalise an economic and cultural network to suit multinational corporations. In South Africa, provided that 50 % of a film with a minimum budget is shot within the country, incentive policies offer a cash rebate of up to 35 %.[57] Some of the states in the USA have also sought to attract Hollywood producers thanks to tax loopholes and subsidy systems. In addition, large cities promote motion picture production. For example, New York financially encouraged the shooting and production of films in the city, while London has an agency specifically in charge of promoting cinema and television investment.[58] Such competition aims to maintain the attractiveness of national economies. But by no means is the state the only actor involved in the economic competition among regions.[59] Following our observations, this logic may be applied to any public entity, inducing major studios to relocate their production activities periodically.

Major studios are free to change sites according to variations in costs, currency exchange rates and national regulations and constraints, since public authorities make the heavy investments in infrastructure. Regularly, Hollywood producers change locations all the while maintaining relations with many foreign subcontractors, so the balance of power plainly lies in the hands of major studios. Indeed, they profit from the competition as workers vie to collaborate with them. On this subject, René Bonnell observes that 'when French workers fight each other to get a $100,000 deal with studios for special effects like in the case of Duran Duboi, you need to understand that they are fighting for their survival'.[60] In animation, creation centres are also vulnerable to companies' strategic redeployments. As an example, Walt Disney Feature Animation closed each of its sites in Florida, Montreuil (Paris), Sydney, Tokyo and Vancouver between 2003 and 2006. The studio preferred subcontracting to other companies in search of flexibility and cost effectiveness. For example, in the 2000s, Disney increasingly resorted to the Toon City Animation studio in Manila. Created in 1993, Toon City first produced for Walt Disney Television Animation and then got involved in direct-to-video sequels, such as *Tarzan II* (2005), and the prequel *Little Mermaid III* (2008), all the while working on TV shows for other studios, such as Warner Bros.' *The Looney Tunes Show* (2011). Indeed, new technologies have made 'outsourcing more practical than vertical integration. With Internet, one can send files in less than a second to Warsaw or Bangkok. Under these conditions, Disney no longer needed permanent teams in Paris'.[61] However, it appears more difficult to relocate facilities for producing quality cartoons because a long training period is required to master technical and artistic know-how and dexterity, and long-term public policies are needed to ensure it takes place. Investments such as the subsidy mechanism and the building of infrastructure presuppose the existence of a creative pole. As Steve Hulett has declared, 'a studio animation takes five to six years to become operational, the time for animators to acquire knowledge and experience'.[62]

As we have just seen, outsourcing of the productive process results in a structural change in the Hollywood centre and in the international configuration of motion picture sectors. But far from reducing the power of Hollywood, world fragmentation of the productive process strengthens its central position because the hierarchy of world cinema does not change. Interdependences remain strongly asymmetrical between Hollywood firms and national centres. Movie production centres are no longer autonomous since they are increasingly dependent on what Hollywood orders.

Hollywood companies benefit from this competition resulting from global compression in the sector. This global division of labour leads national centres to specialise in areas of production corresponding to their expertise. In other words, they lose their autonomy, remaining dependent on decisions from abroad on whether or not to produce films. Major studios remain world producers since they decide in Los Angeles on whether such-and-such a production will be given the 'green light' and where it will take place. They centralise there the 'dailies',[63] financial capacities, and symbolic attributes as well as the film's copyright. Finally, although major studios employ foreign workers, this outsourcing does not contribute to the prosperity of the sector as a whole—denying national production companies opportunities for turnover and profit does little to strengthen the industry.

Hollywood also deals with the definition of the film project which forms the primary stage. As Igor Khait said, 'once you come up with an idea, the rest is manufacturing'.[64] The key choices about projects—including an enthralling story, a scenario, the cast and funding—are made in California. Regarding traditional animation, American artists dominate the phases before direction, comprising script-writing, storyboard production and the exposure sheet.[65] Then, the drawing, colouring, inking, painting and photography can be done abroad. However, these tasks have been dramatically reduced owing to computer-generated animation. In other words, Americans coordinate the cinematographic process at the world level. They represent the true project supervisors. They centralise the decisions at every stage, having the money, the necessary contacts and the cultural knowledge.

The American centre of world cinema is fully in charge of the key stages of creation, while other phases are delegated to foreign sites controlled by the major studios. In fact, these phenomena are observed in all transnational processes—where leadership and innovative research are centralised, companies resort to sub-contracting and subsidiary entities for other functions.

The Studios at the Heart of the World-Economy

An Unfinished Strategy of Global Expansion

In addition to their central role in audio-visual sectors, the studios retain a strategic place in economic spheres. They market influential business symbols and narrative universes, which makes them attractive to other multinational companies. Hollywood companies disseminate their content globally thanks to multimedia structures. The following analysis of their activity will highlight their preponderance in entertainment sectors despite the international rather than global mindsets of their managers. The discussion will subsequently show their integration into global mass-markets and the specificity of these companies which are shaped by creative innovation.

The considerable flow of TV programmes from California to the rest of the world makes up a major part of international trade in this business sector—in fact it is very much one-way traffic. Hollywood does not replace nationally produced content, but its movies are often the only foreign option in many markets.[66] As discussed earlier, prime-time television programmes are either American or nationally (home) produced. This is the reason why national channels vie fiercely for new releases from the major studios. High-income regions import many productions from Hollywood. Even in countries such as France or South Korea, where national production receives significant government support, programmes are mostly for internal consumption—their exports represent only a small share of foreign box office.[67]

Structural power makes it possible for major studios to accumulate colossal profits from the commodification and multi-media roll-out of their films. Indeed, many different ways of disseminating films have become available since the 1950s. The expansion of television marked the beginning of media abundance. Admittedly, the small screen still remains central, whether transmitted via digital, analogue, video, satellite or cable technology. In addition to the diversity of formats, a series of factors, such as channel privatisations and deregulation, has contributed to increasing demand. All these transformations have brought about substantial income for major studios, which, according to Hal Richardson, was unexpected.[68] Hollywood firms played a key role in the expansion of audio-visual sectors around the world. They forcefully invested in national broadcasting. In each country where they affirmed their presence, they contributed to expanding the markets, thus encouraging additional outlets and formatting new behaviour. They particularly promoted individual consumption: all the offers converge from now on to offer greater choice and flexibility in the use and the quality of programmes. Thus, current opportunities deal with dissemination through a number of ever smaller and more mobile screens: electronic home video services are new channels which accompany already established pay TV, physical home video and TV networks.[69] In this respect, the Disney Company under the current CEO, Robert Iger, appears as the spearhead of digital Hollywood. As soon as he became the head of Disney in 2005, Iger signed a deal with Apple to put TV shows and then movies on iPads.[70] Disney also got a head start in clinching deals on online diffusion and in developing online businesses. In 2014, it launched an application called 'Disney Movies Anywhere', allowing people to watch its contents literally anywhere. At the same time it started a partnership with Netflix to produce online-only content.[71]

The prospects for growth are very high in newly developed areas. The Asia Pacific zone in particular remains largely privileged by major studios insofar as emerging middle classes represent most of the world growth potential.[72] In 2014, the turnover of Disney in this region amounted to only $3.9 billion, whereas it reached $36.8 billion in North America and $6.5 billion in Europe.[73] Despite small sales, the firm has invested in all sectors of entertainment. For example, since the 1990s, the Walt Disney Company has kept on investing in Asia year after year. From 1993 to 2003, its motion picture distribution division set up facilities in south-east Asian countries such as South Korea and Taiwan, and also in Australia and New Zealand—it distributed 250 films in ten years to those countries.[74] Since the Disney Channel was launched in 1995 in Taiwan, it has quickly developed throughout most of south-east Asia, reaching eight million subscribers in a few years. To achieve this, Disney significantly increased advertising and promotion of its brand, platforms and services operating within the national telecommunications and broadcasting sectors of the region.[75]

India and China form two continental countries in which major studios have invested strongly, being aware of their colossal potential for growth. However, the structural supremacy of Hollywood appears limited by factors which prevent major studios from imposing their commercial logic. Such obstacles come from legal and political agreements as well as from the lack of cultural socialisation. As in any sphere of knowledge, Hollywood imageries must adapt to national cultures and integrate with collective imaginaries. The arrival of major studios in these countries worries national operators competing in the same markets.[76] In China, tensions have arisen revealing reluctance towards adopting imported programmes. Protectionist measures have kept Western operators from acquiring a strong position. Indeed, Hollywood distributors are confronted with a quota system for foreign films, which is nevertheless slowly softening. In addition, they also face censorship and arbitrary measures. For instance, in June 2006, the Chinese government suddenly ended screening of the film *The Da Vinci Code* (2006) as Hollywood companies reached more than half of the national box office.[77] Public authorities also wanted to take advantage of the anniversary of the ruling regime to promote domestic movies. Some restrictions have been imposed over successful programmes. The Nickelodeon channel aggressively marketed imported content through the China Central Television (CCTV) channel. As a result the Chinese government forbade them from broadcasting during prime-time hours.

As for Disney, it has avoided discriminatory measures by engaging with national partners for TV programmes such as *Dragon Club*. Since it is limited by quotas for films as is any other foreign studio, Disney invested in all domestic entertainment sectors through partnerships with national firms. It partnered with Shanda Interactive Entertainment in online video games while co-producing animated films such as *The Magical Brush* (2014). Disney deepened relations with Shanghai Media Group for the children's animation series and other television productions. However, the most crucial initiative was the launching of Disney theme parks—Hong Kong Disneyland opened in 2006 and Shanghai Disneyland in 2016.

In India, the challenge for Hollywood companies is of a different kind, one consisting of economic competition and cultural adaptation. This country has the largest movie industry in terms of production, with more than one thousand feature films released every year in 30 dialects.[78] Its theatrical market reaches 2.6 billion admission tickets annually but only amounts to a box office of $1.6 billion.[79] Overseas theatrical revenues remain low, accounting for 6 % of overall film revenues.[80] Thus, major studios are competing with a vast and successful domestic industry. Their market share is estimated at just 10 %.[81] Disney has invested heavily in its Indian subsidiary. Since 2004, the Disney Channel have been active in India through cable and satellite networks. In 2006, Disney bought out Hungama TV, a channel devoted to children's broadcasts. At the same time, it co-produced with the UTV Communications group which it eventually acquired in 2011.[82] The latter is a diverse group engaged in TV and movie production, broadcasting and gaming. Estimates show that Disney networks reach 71 million Indian households and its programmes around 145 million.[83]

By diffusing their feature films in audio-visual format, cultural capitalists have initiated consumer practices on an international scale. Globalisation of their programmes remains unfinished, however. Although they are allegedly most committed to the globalisation of the audio-visual sector, Hollywood producers remain very United States-centred and only partially internationally minded.

Many producers have declared that from the very start of the creative process, they think not only of American audiences but also of global audiences. According to Michael Taylor, this mindset is specific to the Hollywood sector: 'Hollywood has always meant to be an international business [...] I try to find stories that I think have universal appeal and will play all over the world'.[84] However, several statements show an orientation which weakens such a global engagement. Indeed, Hal Richardson, senior executive in charge of distribution at Paramount, mentioned contradictorily on this subject, 'I can tell the production folks my thoughts [to make it easier to sell the film internationally] but that might make the movie less successful domestically'.[85] Hal Richardson's statement reveals the central place that the US market occupies from his perspective. However, as Bill Mechanic points out very pertinently, 'the US as good as it may be represents only 5 % of the world population. I have always thought that the opportunities were greater overseas'.[86] Moreover, the environment in which Californian employees work remains very US-centred. Thus, articles and deeper analyses deal with advertising, marketing and distribution by means of national estimates, appraisals and data. The area of attention is usually confined to North America. This is highlighted by articles published in the trade press which limit most of their indicators and articles to domestic or North American issues concerning promotion, licenses, home video and box office.[87] It's true, certain international estimates and appraisals are arguably hard to produce and are less likely to be reliable, but by no means is this an appropriate approach for a global industry. Besides, opinions with regard to foreign audiences often remain rudimentary. The only assumptions are that international audiences appreciate action and adventure films with special effects and well-known actors. In other words, the perception of the industry sector is far from being global.

The international distribution of film productions results in an uneven strategy of global development. Even if the leaders of studios want to invest fully in the global sphere, practices are far removed from achieving such a goal. An ideal type for such a global strategy would suppose that production be directly and transnationally managed from the profits that it makes and the costs that it incurs worldwide. Budgets would be allocated in the light of worldwide revenue expectations: 'every substantial production should be based on the prospect of global success'.[88] In this case, the Los Angeles headquarters would manage distribution networks with the support of their affiliated national companies. The studio would completely accept failures and successes. This strategy would lead to another film-making configuration than the one presently characterising the sector. Currently, the largest budgets are allocated to projects integrating well-known themes and actors, while less substantial financing is invested in films with more ambitious scenarios and style. In the case of true Hollywood globalisation, a global type of production would be adopted: productions likely to attract world audiences would get the largest budgets; content designed for certain transnational audiences would receive less funding; while productions only aimed at the national public would be reduced. For example, full-length films dealing with sports specific to the United States (American football or baseball, for example) would receive less money, and films dealing with truly global sports, such as football, would receive strongly increased financial support.

Unfortunately, this type of rationale appears to have minimal support in the studios. Before green-lighting a film, production executives should systematically ponder on possible successes outside America. In fact, Bill Mechanic said in 2006,

> Hollywood producers think too little of international markets. If I was questioning Warner Brothers making *Superman*, I would say that *Superman* is not a movie that can travel. *X-Men* can travel, *Superman* cannot travel because he wears red, white and blue [...] The world does not want Americanism [...] Any big budget should be justified by its vision of the world and that's why I would also recommend international directors.[89]

In other words, the global dimension is certainly taken into consideration, but it is not systematically at the centre of corporate strategy.

Observed practices of major studios simply reveal an international vision, rather than a global one. They often exploit their works in the domestic market, while they frequently sell the foreign distribution rights to other entities. They can give them to foreign counterparts or to another studio in order to reduce risk. Illustratively, two major studios have financed and distributed the long-time top-grossing blockbuster *Titanic* (1997). Indeed, when 20th Century Fox started to produce the film, it preferred to give international distribution rights to another major studio, Paramount. The film made $600 million from US domestic sales and grossed more than $1.2 billion worldwide. Major studios also co-finance films with smaller entities such as Carolco Pictures and Spyglass Entertainment, companies mentioned in Chap. 2. These practices also bring to light a national tropism which considers the domestic market to be the safest. Pre-sales have become common in the audio-visual sphere, which have led Hollywood to produce movies for the rest of the world. Frederick Wasser identifies such phenomena with the 'transnationalisation' of the sector, reusing the pioneer phrase of Dino de Laurentiis.[90] With hindsight, real global management would suppose direct distribution of the films. In this respect, the Disney studio occupies a special place. Marked by its founder Bill Mechanic, Buena Vista, now called Walt Disney Studios, instilled the company with a global vision of distribution during the 1990s and 2000s.[91]

Moreover, major studios cyclically withdraw from certain markets. They disengage from some while concluding new arrangements with others. This illustrates the lack of any systematic strategy of world development. Bill Mechanic reacted against such short-term calculations by creating Buena Vista International. He is in favour of sustainably investing in national sectors, which would mean distributing national films in order to obtain indisputable authority.[92] In fact, Jean-François Lepetit rightly underlines the permanent swing of the pendulum for major studios between establishing a national subsidiary after a series of successes on the one hand, and contracting a convenient alliance with a national partner after a series of failures on the other.[93] The first option increases fixed costs—and the risk—while the second one lowers the risk. However, in the second case, Hollywood capitalists also share the gains of film successes. Finally, this ambivalence further shows the lack of any global and systematic strategy for durable expansion.

The conglomerate logic ethos into which the major studios have entered slows down the dynamic of world cinema. It may streamline the sector, but it contributes also to the development of short-term risk management. Reducing risk implies sharing the production and distribution of films. Consequently, major studios often rely on external financing and other distributors because they are driven by 'an excess of caution and a lack of passion, creativity and conviction'.[94] They are also tempted to decrease the risks of creation in order to protect their finances. Thus, Hollywood decision makers reduce transnational motion picture phenomena by remaining state-centred and avoiding risky investments. Arguably the scale of US domestic sales within major studios' turnover suggests a lack of real global initiatives rather than an inability to succeed abroad. On this point, many big-budget films are intended primarily for America. As Bill Mechanic said in 2006, 'no national cinema exists solely inside their domestic border. The costs of making movies are too great'.[95]

The lack of global focus has nonetheless been slowly changing. As previously discussed, 70 % of the box office of major studios comes from foreign markets. In addition, many specialists estimate that major studios have adapted their strategy to favour an increase in the receipts coming from abroad. The rise of large adventure-type blockbusters with superheroes and special effects is associated with this internationalisation of Hollywood and the rise of markets such as China. The conquest of Chinese markets pushes Hollywood to locate a part of its production in China and to hire Chinese actors with pro-Chinese stories.[96] Consequently, one can agree with Hal Richardson that 'from mid-1990s on, international business has been huge [...] the international business has come into its own and become a much more focused part of the studio portfolio'.[97] But under no circumstances does it mean a real change in mindset from international to global.

Therefore the existence of the transnational capitalist class—to which Hollywood executives would belong—deserves to be reconsidered in the light of behaviour and practices. One may question its ability to 'have global rather than local perspectives on a variety of issues'.[98] If US studios were 'in the process of denationalizing, redefining [their] ties to [their] place of birth, and forging new ties with global markets and partners',[99] they would have a global vision. Admittedly, these leaders hold the majority of world production resources under their control and they are involved in global entertainment on many fronts. But, under no circumstances have they overtaken their national tropism.[100] They have difficulties in adopting a multinational viewpoint and yet paradoxically they commit substantial funds to globally distributed productions.

The Immersion of Cultural Capitalists into the Rest of the Economy

Hollywood companies take on economic and cultural dimensions since their business is based on the commercial exploitation of their creative content. They form colossal entities whose creative departments remain closely linked to the economic sphere. Major studios are immersed in the rest of the economy via the control of their shareholders, their executives and the economic and cultural alliances they form with other large companies. But a closer look at the careers of the top managers at Disney leads us to make a number of specific observations and conclusions.

The US financial and economic milieu keeps very close tabs on Hollywood's financial results. The first weekend box-office returns play a key role in assessing the potential of new productions. Business experts forecast future income at the box office and on ancillary markets, foreseeing the 'legs'[101] that the movie will have.[102] Thus, quotations of the studios on the stock market react to these performances. In addition, new projects are closely scrutinised—analyses compare previous films to projects of the same genres, and costs and revenues along with the release date are reviewed and analysed.[103] As for other studio divisions, they examine the quarterly income reports and the outcomes of any particular activity or event, such as the makeover of an attraction in a theme park.[104]

Large departments aim at diffusing films rather than at creating them. The marketing, distribution and home video departments are in charge of their dissemination. This study, based on the career paths and the trajectories of Disney executives, distinguishes different profiles.[105] Production executives move from one to another company and take up creative functions such as producers. Indeed, it is worth mentioning that interviewees with this profile gain multiple levels of experience by working for various companies. Robert Cort and Adam Leipzig both worked in various societies as independent producers and production supervisors. A study of the Disney staff confirms this report since it shows that a great number of its production Vice Presidents had already taken up similar responsibilities in different, independent entities—compared with their colleagues in different positions, production executives having a high chance of becoming producers. Previously they had worked in film and TV production (39 % and 23 % respectively) or in entertainment (11 %). More than one third of them had achieved a direct task in creation. After working for Disney, two thirds of them took on a direct role in motion picture creation mostly as producers.[106]

Other executives are much less integrated in the Hollywood creative milieu. Coming from many different sectors, they either continue working in a similar type of business or completely change career direction upon leaving the Disney Company. Very few of them choose to go into artistic creation. However, they play a major role in Hollywood firms, even in negotiating new production contracts. After they left the studio, only 50 % remained in the audio-visual industry, often taking on similar functions elsewhere. Furthermore, a third of these executives completely changed their career paths, moving into totally different sectors. In the end, the analysis revealed that these executives did not feel personally attached to the motion picture industry. It also revealed that employers in other economic sectors regard people coming from the movie sector as valuable. A job at a major studio can represent a valuable experience for a lawyer or a businessman—he or she can then easily find a higher position in another commercial activity.

Distribution executives remain more related to sectors other than film production. Before being employed by the Disney Company, only 5 % of them were directly involved in creative production and 10 % in production supervision, while half came from the audio-visual sphere and a third from distribution. After their employment at Disney, none of them assumed responsibilities in movie production except for Bill Mechanic and Ann Daly. Furthermore, only 18 % moved on to a creative activity.

The executives in charge of distribution and marketing represent the backbone of the firm. Their profiles clearly differ from those of other executives because they remain in the company longer. Indeed, over 38 % in these functions remained at Disney for the entire two-decade period of my study. In addition, from 1986 to 2006, distribution and marketing executives retained their positions on average for more than 17 years, whereas production supervisors only remained for 11 years. This differential was likely only to increase since many distribution and marketing leaders were still in charge at the end of the period under study. In addition, these analyses deal with leading managers, comprising the positions of senior vice presidents, executive vice presidents and presidents. Concerning simple 'veep' production (contraction of Vice President), the turnover is much higher. They generally remained no longer than four years. There is an inherently quicker rotation among managers supervising creative talent.

Outside the audio-visual sectors, major studios have developed enormous non-creative departments whose activities are diversified. Theme park divisions have substantial relations with sectors other than the audio-visual industry. In this respect, they remain closely dependent on living standards of the general public as the financial problems of Disneyland Paris have highlighted. The park required specialists in building, catering and accommodation engineering. For instance, along with the parks, the Walt Disney World Resort consists of 18 hotels, comprising 23,000 rooms and employing 60,000 people.[107] The Imagineering departments, which are in charge of attractions, deliberately recruit managers outside the film sector and in close contact with external partners.

In a nutshell, with regard to individual careers, we can thus make the case for three profiles in the movie and entertainment business: first, creative profiles, such as actors, directors and producers. As discussed previously, they rapidly change jobs according to their cultural affinities, creative opportunities and previous successes. This flexible and mobile employment strategy differs substantially from the classical era of the Hollywood studio system. Second, production managers are less mobile than the creative talent in the first profile, even though they do have artistic priorities and aspirations, which lead them to change employment at times. Third, the final profile comprises people in charge of marketing, promotion, business affairs and distribution. They remain in company for a longer time than the first two categories. This prevalent organisational stability accounts for Hollywood's success and durability in Western commercial markets since the 1920s. These executives work to manage commercial partnerships, negotiate promotion deals and coordinate the activities of the whole group, maintaining close ties with the economic sectors. Business ethics, much more than artistic objectives, drive their behaviour. Hal Richardson asserts very clearly that

> the theory I have always had as a television salesman is you guys [production executives] make the movies, that's your job. My job is to figure out how to sell every movie you make [...] At the end of the day, my job is to sell the stuff and your job is to make the stuff.[108]

Thus, cultural industries are integrated into economic domains with executives standing away from artistic input. Creative branches remain however—to a different extent—influenced by creative tensions. Moreover, the functions of production continue to be deeply impacted by the haphazard character of art and the unforeseeable nature of success. Successful creative formulas always appear shifting and temporary, which explains the rapid turnover amongst creative artists.

After this analysis at the individual level, the close commercial links the studios maintain with other multinational corporations will be examined. Indeed, the studios' position at the centre of the world-economy arises because of these very links. Their global success influences generations culturally and emotionally through emotive association, which other companies want to benefit from. In this respect, cultural capitalists can be compared to 'the transnational capitalist class'[109] which purportedly disseminates consumerism and attempts to commodify the world. Also, Hollywood appears at the top of creative economies.[110] For film companies, these commercial associations are a source of financing all the more crucial as production and distribution costs have increased enormously since the late 1990s.

This promotion takes place in the context of the information society wherein knowledge and collective representations are fundamental for markets. Cross-promotion partnerships profit from the advantageous investments of both parties. Corporations associate their products with popular imageries through creative contents, while studios obtain maximum media coverage and financing for their film releases. According to Arjun Appadurai, imagination cannot be reduced to a pure daydream or to a simple escape. Far from being limited to a cultural fact, imaginaries form fields with their own social practices and types of work. Subjectivities change by stimulation, imaginative activity and mediatisation, all of which represent high sociocultural and economic stakes. Appadurai states precisely that the present world is marked not so much by 'technically new forces' but by 'ones that seem to impel (and sometimes to compel) the work of imagination'.[111]

Commercial partnerships link Hollywood companies with the rest of the economy, an old practice and one that has increased substantially of late. The films *The Yellow Rolls-Royce* (1964) and *The Love Bug* (1968) are remarkable examples of a film whose plot is based around a car.[112] Not to be forgotten is Reese's confectionery products whose sales grew by 85 % after the success of *E. T. the Extra-Terrestrial* (1982).[113] In the 1990s, product placements already amounted to several million dollars, which Bob Levine—at the time head of marketing of Walt Disney Pictures—analysed as a strategic support: 'I believe it's a long-term relationship that's now going to exist [between] the movie industry and product marketers'.[114] In 2013, product placement represented an estimated of $1.8 billion for the US movie industry.[115]

Organisations such as Creative Entertainment Services have specialised in these practices. They review hundreds of scenarios a year, looking for opportunities for commercial insertions: they identify stories and [illegible] moments when products could be placed. They prefer to use them in action-based film scenarios, which makes their visibility more crucial than a simple placement.[116] In this case, they may propose modifications to the plot and even condition their financing to these modifications.[117] Holding a long-established and well known label, the Disney Company maintains close relationships with other corporations. The studio produces family-oriented animated films which provide an enormous potential of promotion for any business. In the fall of 2004, Disney earned $360 million from advertising associated with the release of the films *National Treasure* and *The Incredibles*. Its partners were corporations such as SBC, Verizon and Procter & Gamble. The financing materialised through TV spots, games, postings in stores, special packaging, premium by-products, mail and email advertising.[118]

When such economic and symbolic alliances extend over several years, they contribute to the association of certain products with specific collective narratives and imageries. In this way, product attractiveness is increased for the general public, which the McDonaldisation theories have neglected.[119] Large corporations take great care when utilising Hollywood films as a vehicle for their products, ensuring that lucrative agreements embody positive values.[120] For instance, Visa united with Disney to produce a Disney Visa credit card, and McDonald's concluded a 10-year exclusive global partnership with Disney in 1996. This latter agreement was not renewed in 2006, however, since McDonald's wanted to ally with other rising studio competitors of Disney as well. In addition, Disney and Pixar were concerned with the unfavourable image often associated with fast-food companies.

On a global level, cultural companies maintain symbolic and business relations with economic operators which go beyond sectors aimed exclusively at children. The release of films in particular provides lucrative opportunities to expand commercial relations. Illustratively, for the release of *Cars* (2006), commercial tie-ins brought a total of $125 million in addition to the $50 million obtained in television spots. Promotional contracts have included companies which sell products for adults, such as State Farm Insurance, Hertz, Goodyear and Porsche. It is also worth underlining that 'only four of seventeen associations [sold] products or [developed] promotion programs towards children'.[121] Some alliances, notably regarding the automotive sector, made good sense and fit in with the subject of the film. Since its 2006 release, *Cars* has become one of the major Disney franchises, reaching $8 billion in global retail sales by 2011 even before launching its sequel, *Cars 2*.[122] The following year, the franchise had earned more than $11 billion of which only $1 billion came from worldwide box-office returns.[123]

Moreover, the studios are accepting more control and coordination as a price worth paying for commercial partnerships since they are aware of audience sensitivities to mercantile promotions. In this respect, cross-promotions for *The Chronicles of Narnia: The Lion, the Witch and the Wardrobe* (2005) stuck to the literary legacy of the British novel, published in 1950. The Disney Company avoided over-commercialisation of the film with noisy and blatant advertisements. Buena Vista Pictures Executive Vice President for marketing Brett Dicker has commented: 'we worked with our partners and monitored everything very carefully. We wanted everything to reflect the wonderment of the book and the film and to be as magical as possible'.[124] Profiting from the reputation of Walden Media, Disney even distributed didactical presentations of C. S. Lewis's work to many US schools.[125]

This commodification also appears in other divisions of the studio companies. In 1992, the opening of Euro Disney paved the way for financing agreements with 12 firms such as Coca-Cola and Banque Nationale de Paris (BNP). Contracts were reportedly worth hundreds of millions of francs. At the time, the car manufacturer Renault decided to promote its brand by financing the design of a visionarium which would project future car models on 360-degree screens. The company deemed it wise to invest in such an attraction that millions would visit. In exchange for this considerable publicity, 650 of its cars were offered to Disney employees. And, during their promotional journey across Europe, Mickey, Minnie and the ambassador of the park travelled in a convertible Renault car.[126]

The Disney studio had already resorted to similar sponsorships for their previous parks. In fact, contracting companies of such partnerships expect added value for their products. General Electric, for example, contributes to developing Progressland at Disney World. PepsiCo does likewise for the attraction It's a Small World and Ford for Magic Skyway.[127] 'Alliance capitalism'[128] which was observed in research and development as well as in the organisational and reticular resources—is also present in symbolic and narrative domains. When the Disney Company repositioned its label in 2006, it refocused on its core contents and symbols which were easily usable in every division of the company. This is why an anonymous producer pointed out at the time that '[the Disney studios] will now prefer to take less risk with family films'.[129] In fact, over the following decade, the Studio Entertainment division (movies) accounted on average for below 20 % of company revenues and for only 15 % of operating income whereas the Media Networks and Consumer Products divisions amounted to 46 % and 8 % respectively of Disney revenues with operating income well above 25 %.[130] In addition, the last two divisions mobilised fewer assets and working capital than movies. As a result, they have a much better return on invested capital. Under these conditions, corporate strategy favours media- and consumer-related activities over films in order to optimise value creation for shareholders.

As discussed previously, conglomerate logic has restructured the motion picture industry significantly. Having examined sectoral and individual dynamics in the major studios, the interactions and interdependences at work within conglomerates through the case of Disney animation can be analysed. Thomas Schatz spoke of 'the new Hollywood' to name the change of configurations specific to the industry, such as the rise of home video, pay television, blockbusters and the resulting increase in marketing and production costs.[131] It is worth pointing out that movie departments have become submitted to many others whose activity depends on the success of movie narratives and imageries. Animated films are a good case in point of this commercial logic because of their costs and their potential promotion. Indeed, they require several years of development and production and their narrative universe also allows a much more intense economic promotion. On this subject a former Disney executive underlines that all Disney departments are involved in the creation process:

> marketing people must be on board and feel that they can sell that movie [...] It needs to be something that the theme parks can get excited about and feel that it will have a family appeal [...] There are a lot of divisions of the company that are involved early on and that determine whether they [Disney people] are going to go ahead and make the movie.[132]

After preproduction, enormous investment is committed to all appropriate divisions. This is why studio values scenario. Once the film project is green-lighted, the scenario is sent to all the divisions, which then prepare for the release by organising toy and gift product lines and vast promotion campaigns. On this point, working at Disneyland Paris in consumer products, Claudine Reynes remembers, 'In the process, the studios would launch a movie and we would be informed very quickly about it through the script and the characters of heroes. Before the animated film was made and cut, we should work on consumer products and ask the film designers for their approval'.[133] New films are presented in advance to company partners in order to conclude licensing agreements and synchronise marketing of the merchandise with the movie's theatrical release.[134] In this context, the total value of a film lies in its commercial intertextuality—its capacity to adapt to and interact with other business activities. Every movie project contains a line of multimedia production in which lies the intertextuality. In other words, it is necessary to treat each film as a text as well as a product. Also, with the example of *Batman* movies (1989, 1992, 1995, 1997 and 2005), Eileen Meehan concludes that 'decisions about movies are increasingly focused on the potential profitability of a wide range of products'.[135]

Walt Disney established his patronym as an intertextual legacy, which is today the most valuable in American cinema. He actually set up a franchise of himself, which his successors have cautiously preserved. This is why the firm lobbied fiercely to prevent its most intangible assets, such as Mickey Mouse, from falling into the public domain. The Sonny Bono Copyright Term Extension Act signed in 1998 increased corporate authorship by 20 years, pushing it from 75 to 95 years after the release date.[136] At the global level, Hal Richardson stressed that Disney is

> the only motion picture brand that on a worldwide basis means anything [...] And that's a huge advantage. Today, in most regions of the world, when you release a Disney animated movie, there is a built-in level at the box office, no matter how good, bad or indifferent it is. There are people that are going to see it, that first week end, regardless of what it is about. All you have to do is to have that signature Walt Disney on it.[137]

Indeed, Walt Disney is ranked number 11 on the *Forbes* world's most valuable brand list.[138] No other brand in entertainment sectors holds such a power.

The promotion of Disney content comprises regular re-releases of its animated films in order to ensure that its symbolic attributes are integrated by successive younger generations. The studio has implemented a policy which spawns intergenerational and international franchises. Although Disney slowed down its content creation during the 1970s, it always took care to keep its imageries and narratives popular by periodically re-running films. Released in December 1937, *Snow White and the Seven Dwarfs* was re-released eight times in movie theatres between 1944 and 1993. Since the 1990s, Disney releases have continued through home video. *Snow White* was launched in video format in 1994. In 2001, one million DVD copies of this film were bought in less than 24 hours and fourteen years later, 26 million units of home video editions have been sold, including 18 million on DVD format.[139] In 2009, the Blu-ray edition was released. The film received ultimate recognition in 1989 when it was classified among films judged by the library of the Congress to be 'culturally, historically and aesthetically important'.[140] Disney implemented a similar patrimonialisation with classics from the Eisner/Katzenberg period. They were released in home video format; many sequels were made out of their narratives and they were adapted for live theatrical shows.[141]

Audiences welcomed this intergenerational policy by taking their children to cinema theatres to watch the Disney classics. As Hal Richardson has affirmed, the Disney brand prevails because 'Walt Disney created a culture behind animation and instituted the concept of the feature animated picture [...] and for a long time he was the only person doing this [...] Since the thirties, parents have taken their kids to see Disney animated movies'.[142] Consequently, the firm takes advantage of a traditional legitimacy which can be found among the interviewees who participated in this study: 'How can we escape from Disney when we have children?'[143] Other researchers found the conformist injunction, which a young US mother termed as, 'How can you not expose your kids to Disney? It's not realistic to think you can avoid Disney... I wouldn't want to rob [them] of [their] childhood'.[144]

Specialists have often decried this manifold commodification of films which reinforces the mercantilism in the film production process. Producers have stated that they decide to take on movie projects without thinking of any of the mercantile opportunities. Such a statement appears doubtful given the increasing pressure coming from booming budgets.[145] Far from only representing a bonus, practices such as product placement are integrated into the production process since such commercial deals are integrated into financing plans.

Although Hollywood has always resorted to these practices, they have lately intensified. Inflation of costs and the attractiveness of this 'genuine folk art',[146] movies, make up fundamental elements in their cultural interfirm relations. Moreover, global successes have increased opportunities for more promotional insertions. If universality remains a condition of art, then only Hollywood creations could fill this criterion. Indeed, the majority of other artistic forms are cut from the general public, being appreciated now only by restricted elites. As Panofsky has explained,

> commercial art can be defined as all art not primarily produced in order to gratify the creative urge of its maker but primarily intended to meet the requirements of a patron or a buying public. It must be said that non-commercial art is the exception rather than the rule, and a fairly recent and not always felicitous exception at that. While it is true that commercial

art is always in danger of ending up as a prostitute, it is equally true that non-commercial art is always in danger of ending up as an old maid.[147]

Consequently, commercial and creative dimensions should not be opposed but regarded as integral parts of cinema—it seems that Hollywood capitalism reconciles these two aspects, ensuring the prosperity of its worldwide activities.

A genuine civilisation of leisure has emerged from the global activity of cultural capitalists, producing movies and complete entertainment packages and distributing them as original content, sequels, spin-offs, merchandise and so on. It is important to analyse the formation of imageries and the factors affecting their production, without forgetting to examine their appropriation by the public. To achieve this it will be necessary to study attitudes towards symbolic attributes in foreign societies, to analyse their effect on media consumption and to judge the extent to which they modify individual behaviour.

Notes

1. PricewaterhouseCoopers (2015) *Global Entertainment and Media Outlook 2015–2019*, available at <http://www.pwc.com>.
2. PricewaterhouseCoopers (2014) *Global Entertainment and Media Outlook 2014–2018*, available at <http://www.pwc.com>.
3. PricewaterhouseCoopers (2014) *Global Entertainment.*
4. D. Smith (1998) *Disney A to Z. The Updated Official Encyclopedia* (New York: Hyperion), p. 152.
5. D. Gomery (2005) *The Hollywood Studio System: a History* (London: British Film Institute), p. 265.
6. M. Goold and A. Campbell (1998), 'Desperately Seeking Synergy', *Harvard Business Review*, September–October, 130–43.
7. L. Miles, A. Borchert and A. E. Ramanathan (2014) 'Why Some Merging Companies Become Synergy Overachievers', Bain & Company, available at: www.bain.com
8. J. Wasko (2007) 'Can Hollywood Still Rule the World?' in D. Held and H. L. Moore (eds.) *Cultural Politics in a Global Age: Uncertainty, Solidarity and Innovation* (Oxford: Oneworld Publications), pp. 187–95.
9. S. Watts (1997) *The Magic Kingdom: Walt Disney and the American Way of Life* (Boston: Houghton Mifflin), p. xx, 23; J. P. Telotte (2004) *Disney TV* (Detroit: Wayne State University Press). See also J. M. Barrier (2007) *The Animated Man: a Life of Walt Disney* (Berkeley: University of California Press).

10. T. Risse-Kappen (1995) (ed.) *Bringing Transnational Relations Back in: Non-State Actors, Domestic Structures and International Institutions* (Cambridge: Cambridge University Press). For more information on the structure of feelings, see R. Williams (1961) *The Long Revolution* (New York: Columbia University Press), p. 48 *ff.*
11. Smith, *Disney A to Z*, pp. 362–63.
12. Smith, *Disney A to Z*, p. 34 and pp. 36–8 (Supplement to the 2006 edition)
13. M. Garrahan (2015) 'Violetta's Teenage Angst Grips a Global TV Audience', *Financial Times*, 11 January.
14. See The Walt Disney Company, *2004–2014 Annual Reports*, available at <http://www.thewaltdisneycompany.com> and <www.sec.gov>. See Appendix 4.
15. See The Walt Disney Company, *The 2013 Factbook* and <http://www.disneyabcpress.com>.
16. M. Graser (2013) 'How TV Has Replaced Films as Disney's Biggest Brand Ambassador', *Variety*, 15 March.
17. Interview with C. Nelson, former Vice President Advertising in the Disney studios, 19 August 2006. For more information, see Appendix 5.
18. For more information, see the corporate websites and the annual reports of the Walt Disney Company. See also, Smith, *Disney A to Z.*
19. On the global phenomenon of concentration and its implications for democracy, see R. W. McChesney (2015) *Rich Media, Poor Democracy. Communication Politics in Dubious Times* (New York: New Press); N. Lear and R. W. McChesney (2007) 'Does Big Media Need to Get Bigger?', *Los Angeles Times*, 5 August, B17.
20. N. Continet, F. Moreau and S. Peltier (2002) *Les Grands groupes des industries culturelles. Fusions, acquisitions, alliances: les stratégies des années 1980–2000* (Paris: Ministère de la culture et de la communication).
21. With 21.5 million subscribers in the United States, Comcast is the leading cable provider, offering high speed internet connection, video and phone. On the Comcast bid, see N. D. Beaulieu and A. M. G. Zimmerman (2005) 'Saving Disney', *Harvard Business School Cases*, Brighton, MA: Harvard Business Publishing.
22. J. Holt (2001) 'In Deregulation We Trust. The Synergy of Politics and Industry in Reagan-era Hollywood', *Quarterly Film*, 55 (2), winter, 22–39.
23. J. Hartley, W. Wen and H. Siling (2015) *Creative Economy and Culture. Challenges, Changes and Futures for the Creative Industries* (London: Sage); J. Hartley (2005) (ed.) *Creative Industries* (Oxford: Blackwell)
24. See PricewaterhouseCoopers (2015) *Global Entertainment.*

25. The return on investment of movie production would vary thus from –20 % to +20 %, excluding televisual divisions and ancillary markets. See H. Vogel (2004) 'Analyzing Movie Companies' in J. E. Squire (ed.) *Movie Business Book* (New York: Fireside), p. 143; P. Dekom 'Movies, Money and Madness' in Squire, *Movie Business Book*, p. 102.
26. Vogel, 'Analyzing Movie Companies', p. 144.
27. Interview with a senior producer who had close ties with the Disney Company, 20 August 2006.
28. C. Littleton (2013) 'Major Film Studios Prosper on the Margins', *Variety*, 18 April.
29. B. Lang (2015) 'Disney Set to Dominate as it Unleashes Full Power of Pixar, Marvel and 'Star Wars'', *Variety*, 22 April; J. Kroll (2013) 'Disney Takes Over Rights to 'Indiana Jones' Franchise', *Variety*, 6 December.
30. B. Fritz (2015) 'How Disney Milks Its Hits for Profits Ever After', *The Wall Street Journal*, 8 June. See the growth of Disney Company's operating income in Appendix 4, Graph 2.
31. See Appendices 3 and 5.
32. Interview with B. Mechanic, former leading executive at Buena Vista and then Fox, 4 August 2006. For more information, see Appendix 5. On the Hollywood studios absorbed into larger companies, see M. Wolf (1999) *The Entertainment Economy: How Mega-Media Forces Are Transforming Our Lives* (New York: Times Books/Random House).
33. T. Miller, N. Govil, J. McMurrin, R. Maxwell and T. Wang (2005) *Global Hollywood 2* (London: British Film Institute), p. 111 *ff.*
34. S. Sassen (2003) 'Globalization or Denationalization', *Review of International Political Economy*, 10 (1), February, 1–22.
35. On the dichotomy between organic solidarity and mechanical solidarity, see E. Durkheim (1998/1893) *De la Division du travail social* (Paris: PUF).
36. Durkheim, *De la Division du travail social*, p. 238.
37. Interview with Michael Taylor, independent producer, 3 August 2006. For more information, see Appendix 5. See also C. K. Yale (2010) *Runaway Film Production: A Critical History of Hollywood's Outsourcing Discourse*, Ph.D, University of Illinois.
38. J. A. Lent (1998) 'The Animation Industry and Its Offshore Factories' in G. Sussman and J. A. Lent (eds.) *Global Productions: Labor in the Making of the Information Society* (Cresskill: Hampton Press), p. 246.
39. Interview with S. Hulett, former animator and Business Representative at the Animation Guild, 1 July 2006. For more information, see Appendix 5.
40. Lent, 'The Animation Industry and Its Offshore Factories', p. 244.
41. G. Elmer and M. Gasher (2005) (eds.) *Contracting Out Hollywood: Runaway Productions and Foreign Location Shootings* (Lanham: Rowman

& Littlefield), pp. 8–9. The *X-Files* series was mainly shot in British Columbia, Canada.

42. Elmer and Gasher, *Contracting Out Hollywood*.
43. M. Osborne (2003) 'Picky Disney Bows Kids Block', *Variety*, 391 (10), 28 July, 1 (25).
44. Interview with J.-F. Lepetit, French producer who worked on projects and films with Disney, 1 June 2006. For more information, see Appendix 5.
45. Interview with I. Khait, producer and production manager at the Walt Disney Studios, 6 September 2006. For more information, see Appendix 5.
46. Interview with S. Hulett, former animator at Disney and now Business Representative for the Animation Guild, 1 July 2006. For more information, see Appendix 5.
47. C. DiOrio (2006) 'Runaway Prod'n Costs U.S. Dearly', *The Hollywood Reporter*, 1–7 August, 3 (62).
48. G. Freeman, J. Kyser, N. Sidhu, G. Huang and M. Montoya (2005) *What is the Cost of Run-Away Production? Jobs, Wages, Economic Output and State Tax Revenue at Risk When Motion Picture Productions Leave California* (Los Angeles: Los Angeles County Economic Development Corporation), p. 15.
49. FilmL.A. Research (2015) *2014 Feature Film Study*, available at <http://www.filmla.com>, p. 2. On this subject, see also C. Cooper, S. Sedgwick and S. Mitra (2014) *California's Film and Television Tax Credit Program: Assessing Its Impact*, Los Angeles County Economic Development Corporation, March, available at <http://www.scag.ca.gov>, p. 11.
50. FilmL.A. Research, p. 12.
51. J. Tracy (1999) 'Whistle While You Work: The Disney Company and the Global Division of Labor', *Journal of Communication Inquiry*, 23 (4), October, 385.
52. 'Canadians Riding Out Film-Production Crisis', *The Hollywood Reporter*, 23–9 November 2004. See also Yale, *Runaway Film Production*.
53. For example, Universal's Illumination Mac Guff studio was successful with the *Despicable Me* series (2010, 2013) and *Minions* (2015). The studio is based in Paris and Los Angeles. On the subject, see N. Luciani (2015) 'Illumination Mac Guff, riche à Minions', *Le Monde*, 7 July.
54. J. Wasko (1998) 'Challenges to Hollywood's Labor Force in the 1990s' in Sussman and Lent, *Global Productions*, pp. 173–90; M. J. Pendakur (1998) 'Hollywood North: Film and TV Production in Canada' in Sussman and Lent, *Global Productions*, pp. 213–39; B. Kelly (2003) 'H'wood Studios May Quit Quebec', *Variety*, 13 November.
55. See J. A. Lent (1998) 'The Animation Industry and Its Offshore Factories', p. 240.
56. 'You Can Click But You Cannot Hide', *Screen International*, 7 January 2005, 17–20.

57. L. Glickman and M. Rothschild (2012) *Tax Credits and Other Film and TV Incentives: The World Outside Canada and the United States, the American Bar Association Forum on the Entertainment and Sports Industries, Annual Meeting*, Las Vegas, Nevada, 6 October. See also M. Taylor (2014) Film and Television Production: Overview of Motion PictureIndustry and State Tax Credits, Legislative Analyst's Office, April 30. http://www.lao.ca.gov.
58. See S. Kemp (2004) 'London Offers Film-Friendly Base', *The Hollywood Reporter*, 23–5 April, 13 (20); R. Armbrust and I. Mohr (2004) 'N.Y. Tax Incentive Likely', *The Hollywood Reporter*, 19 August, 1 (23).
59. P. G. Cerny (2000) 'Restructuring the Political Arena: Globalization and the Paradoxes of the Competition State' in R. Germain (ed.) *Globalization and its Critics, Perspectives from Political Economy* (Basingstoke: Macmillan), pp. 117–38.
60. Interview with R. Bonnell, former President Cinema at the Canal+ Group, 8 June 2006 (for more information, see Appendix 5). The Duran Duboi Company went bankrupt in 2011.
61. Interview with R. Bonnell.
62. Interview with S. Hulett.
63. 'Dailies' are the unedited footage shot during the production of a film. They are viewed by the director, other staff members and other people such as the producer and studio executives.
64. Interview with I. Khait.
65. The exposure sheet contains all the information which the animator needs for his or her drawings.
66. European Audiovisual Observatory (EAO) (2012), *Yearbook. Television, Cinema, Video and On-demand Audiovisual Services in Europe*, vol. 2 (Strasbourg: Council of Europe), p. 124; on the local productions remaining important, see PricewaterhouseCoopers, *(2015) Global Entertainment.*
67. CNC (2015), 'Bilan 2014', *Les dossiers du CNC*, 332, May, 10, 175.
68. Interview with H. Richardson senior executive for distribution at Disney studios, DreamWorks and then Paramount, 11 August 2006. For more information, see Appendix 5.
69. PricewaterhouseCoopers (2015) *Global Entertainment.*
70. 'Disney Downloads iTunes Deal', *Variety*, 9 January 2006, 6 (1).
71. M. Lev-Ram (2014) 'Disney CEO Iger's Empire of Tech', *Fortune*, 29 December.
72. S. Tripathi and A. Rimmer (2012) *Profitable Growth Strategies for the Global Emerging Middle. Learning from the 'Next 4 Billion' Markets*, PricewaterhouseCoopers, available at <http://www.pwc.com>.
73. The Walt Disney Company (2015) *2014 Annual Report*, available at <http://www.thewaltdisneycompany.com>, p. 72.

74. 'Who's Getting What at this Year's Confab', *Variety*, 17 November 2003, A2 (1).
75. J. Stein (2006) 'Dis New Media Pitch Hits Asia', *The Hollywood Reporter*, 20–6 June, 76 (80).
76. 'Par's Passage to India', *Variety*, 402 (6), 27 March 2006, 2 (1).
77. See J. Landreth (2004) 'B'day Ends China's 'Da Vinci' Run', *The Hollywood Reporter*, 9–11 June, 70 (8); J. Landreth (2006) 'H'wood Tops Chinese B.O', *The Hollywood Reporter*, 27 July, 17 (4).
78. CNC, *Bilan 2008*, p. 11; S. B. Iyer (2005) 'Event Gives India Global Frame of Reference', *Variety*, 398 (6), 28 March, A2 (1).
79. N. Bhushan (2015) 'Local Film Revenues Stagnate in India', *The Hollywood Reporter*, 25 March; N. McCarthy (2014) 'Bollywood: India's Film Industry By The Numbers', *Forbes*, 3 September. See also A. Punathambekar (2013) *From Bombay to Bollywood: The Making of a Global Media Industry* (New York: New York University Press) and C. Deprez (2010) *Bollywood: Cinéma et mondialisation* (Villeneuve d'Asq: Presses Universitaires du Septentrion).
80. The Indian industry has begun exporting with its diaspora; see H. Tyrrell (1999) 'Bollywood Versus Hollywood: Battle of the Dream Factories' in T. Skelton and T. Allen (eds.) *Culture and Global Change* (London: Routledge), pp. 260–73.
81. Bhushan, 'Local Film Revenues Stagnate in India'.
82. N. Bhushan (2006) 'Disney Buys Into India TV Buzz', *The Hollywood Reporter*, 26 July, 9; S. B. Iyer (2004) 'Rivals Squeak at Mouse Bow: Channels Try Tricks to Keep Kiddie Auds', *Variety*, 397 (6), 27 December, 13 (1); J. Leahy and S. Tucker (2006) 'Disney Switches On to Hindi Market', *Financial Times*, 13 September, 2; G. Szalai (2011) 'Walt Disney Offers to Buy Full Control of India's UTV Software', *The Hollywood Reporter*, 26 July.
83. H. Venkatraman (2010) 'We are here to build Indian Walt Disney: Walt Disney India MD', *Economic Times*, 3 May.
84. Interview with M. Taylor.
85. Interview with M. Taylor.
86. Interview with B. Mechanic.
87. General comments on the activity of the industry are usually based on domestic figures. For example, on home video, see A. Wallenstein (2016) 'Why 2015 Home Entertainment Figures Should Worry Studios', *Variety*, 6 January ; and on TV advertising spend, see ''Godzilla' Warner Bros. Lead the Year's Top TV Ad Spend for Movies', *Variety*, 3 January 2015.
88. Interview with B. Mechanic.
89. Interview with B. Mechanic.

90. F. Wasser (1995) 'Is Hollywood America? The Trans-nationalization of the American Film Industry', *Critical Studies in Mass Communication*, 12 (4), December, 423–37.
91. In the 1990s and 2000s, Buena Vista International used to retain a maximum of foreign copyrights even for co-financed movies such as *The Sixth Sense* (1999), *Mission to Mars* (2000) and *Instinct* (1999). The major studio bought out Universal's *Ends of Days* (1999) and *The Hurricane* (1999).
92. Interview with B. Mechanic.
93. Interview with J.-F. Lepetit.
94. Interview with a senior producer who had close ties with the Disney Company, 13 August 2006.
95. Interview with B. Mechanic.
96. A. Smith (2014) 'The Rise Of The Chinese Box Office Is Staggering, And It's Transforming Hollywood', *Business Insider*, 26 July; MPAA (2015) *2014 Theatrical Market Statistics*, <http://www.mpaa.org>.
97. Interview with H. Richardson.
98. L. Sklair (2002) *Globalization: Capitalism and Its Alternatives* (Oxford: Blackwell), p. 98.
99. L. Sklair (2001) *The Transnational Capitalist Class* (Oxford: Blackwell), p. 256; see K. Van Der Pilj (1998) *Transnational Classes and International Relations* (London: Routledge).
100. Sklair, *The Transnational Capitalist Class*, p. 295.
101. The 'legs of a film' is a phrase used for movies continuing to return large box-office figures over many months.
102. J. Friedman (2006) 'Nice Movie Opening, But Did You Beat the Forecast?', *Los Angeles Times*, 6 August, C1 (C6); B. Fritz (2015) "Avengers' Overpowers the Box Office', *The Wall Street Journal*, 3 May; E. Schwartzel (2015) "Avengers' Sequel Continues Box-Office Reign', *The Wall Street Journal*, 10 May.
103. See C. DiOrio and J. Goldsmith (2000) 'Conglom Crunch', *Variety*, 13 November, 9.
104. B. Fritz (2015) "Frozen Ever After': An Exclusive Look at Disney's Upcoming Attraction', *The Wall Street Journal*, 9 June.
105. The study focuses on the production, distribution and marketing departments of the Walt Disney Studios. See Appendix 3.
106. On executives such as B. Mechanic, see S. Galloway (2002) 'Greener Pastures', *The Hollywood Reporter*, 19–25 November, 18–19.
107. See figures obtained on the corporate website at <http://wdw.disneycareers.com>; The Walt Disney Company (2015) *2014 Annual Report*, available at <http://www.thewaltdisneycompany.com>, p. 9.
108. Interview with H. Richardson.
109. Sklair, *Globalization*, p. 108, 164.
110. Hartley, *Creative Industries*, p. 31.

111. A. Appadurai (1996) *Modernity at Large. Cultural Dimensions of Globalization* (Minneapolis, U.S.: University of Minnesota), p. 4.
112. In *The Yellow Rolls Royce*, released in 1964 by MGM, the multiple lives of this automobile form the heart of the plot during which its resistance, faithfulness and attractiveness are put to the fore. In addition, Walt Disney Studios produced a series of films on the adventures of Herbie, an anthropomorphic Beetle car—the first movie is entitled *The Love Bug*.
113. J. Wasko, M. Phillips and C. Purdie (1993) 'Hollywood Meets Madison Avenue: the Commercialization of US Films', *Media, Culture and Society*, 15 (2), April, 274.
114. Wasko et al., 'Hollywood Meets', 277.
115. G. Beltrone (2014) 'A By-the-Numbers Look at Hollywood's Marketing Machine, Media spend and Agencies of the Biggest Studios', *Adweek*, 24 February.
116. Beltrone, 'A By-the-Numbers Look', 274.
117. Illustratively, Jeff Bell—Vice President at Chrysler/Jeep—declared that 'we always want our vehicle to play a role in the film'. See G. Schiller (2005) 'Warfare', *The Hollywood Reporter*, 10–16 May, S4.
118. G. Schiller (2004) 'Record Promo Dose for Disney's Fall Duo', *The Hollywood Reporter*, 22–24 October, 84 (1).
119. G. Ritzer (1993) *The McDonaldization of Society: An investigation Into the Changing Character of Contemporary Social Life* (Newbury: Pine Forge Press). For a criticism, see B. Smart (1999) (ed.) *Resisting McDonaldization* (London: Sage).
120. On '*the experience economy*', see J. Pine and J. Gilmore (1999) *The Experience Economy: Work Is Theater & Every Business a Stage* (Boston: Harvard Business School Press).
121. G. Schiller (2006) 'Brave New World for Summer Tie-ins', *The Hollywood Reporter*, 30 May–5 June, 51 (1).
122. G. Szalai (2011) 'Disney: 'Cars' Has Crossed $8 Billion in Global Retail Sales', *The Hollywood Reporter*, 14 February.
123. See 'Les franchises Disney les plus lucratives', *L'Expansion*, 31 October 2012.
124. On Disney's Narnia movie, ten partnerships were established on 80 brands including 71 from Unilever and General Mills, totalling a value of $100 million. See G. Schiller (2005) 'Promos by the Book on 'Narnia'', *The Hollywood Reporter*, 18–20 November, 9 (1).
125. P. McClintock (2005) 'Kids Get Muscled by Marketers: H'wood Goes Back to School With Tie-ins that Promo Recent Releases', *Variety*, 399 (5), 20 June, 2 (8).
126. A. Feitz (1992) 'Euro Disney: Dissection d'un lancement', *Médias*, (327), April, 28–9.
127. A. Bryman (1995) *Disney and His Worlds* (London: Routledge), p. 13.

128. J. H. Dunning and G. Boyd (2003) *Alliance Capitalism and Corporate Management: Entrepreneurial Cooperation in Knowledge Based Economies* (Cheltenham: E. Elgar).
129. Interview with a senior producer who had close ties with the Disney Company, 20 August 2006.
130. See Appendix 4, Graph 2.
131. T. Schatz (2004) 'The New Hollywood' in T. Schatz (ed.) *Hollywood. Critical Concepts in Media and Cultural Studies*, vol. I (London: Routledge), pp. 285–97.
132. Interview with I. Khait.
133. Interview with C. Reynes.
134. Interview with L. Besson, former executive at the French toy company, Smoby. For more information, see Appendix 5.
135. E. Meehan (2004), 'Hollywood Commodity Fetish, Batman!' in T. Schatz (ed.) *Hollywood. Critical Concepts*, vol. IV, p. 314; J. Gilmore and M. Stork (2014) (eds.) *Superhero Synergies: Comic Book Characters Go Digital* (Lanham: Rowman & Littlefield).
136. B. Boliek (2002) 'Copyright Law Goes to High Court', *The Hollywood Reporter*, 8–14 October, 3 (108); P. McClintock (2002) 'Challenge Threatens Mouse Copyright', *Variety*, 386 (2), 25 February, 1 (6); J. Wasko (2001) *Understanding Disney: the Manufacture of Fantasy* (Cambridge: Blackwell), p. 85.
137. Interview with H. Richardson.
138. Disney's brand value is estimated at $35 billion in a ranking where the top ten is dominated by computer and Internet companies such as Apple, Google and Samsung. For more analysis, see K. Badenhausen (2015) 'The World's Most Valuable Brands 2015: Behind The Numbers', *Forbes*.
139. D. Groves (2001) "Snow White' DVD Dwarfs O'seas Records', *Variety*, 25 November; Smith, *Disney A to Z*, p. 509.
140. Smith, *Disney A to Z*, p. 110.
141. Smith, *Disney A to Z*, p 52.
142. Interview with H. Richardson.
143. Quote collected during the questionnaire. See Appendix 3
144. E. Meehan, M. Phillips and J. Wasko (2006) (eds.) *Dazzled by Disney? The Global Disney Audiences Project* (Leicester: Leicester University Press), p. 49.
145. Wasko et al., 'Hollywood Meets', 275.
146. E. Panofsky (1966/1934) 'Style and Medium in the Motion Pictures' in D. Talbot (ed.) *Film: An Anthology* (Berkeley: University of California Press), p. 16.
147. Panofsky, 'Style and Medium', p. 30. See F. Montebello (2003) 'Les deux peuples du cinéma: usages populaires du cinéma et images du public populaire', *Mouvements*, 27–8, May–August, 113–19.

CHAPTER 4

A Vulnerable Civilisation of Leisure

An Economic-Cultural Domination in Global Entertainment

The Global Constitution of Commercial Symbols and Products

Cultural capitalists have developed entertainment spheres thanks to intense diversification. Based on cultural synergies among intertwined sectors, they disseminate their narrations and practices throughout society globally. They propose heterogeneous activities and productions—interactive as much as didactic—whose cultural, emotional and artistic dimensions are highly valued. By doing this, they introduce, at the world level, living standards and consumer behaviour which favour the growth of multinational corporations. In this sense, they spread the American way of life which consists just as much of products as of symbols. And Hollywood companies have to periodically renew their symbols and adapt to socio-economic mutations.

Proposing a range of entertainment activities, studios have based their prosperity on leisure time which has grown at a rapid pace in developed countries.[1] Defined as 'a set of occupations in which individuals can fully indulge in entertainment [...] after freeing themselves from their work, family and social obligations',[2] leisure forms 'a central element of the culture lived by millions of workers [...] not only as an attractive possibility but also as a value'.[3] Indeed, a combination of decreased working time

A. Bohas, *The Political Economy of Disney*, International Political Economy Series, DOI 10.1057/978-1-137-56238-8_4

and an increase in life expectancy offer many moments which are based on 'new morals of happiness [and] of amusement'.[4]

What are the cultural implications of Hollywood products, including the non-audio-visual type? They also drive behaviour and diffuse imageries and narratives. Actually, like feature films, they also provoke strong emotions and represent high economic stakes. As already mentioned, in 2014 the global entertainment and media markets earned $1.7 trillion in revenue, a figure that could easily increase to $2.2 trillion by 2019, at an annual average growth rate of 5 %.[5]

These domains often remain minimised. As Joffre Dumazedier has pointed out with some regret, leisure as consumption suffers from disrepute in academia. Entertainment is regarded as external to artistic spheres. According to certain scholars, the commercial use of films would result in the degradation of the latter. In addition, consumption has only been recognised lately as structuring identities and cultures. Although consumption, like work, is central in Western societies, it has only become a domain of academic study since the 1960s thanks to the School of Birmingham.[6] Formatting identities, consumer behaviour indeed remains a privileged way of self-definition. As scholars, especially Norbert Elias and Thorstein Veblen, have underscored the power dimensions of socio-economic activities at the Court of King Louis XIV or at the end of nineteenth century,[7] similar phenomena are at play in present mass markets.[8] On this point, marketing has been brought to rely increasingly on emotional rather than rational appeal. Traditionally, marketing managers attempt to differentiate their products from one another through functional insights, benefits and technical reasons, appealing to the consumer's logic. However, in mature and over-affluent markets, they have turned more and more to consumer emotions such as fear and happiness to sell their products.[9] In this context, this analysis highlights the impact Hollywood companies plainly have on consumer behaviour.

The Hollywood leisure industry has contributed to a worldwide expansion of the American way of life. This expansion has had a critical impact on economies and societies, taking on a civilisational dimension by shaping 'collective mentalities which orient prejudices, attitudes and choices of the populations'.[10] Not only does it frame production and economic infrastructure, but it also shapes world-economies by orienting consumer behaviour and supply. Hollywood entertainment instils symbolic attributes and imageries conducive to practices, behaviour and living standards. Composed of objects and symbols, these meaningful elements are linked to Western living standards. According to regular reports,[11] the exports of copyright industries ($142 billion), to which Hollywood studios belong, would exceed *sensu lato* those of major US industries such as aerospace ($106 billion). Moreover, export forecasts in the Asia Pacific zone are huge with an estimated four billion people being in a position to access leisure activities in the coming decades. Having in common their middle-class incomes, they enter the consumer society which spurs rapid growth of leisure activities.[12] Despite the economic slowdown of emerging markets, consumption by middle and upper middle classes is growing rapidly. In China, over the past decades, Western companies have relied on the sales of luxury products to the wealthy people of the east coast. Now, the most promising regions are the inland lower-tier cities which house a concentration of new customers with rising purchasing power. They represent a much larger consumer spending opportunity and are eager to endorse the American way of life. Growth of urban private consumption in China is expected to rise from $3.2 billion in 2015 to $5.6 billion in 2020.[13] This explains the opening of Disneyland in Shanghai but also Disney's partnership with Uniqlo—based on mainland China, the Asian retailer owns 360 stores and sells clothes at an affordable price. Betting on the rise of the new middle class, Uniqlo plans to open one hundred new outlets per year.[14]

Over the last few years, the Disney Company has invested in many growing markets, achieving considerable expansion of its activities. It took strategic advantage of compelling narratives and successful products and maximised their potential within the entertainment industry. While Disney's consumer products departments develop its merchandising, other companies generate royalty income for the company by using its imageries, logos, artwork and themes for their own products. Consumption patterns and lifestyles are oriented by brand presence and advertising. Disney is the number one global licensor in the sector of consumer products, accounting for $45 billion of licensed sales in 2014 in a market of $[illegible] billion. The studio consists of 11 key franchises which generate more than $1 billion in annual sales.[15] The reliance on brand and narrative licensing is common and is complementary to in-house activities. For instance, in the publishing sector, Disney develops licensing while claiming also to be the world's leading children's publisher.

Cultural capitalists benefit from profitable and growing entertainment spheres which combine social practices and cultural consumption synchronised with modern life and the market economy. As Fernand Braudel has posited, far from merely reducing risk, economic diversification is inherent in global capitalism, which 'diversifies since no branch is large enough to absorb all its activities [...] If it so often changes activity, it is because the greatest profit relentlessly changes sectors'.[16] On this point, the French historian added, 'capitalism is of a short-term nature. Today, one of its great forces is still its ability to adapt and restructure easily'.[17]

Positioning itself as a basis for differentiation, Hollywood cinema represents for leisure activities a powerhouse for fashion and for new sociocultural practices. In fact, from the very beginning, Mickey Mouse appears in cartoons dealing with jazz music and self-fulfilment through various festivals and recreations, such as in *The Whoopee Party* (1932).[18] For this reason, this character arguably diffused contemporary ideals—even avant-gardist for the time—if we consider the current value of entertainment. In the same way, television programmes for children accompanied, or announced, the rise of a new social category—youth.

The vast productions of the Disney Company offer different experiences which complement one another. In line with the rising interest of marketing practitioners for customer experience,[19] a more encompassing view will be adopted to identify the diversity of consumers' experiences proposed by Disney entertainment. In terms of communications, it corresponds to an integrated marketing management[20] which aims to deliver a consistent cross-channel message. To do so, it considers all the touch-points between the customer and the company in order to improve the corporate image, identity and reputation.

This experience of a 'civilisational' nature can be considered with two criteria. The first takes into account the quantity of information which the medium delivers. Based on this parameter, Marshall McLuhan distinguished 'cold' media from 'hot' media, depending on information density. Hot media are 'well filled with data'.[21] The density of information appears so significant that they 'do not leave so much to be filled in or completed by the audience'.[22] The second criterion clarifies the level of interactivity within narrative universes. In these activities, people enter into the imageries and narrations. They become fully fledged actors, which represents for them a powerful cultural experience. Consequently, these two criteria can be subdivided into four types of goods or activities designed by the studios (Graph 4.1).

In the first category, theme activities have individuals participate in the narrative, while diffusing knowledge. People live for several hours—even for several days—in theme universes. This type of activity provides people

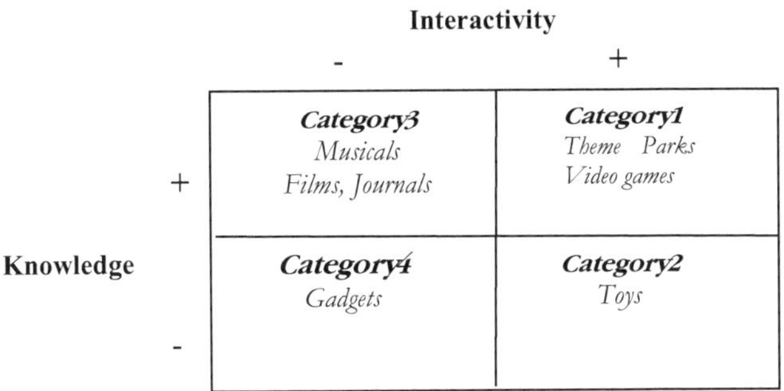

Graph 4.1 The categories of Disney entertainment

with an opportunity to live through an interactive experience with the narrative. It only requires a minimum level of knowledge. For example, in theme parks, visitors are entertained by the imageries as much as by the feelings that they experience. The latter consist of 'a blend of kinetic, visual, aural, tactile and electronic experiences [which are] indispensable to Disney's celebrated synergy, the overlap of marketing, advertising and content has become the very essence of media profitability'.[23] The parks do indeed form 'a new kind of mass medium [...] part of a process of mass cultural production'.[24]

For several days, guests remain in contact with characters and are in close proximity to various imageries. These attractions represent an outstanding experience for visitors because their collective and all-encompassing aspects combine to entrench Disney's symbolic attributes in people's imaginaries. The celebratory atmosphere, the omnipresence of the Disney label and the daily contact with legendary heroes generate a religiosity which is close to the totemism described by Emile Durkheim. All this explains why the participants are stimulated by the festive nature of these gatherings.[25] Revealingly, Hal Richardson states

> that it is actually a world [...] you go there and you are in that world for the entire time you're there [...] it is as if you get dropped into this black box of Disney. It is staggering to me. That's where the whole thing comes together. You meet the characters at breakfast, they sign autographs [...] and the kids go crazy with what they do in the parks.[26]

Video games correspond to this category, although they only focus on one universe. They only require very little information to use, giving the opportunity to extend the narrative beyond simply watching the contents.

In the second category, the traditional toy requires preliminary knowledge of the narratives. Indeed, compelling differentiation comes from an a priori familiarisation with Disney imageries. Concerning the Pixar franchise *Cars* (2006, 2011), the radio-controlled Lightning McQueen car is of particular interest only if the child knows the narrative beforehand. Such goods represent 'reverse product placement', where products previously only available in a virtual world are created for the real world.[27] They convey strong connections to virtual worlds, fictional characters and other consumers-spectators.[28]

The third category includes films, TV fictions, newspapers and stage performances, all of which are didactic since they inform audiences through multimedia content. But the spectator or the reader does not play an active role. In this respect, there is a gradation in the informative quality of the contents: films remain richer than newspapers, while live shows supplement the film experience by putting the world of Disney on stage. For example, Disney has developed, since the 1930s, a branch dedicated to books and journals, Disney Publishing Worldwide. This division has three main dimensions: first, it claims to reach 100 million readers monthly thanks to the translation of its content into 85 languages and a presence in 75 countries.[29] Second, as early as in 2009, it launched its digital publishing business. Since then, 170 applications, more than 1,500 comics and hundreds of magazines have been digitalised. Third, Disney publishing has expanded in curriculum-based content with Disney Educational Productions and Disney English. In China, in 2008, Disney entered the English language-learning market through quality courses and home study material. It now consists of 800 titles and ten applications.[30]

Finally, the last category of Disney products offers little activity and information but simply points to Disney imageries by its graphics, logos and symbols. This type has spread to domains such as the clothing industry. As Melissa Utsler showed in her analysis of Disney light bulbs, these purchases are based on what geographer Yi-Fu Tuan calls 'the urge to reify experience, to give those fleeting moments of pleasure and pain a narrative outline or a visual shape'.[31]

This Hollywood civilisation can lead us to rethink the level of risk involved in cultural productions. Many economists underline this inherent aspect of the motion picture industry whose income always remains random. In this respect, Arthur De Vany states: 'movie revenue dynamics are so complex that they are nearly chaotic [...] every actor, director and studio executive knows that their fame and success are fragile and they face the imminent threat of failure with each film they make'.[32] In fact, neither actors nor narratives or technological innovations can guarantee success. In addition, all the profits are concentrated in a few films. According to Vogel's estimate, '5 % of movies earn about 80 % of the industry's total profits. Exhibition on a large number of screens can just as easily lead to rapid failure as to quick and great success'.[33] All the while promotion and production costs have skyrocketed.

However, the box office represents only one negligible part of financial revenues. Indeed, Hollywood firms secure return on their investments in other markets, which are home video, TV, video on demand and non-audio-visual markets. For the disney Company revenue generated by the Studio Entertainment division reached $7.2 billion out of a total turnover of $48.8 billion in 2014.[34] Gross from box office amounted to $2.4 billion, in other words less than 5 % of the turnover during an outstanding year.[35] Thus productions other than cinema theatres account for the bulk of revenue.

The Power of Goods-Symbols: By-Products Reconsidered

By-products consist of a myriad of goods and activities, which include primarily consumer merchandise and theme park attractions. Their power and influence have grown independently from films and they possess a strategic strength of their own—their cultural aspects reinforce narrative universes in collective imaginaries. Stemming from creative work, they represent goods-symbols which generate profits and diffuse imageries.

Traditionally, the success of full-length films is regarded as a determining factor for the success of sales in other product areas. But spin-offs have a life of their own—the link between by-products and audio-visual content is irreducible to a simple dependence of the former on the latter. In this respect, movie specialists have studied the business activity related to these films but often underestimated the properly creative aspect of the by-products themselves. For example, Janet Wasko considers that 'film plays a key role in these synergistic efforts [...] corporations, such as the Walt Disney Company, build product lines that begin with a film but continue through television, cable, publishing, theme parks, merchandising and so on'.[36] Although audio-visual creations prove to be key in the development of consumer products, more complex relations exist between films and the latter which generate in turn their own consumption cycles. One can first note that Disney's unsuccessful movies in the 1970s did not bring about a collapse in consumer sales. Admittedly they provoked a deceleration of expansion and a drop in profitability, but, by no means did they bring about a substantial reduction in revenue.[37] In other words, creative by-products induce an additional demand by introducing new narrations, spawning their own spiral of purchasing.

Disney consumer products divisions have experienced many developments. The first by-products came simultaneously with the earliest animated films adding a way of disseminating narrations and generating streams of revenue. As early as 1927–8, pins, candies and painting kits accompanied the release of the 26-episode *Oswald the Lucky Rabbit* series.[38] Concerning Mickey Mouse, Walt Disney agreed to brand pencil boxes with this character in 1929 and licensed comic strips a year later.[39] Herman Kamen then organised the spectacular development of Disney in this field. In the mid-1930s, approximately 75 merchandising contracts already existed in the United States, 20 in Canada, 45 in the United Kingdom and six on mainland Europe.[40] Between 1933 and 1934, sales estimates of consumer products amounted to $20 million of which Disney took royalties ranging from 2.5 % to 10 %. At the time, the giants of American industry such as RCA Victor, General Foods, National Dairy Products and Emerson Radio Corporation held the majority of licensing deals with Disney. The early development of consumer products casts new light on the commercial aspect of art.

Sales originated from the success of full-length films as well as other non-audio-visual activities. The latter brought about intense emotions, strong memories and a similar type of consumer behaviour to movie-goers' bonding with film narratives and characters. Set up in 1929 by Harry Woodien in California, the Mickey Mouse Club numbered 500 associations and 500,000 members in 1932. Several decades later, Disney chose the same name for a TV broadcast, perpetuating symbolically a type of children's community. This club would be a precursor to future theme parks since it already formed extra audio-visual activities where children met on a weekly basis to watch cartoons and to play together. Leaders were elected among the kids and every meeting began by reciting the club creed.[41] These activities stimulated the sales of Disney products, the success of its films and the brand loyalty to the label.[42] The company launched its first retail outlets outside theme parks under the name Disney Stores in the late 1980s, the years during which Eisner was CEO of the company.[43] In this respect, the diffusion of Disney imageries parallels the development of diverse sales, indicative of the role of goods-symbols in the maintenance of imageries.

In the same way, the success of the narratives triggered the development of series and sequels. The use of pre-existing and well-known universes makes these creative enterprises less risky and less demanding. They profit from the notoriety of the previous films, which results in higher revenues. For example, the box office of *Pirates of the Caribbean: The Curse of the Black Pearl* (2003), the first episode, came to $654 million while all the subsequent three episodes of the series exceeded this result. Total revenue of this franchise has reached $3.7 billion at the worldwide box office.[44] Intense merchandising has accompanied the movie theatre and home video releases.

The Disneyland Parks play an inescapable role in Disney universes. Borrowing from world fairs, they attract massive numbers of visitors—in total in 2014 Disney parks and resorts welcomed 134 million visitors.[45] As Hal Richardson claims, 'the Disney park was a hugely wonderful idea as far as keeping the brand alive [...] when there was no [audio-visual] entertainment other than the old stuff being recycled [after the death of the founder Walt Disney and the subsequent decline of film creation]'.[46] Indeed, through this medium, visitors deepen their knowledge of Disney narratives and increase their sensitivity to Disney symbols. In addition, these parks have international customers. In Disneyland Paris, foreigners made up the majority of 2014 visitors—only 49 % of whom were French.[47]

The parks contribute fully to the power of media companies by reinforcing the dissemination of narratives, brand acceptance and the development of sales. Before the opening of Disneyland Paris, several parks already existed in France but lacked a strong design concept and visitor numbers—the Sea of Sand attracted only 0.4 million visitors annually, Astérix 1.8 million and Nigloland 0.4 million.[48] In sharp contrast, Disneyland Paris welcomes 14 million people each year, thus representing the primary tourist destination in Europe. In other words, Disney universes drive visitors to attractions.

Consumer products are the result of artistic research. Their success depends on their creative dimensions. Shows, comic strips and attractions, just like films, add emotion and magic to the same narratives, which in turn generate new cycles of consumption. This leads to a reconsideration of the bonds which exist between consumer products and audio-visual works. In this respect, renowned animators have been involved in divisions other than animation. As an example, and highlighting the creative dimensions in this field, Ken Anderson created park attractions such as Peter Pan's Flight, Mr Toad's Wild Ride and Storybook Land while also working in the film production of *Cinderella* (1950), *Alice in Wonderland* (1951), *Peter Pan* (1953), *Lady and the Tramp* (1955) and *Sleeping Beauty* (1959).[49]

Far from only exploiting the magic of a story, consumer products extend the enchantment produced by original creations.[50] For this reason, studios substantially improved the overall quality of products such as sequels—a failed sequel can damage, even destroy, the appeal of a story and consequently its commercial value.[51] On this point, the Disney Company has always been concerned with the protection of its narratives and characters, also taking an autonomous approach in making TV shows. Jeff Holder said that

> if you don't own the distribution, you are relegated to pitching shows and are at the mercy of the network buyer [...] This led to odd network-mandated things like Hanna-Barbera taking a valued character like Yogi Bear and turning him into a bear at a mall with Ranger Smith being mall security.[52]

This failure had some negative effects on the character Yogi and almost destroyed his narrative universe. The Disney Company was anxious to preserve the specificity of its narrative until it ultimately decided to buy out the ABC network and its cable extensions. The same concern has led the major studio to take charge of merchandising. For instance, Disney theme parks conceive exclusive lines of products which differ from the ones sold in high street outlets.[53] Nowadays, video games draw much attention. Developers take care not to compromise Disney's integrity. As an executive of the renowned video game company Square mentioned, Disney people 'don't like if we use the word "attack" too much'. A Disney Interactive Vice President, Dan Winters added, '[characters in the game] don't die, they sort of disappear'.[54]

In a similar way to movies, theme parks reinforce the relation between emotional experience and consumer goods. They also sustain synergistic spirals of purchasing. According to this study, few interviewees stated that they had recently bought films and visited the parks.[55] Generally, the purchase of by-products was combined either with watching full-length films, or with a visit to a theme park, which shows that these last two types of activities imply different cycles of consumption. This can be observed in the financial results of the Disney Company. The growth of the Parks and Resorts division is less dependent on the development of studio entertainment than the growth of consumer products.[56]

Narrative influence has been given a new lease of life thanks to development of the live theatrical performance. Through directly managed production and licensed shows, Disney Theatrical Productions attracts 19 million spectators annually in 50 countries. For example, *The Lion King* on stage has grossed $6.2 billion worldwide. Since 1997, more than 75 million spectators have attended one of the 22 global productions.[57] The show won six Tony Awards and 70 other major art awards. In this respect, its success shows the longevity of this franchise, whose initial release took place 20 years ago. It also reveals the contribution of theatrical productions to maintaining this franchise. Since 1981, the Disney Company has associated with Feld Entertainment for spectacles such as Disney on Ice. In 1994, Disney initiated a rebirth of live shows based on the film *Beauty and the Beast* (1991). In 1997, it contributed to the restoration of the New Amsterdam Theatre and the district of 42nd West Avenue in New York.[58] In 2000, it signed an agreement with Stage Entertainment, which owns more than 22 theatres in Europe and the United States. The company also set up alliances with national partners in Japan, Korea and China. In other words, although Disney revenues still come primarily from Western countries, its cultural influence has taken on a truly global dimension. Indeed, staged performances directed towards families have become global.

Such success challenges Baumol's Law which highlights the constraints inherent in live spectacles.[59] Under this rule, the absence of technological innovations and productivity gains keeps labour costs high, so much so that the performing arts sector, for example, would be irremediably condemned to losing money. However, cultural capitalism and global brand recognition have led to multiple and worldwide replications of shows and vast numbers of spectators attending them, enabling a partial easing of these restrictions.

Beyond doubt, the leading figure and most famous character of the Disney Company is Mickey Mouse. Arguably, his notoriety is presently based on consumer activities and products rather than on audio-visual content, showing that consumer products maintain and develop narratives and imageries. Invented after Oswald The Lucky Rabbit, Mickey Mouse was successful from his first appearance in *Steamboat Willie* (1928).

However, over the last few decades, he has only appeared in re-releases, specials, cameos and direct-to-video films and sequels. Since *The Simple Things* (1953), Mickey has been animated only four times for original movies; *Mickey's Christmas Carol* (1983), *The Prince and the Pauper* (1990), *Runaway Brain* (1995) and *Get a Horse!* (2013). Actually, this character is subject to close attention because using him in new creative contents is risky. Jeff Holder reports on this subject that executives were finally very reluctant about resorting to using Mickey in their TV shows because

> Mickey Mouse is not only a show but the corporate icon, the crown jewel [...] there was an internal debate: if you do it [the programme] and it does not work well, you can pull down a lot. The whole magic kingdom lives around Mickey Mouse. If you have a bad Mickey Mouse show, you pull the whole thing down.[60]

But many products, such as *Le Journal de Mickey* and the TV broadcast *Mickey Mouse Club*, still refer to the famous mouse. Mickey also appears on clothing, toys and figurines. Consequently, by-products are presently a major element in maintaining the icon of the Disney Company.

Moreover, many films have been made after the production of consumer goods—pre-existing items, such as toys, have forged many audio-visual intrigues.[61] These feature films thus reinforce the popularity of the artefacts and introduce a magical element and emotional aspect into ordinary goods. In marketing terms, movies increase their image and notoriety, so to speak their brand power, which results in a competitive advantage in contemporary saturated markets. On this subject, one of the most famous Pixar films deals with toys. Indeed, *Toy Story* (1995) is about a cowboy, Andy, and a cosmonaut, Buzz Lightyear. Despite radical differences between the two characters and their lifestyles, they have to embark together on multiple adventures to re-join their companions. These stories, which stimulate the imagination, can only emerge through artistic creativity that imbues simple inanimate objects with narrative substance and true human depth. Only innovative productions can cause this increase in meaning.

Major studios and other entertainment companies are closely intertwined, developing real collaboration which backs up their creativity and diversifies their topics. For instance, Hollywood firms have been involved in sport. Very early on the Disney Company launched movies showing

Mickey Mouse playing different types of sport. In 1996, Disney acquired part of ESPN, the reference company in sport television, whose leading channel presently has 100 million cable subscribers.[62]

Cultural capitalists endeavour to maximise the value added generated by their creations. To do so, they rely on their critical mass, their involvement in telecommunications and their power over collective imaginaries. Companies' trans-sector investments can accelerate an interest in fashion, for example, or can promote their works through other media. In particular, they have diversified their activities mainly in entertainment. A good story line enhances the appeal of entertainment. This is why non-audio-visual products also contain a narrative element. There is a strategic continuum which extends from direct investment in new activities to the licensing rights given to other companies. On the one hand, any involvement in distant domains supposes additional costs and higher risks, which, in the case of success, can be turned into substantial revenues. On the other hand, licensing distribution via a third party will generate income from fees, which in turn means that the licensing studio will only partially cash in on the cultural appeal of its symbols. This explains why, in the last few decades, many studios have invested in non-audio-visual domains with some disappointing results. The Disney firm replaced its own licensees, becoming involved in extremely diversified spheres. One of the least related domains to Disney's core business has been cruising which it launched in 1998. In 2004, Disney was one of the top ten companies providing sea voyages. It now has four ocean-going ships with 8,000 cast and crew members on board, who welcome 600,000 passengers annually.[63] Thanks to a specific business infrastructure, Disney has contributed to the prosperity of a market sector by attracting families into cruising. Thus the Disney brand encourages individuals to adopt new practices. In other words, through its attractive imageries and narratives, the Disney Company is able to modify or instil social customs and to lead consumers-spectators into targeted markets.

Although Hollywood capitalists did not create theme parks, they promoted and developed this sector by targeting families. Walt Disney initiated attractions that were comfortable for families. The success of Disney theme parks encouraged media companies to invest heavily in this sector, which resulted in several resounding failures. Even though these firms have decreased their direct involvement, they still receive substantial fees from licensing agreements without having to confront operational risk. On this point, the most significant operators remain Disney and Universal Studios, both of whose main resorts are located in Orlando in Southern California and in Japan. Disney is also settled in France, Hong Kong and Shanghai, whereas Universal is established in Singapore and has announced the opening of a new resort in Beijing for 2019.[64]

These attractions are really integrated in the firm's strategy for development where they represent 'entertainment spaces, seemingly limitless opportunities to cross-promote goods and imagery produced in other parts of the conglomerate or acquired elsewhere'.[65] The Disney Company not only incorporates cinematographic themes but also sets up 'thematic environments', to use the phrase of Susan Davis.[66] It needs to co-ordinate multiple services, manage vast organisations and invest heavily in infrastructure, all of which 'requires deep pockets. Temporary and long-term problems demand solutions: traffic flow, design and signing, maintenance and sanitation, interaction between employees and patrons, the quality, tone, style and content of performances, food and drink, souvenirs and concessions, all require continual monitoring'.[67]

As a result, the cultural, emotional and artistic dimensions of Disney symbols structure markets while establishing the supremacy of certain goods. They exert an influence on the habitus of consumers-spectators which have a strong impact on consumption behaviour. But the same key specific advantages provoke vulnerabilities which in the end limit the firm's expansion strategies.

Symbolic Constraints of Major Studios

The Continuous Need for Creative Renewal

Cultural capitalism cyclically loses its symbolic attractiveness due to the uncertainty of creative productions and to sociocultural changes. Its prosperity appears vulnerable to social, cultural and economic contexts since companies have little control over either the success of their creations or the public's response to them. The success of Hollywood capitalists is based on the continuously renewed attraction of their symbols and narratives. However, over time, artists' creativity can be hindered by companies' organisational routines and structural hierarchies.

Many researchers feel puzzled when confronted by consumers' craving for Disney products. Inspired by the Frankfurt School, they disapprove of the processes of commodification which these industries generate. They hold those commercial sectors responsible for the asepticisation of product and accuse them of destroying creative passion.[68] According to these detractors, Disney productions would result only from industrial formulas which would lead to uniformity and stylistic impoverishment. Art would thus be sacrificed to standardisation and serialisation. As for Horkheimer and Adorno, they believe that populations would become gradually alienated under the effect of advertising which would come to be seen as propaganda. Audiences would be transformed into 'an apparatus which even in its unconscious impulses, conforms to the model presented by the culture industry'.[69] According to the same authors, this massification 'is causing the organs which enabled individuals to manage their lives autonomously to atrophy'.[70]

The hostility to cultural capitalists is based on the fear that mass production would degrade works and would debase audiences. There is a strong case for showing that this rejection comes from the underlying assumption that degradation is inherent in popular art. According to the Frankfurt School, the masses are not in a position to appreciate or even recognise true art forms. This reveals the School's prejudice against any contemporary popular art. While famous painters of the past sold their talent and bowed to their sponsors' demands, they were not held in low regard. In contrast, critiques from the Frankfurt School castigate 'culture industries' which, they claim, would take advantage of mass-produced culture, such as cinema, and would threaten authentic art. Appreciated by all social strata, cinema remains 'a genuine folk art'.[71] Whatever the diverse ways of watching movies may be, they always attract vast audiences. Studios do profit from the popularity of movies even if they do not escape from the risk inherent in any creative effort.

Providing a magical experience, cultural innovation plays a decisive role in the success of productions and the competition among companies. Endogenous dynamics of change drive the movie industry. Studios renew the attraction of their symbols and maintain a feeling of amazement among audiences. Rather than a question of inventing radically new content studios demonstrate a sense of 'innovating' in Schumpeter's sense in other words, the adoption of practices, techniques and narratives both familiar and original at the same time. This regeneration can involve various types of internal transformations which come from change in the factors of production due to new usages. Economically this results in the introduction of a new production function.[72]

When an innovation is fundamental, it triggers a new business cycle. Innovative firms are 'upsetting existing industrial structure and heading toward monopoly [and they] are in general precisely those which have set up new production functions and which are struggling to conquer their market'.[73] In other words, innovation generates a new demand which benefits first-mover firms[74] in the innovative process, since they temporarily hold a monopoly. For other companies, on the contrary, these developments accelerate their 'economic death',[75] because of the obsolescence of their production system, induced by this novelty. State-of-the-art progress thus remains crucial so as to postpone cyclic decline and the rise of possible competitors. We are at the heart of 'creative destruction' evoked by Joseph Schumpeter, a 'process of industrial mutation [...] that incessantly revolutionises the economic structure *from within*, incessantly destroying the old one, incessantly creating a new one'.[76] This process takes on a social dimension with capitalists acting as creative entrepreneurs who disturb values and upset power balances inside the movie sector.

According to Schumpeter, competition within the Hollywood milieu does not lie in the efforts to increase margins or supply. To the contrary, production depends on an original combination of invention and tradition which creates its own demand. As Schumpeter affirms,

> it is not that kind of competition [price] which counts but the competition from the new commodity, the new technology, the new source of supply, the new type of organization [...] competition which commands a decisive cost or quality advantage and which strikes not at the margins of the profits and the outputs of existing firms but at their foundations and their very lives.[77]

By analogy, artistic research and development are vital for studios. In the industries of culture, innovation engenders 'new economic space'.[78] On the one hand, it corresponds to narrative universes with diverse creative content, such as films, park attractions and video games. In Baudelaire's words, art 'creates a new world [and] produces the feeling of novelty'.[79] On the other hand, a company with innovating staff and departments will produce a vast array of products, including films and huge ranges of consumer goods. The magical and emotional power of the products results in massive sales and long-lasting profitability. In this context, the value of the content does not come from its use, whatever the product may be. It comes from the associated imagery and narrative, the result of authentic creative acts. What distinguishes an ordinary cup from one branded with the narrative of the film *Frozen* (2013)? The branded cup integrates the symbols, values and emotions related to the adventure of the two sister-princesses, Anna and Elsa. The latter heroine has trouble controlling her icy power and will learn how to do so during the film. In marketing words, the emotional dimension prevails over the functional one. Therefore, the success of Hollywood industries escapes from the ordinary rules of supply and demand since it is based on artistic aspects. In other words, cultural and economic dimensions interweave with one another in the world-economy of entertainment.

The central aspect of creation in the growth of the entire firm can appear in the financial reports of the Disney Company—the more dynamic the creativity of the major studio, the greater the expansion of all its divisions. Between 1984 and 1994, all types of innovation provoked full expansion in the motion picture industry followed by an increase in the business of consumer products and theme parks. The contribution of films to operating income exceeded 40 %. Conversely, at the turn of the millenium, following a slow down in the creative arts' field, this contribution accounted for less than 10 % of the operating income, average operating profit decreasing from 15 % to less than 5 %.[80] These results stress the real decline which started as early as the end of the 1990s.[81] In the last quarter of 2005, Disney's studio division even showed a deficit, losing $313 million from many underperformances.[82] These cinematographic failures were quite alarming since the studio division was expected to push demand for other divisions of the group; the imaginaries were exploited and then maintained for decades. In the 2010s, however, the Studio Entertainment division is experiencing a new golden age after replacing leading executives and acquiring Pixar, Marvel and Lucasfilm studios.[83] The movies *Frozen* (2013) and *Star Wars* (2015) have notably achieved worldwide success similar to that of *The Lion King* (1994).

Technological inventions can result in film breakthroughs provided they are integrated into the production process. Indeed, such inventions contribute to changing the creation and/or the diffusion processes in many ways—they can ease the processes of dissemination; they can even increase the abilities of artists. Major innovations can also disrupt the whole sector. For example, Warner Brothers, followed by other Hollywood studios, initiated talking films with *The Jazz Singer* (1927) then *The Singing Fool* (1928). This conferred a considerable advantage to these firms. In addition, the coming of sound reinforced the supremacy of the major studios, not only in international motion picture domains but also in the entertainment industries.[84] From an artistic standpoint, this innovation allowed artists to develop their talent; for example, according to Marshall McLuhan, a performer could 'transfer [...] the viewer from one world, his *own*, to another, the world created by [...] film'.[85] In fact, narrative depth was increased thanks to a supplementary sense—hearing. This technical innovation induced major sectorial reconfigurations, with in particular the brutal reduction of live theatre performances and the end of silent films. It also implied changes to the careers of actors: some enjoyed highly successful careers while others came to a dramatic end.

In a more limited way, the new team at Disney discovered additional sources of income while innovating in the audio-visual sector. As recalled by Hal Richardson, Bill Mechanic 'discovered and really pioneered' the sell-through consumer business in home video when it was at first only a film rental business. In July 1985, the company sold one and a half million copies of the film *Pinocchio* and one year afterwards, three million copies of *Sleeping Beauty*. Hal Richardson illustrates the competitive advantage of this move: 'Disney discovered this home video business and was first one on this new market segment [...] Consequently, Disney was in a better position to ascertain exactly the number of videos cassettes that they would need'.[86] Thus, by providing the mass markets, the home video segment became—with many generations of formats—the main channel of profitability.[87] Today, the Internet is changing this money-making activity.[88]

Innovation can happen also on the narrative side, through the renewal of a genre which is based on a mix of style, narration and characters. Illustratively, the success of Disney's *Pirates of the Caribbean* franchise renewed the genre of eighteenth-century piracy. In these films, while Orlando Bloom and Keira Knightley represented mainstream actors, Johnny Depp, an outsider, took on the role of the pirate.[89] During the shooting, Johnny Depp was made-up, put on dreadlocks, gold teeth and rings and behaved in an effeminate way. In addition, according to the scenario, his character was a seducer, hanging out with prostitutes and thieves, swearing and behaving in a cowardly manner at times. For all these reasons, the CEO of Disney, Michael Eisner, opposed the project whose marketing intelligence studies disfavoured giving the green light.[90] As Charlie Nelson explained: 'we did not know what we had here. Pirate movies had not been successful since Errol Flynn [in *Captain Blood* (1935)].' By the end of 2003, *Pirates of the Caribbean* had brought in \$300 million at the box office in the United States and \$650 million worldwide for a budget of around \$120 million. Not only did the film 'rediscover' a theme universe, but it also redefined what a Walt Disney Pictures film was: it must entertain the whole family while remaining suitable for kids.[91]

This unforeseen triumph generated even more revenue through subsequent sequels and by-products. Despite forecasts and predictions, successful artistic creation remains irreducibly haphazard.[92] Creative renewal shows the random dimension of the movie business. Neither technical nor financial considerations control art, contrary to the conclusions of the Frankfurt School. Studies on a film project will always appear skewed since they are based on previous successes, taking no account of innovations. As Charlie Nelson posited, Hollywood is 'one of the last places where business decisions involving lots of dollars are still made by gut reactions. We can do some research [...] but it all comes down to the guts [...] There is no science'.[93]

In his time, Walt Disney remained a central figure in the motion picture industry because he constantly maintained the appeal of his productions. Walt capitalised repeatedly on his first-time use of innovations to gain competitive advantage. He introduced state-of-the-art technology in his films to attract audiences, establishing a quasi-monopoly in animated films. Indeed, when he launched *Steamboat Willie* on 18 November 1928, many studios were producing animation such as the adventures of Betty Boop and Popeye.[94] The introduction of sound in this genre spurred international enthusiasm in favour of Mickey Mouse. Then, in 1932, Walt innovated again by inserting colour into his films, for which he received his first Oscar.[95] Decisively, Walt initiated a new type of movie—the animated full-length film. Costing the colossal sum, at the time, of $1.4 million, *Snow White and the Seven Dwarfs* was presented at Carthay Circle Theatre on 21 December 1937. The success was immediate among the general public. Its worldwide box office reached $8.5 million, breaking all-time records in box-office revenues for a feature film. Walt Disney received an honorary Oscar two years later.[96]

The 2007 Parisian exhibition of the Grand Palais depicted the impact of European artists on Disney's art. The creations of Disney studios originated in diverse artistic movements of the medieval and modern epochs. As Bruno Girveau, the general commissary of the exhibition, underlined, Walt Disney's team took inspiration from 'romanticist painters, German symbolists, English Pre-Raphaelites, as much as from Flemish primitives and expressionist cinema'.[97] This multiple source of inspiration revealed the artistic dimension of Walt Disney's work, although he always denied this. In this respect, Bruno Girveau affirmed that Walt Disney was 'the first person to confer an artistic status to animated cartoons. The perfectionism and genius of Walt Disney thus opened up a world audience to animated films'.[98]

After the long decline following the death of its founder in 1966, the Disney studio began a new golden age in 1988. Economic, cultural and technical dimensions at work within the studios interwove—Disney combined the impulses of Katzenberg, the Broadway inspiration from Howard Ashman and the use of new technologies. The new style and narrations appeared first with *The Little Mermaid* (1989). This film brought in $110 million at the box office in the United States and $222 million worldwide. These revenues do not take into account the ancillary markets such as video cassettes for this film where the Disney Company earned $180 million.[99] The studio also received two Oscars for the song *Under the Sea*. But the film *The Lion King* (1994) represented the climax of this period. Produced for only $80 million, it grossed $750 million at the worldwide box office while earning $1.5 billion in sales of consumer products during the ten years following its release.[100] Consequently, the use of this narrative and imagery is a model with regard to cultural synergies made in all the divisions of the Disney studio.

From the mid-1990s onwards, the Disney Company underwent a new phase of decline due to its lack of creativity. As Igor Khait maintained, it missed 'the CGI [computer-generated imagery] turn. It waited too long to start'[101] because it never believed in this technology. In those years its former leader Michael Eisner characterised the efforts of Pixar as 'pretty pathetic'.[102] Consequently, at the end of the 1990s Disney productions such as *Hercules* (1997), *Mulan* (1998), *Tarzan* (1999), *The Emperor's New Groove* (2000) and *Atlantis: The Lost Empire* (2001), failed. Their scenarios were outdated while their technologies still remained 2D. Even the first Disney 3D film, *Chicken Little* (2005), was only moderately successful.[103] Moreover, movie critics regarded it as 'an unprepossessing pic [which] feels second-hand in all respects [...] *Chicken Little* looks recycled inside and out'.[104]

As a result, Disney lost its quasi-monopoly on animated films. Its competitors successfully used technological and narrative supremacy, such as joint collaboration between DreamWorks and PDI and between Blue Sky and VIFX. Disney thus appeared outstripped in its core business with regard to technique and, more importantly, creation. In other words, Disney lacked the intertwining mix of cultural and economic dimensions which were at the heart of its previous successes.

Before being bought out by Disney, the Pixar studio, located in Emeryville, Northern California was one of its competitors. The company, which specialised in computer graphics and stimulating stories, renewed the world of animation. Headed by John Lasseter, Pixar studios came from George Lucas' Industrial Light & Magic, the leading production house in computer-generated imagery, which made the special visual effects for *Star Wars*. Although in 1986 the Disney studio refused to invest some ten million dollars in Pixar, it agreed later to distribute and partly finance the company's animation.[105] Pixar earned global recognition with *Toy Story* (1995). Between 1995 and 2006, the worldwide box office of Pixar films amounted to $3.6 billion, without taking into account revenues coming from consumer products and home video. Disney clearly profited from these successes. And it even became dependent on them because Pixar's full-length films accounted respectively for 97 % and 47 % of Disney's film operating income in 2000 and 2001, with *Toy Story II* and *Monsters*, Inc.[106] Eventually, Disney had no choice but to acquire Pixar studios in 2006, thanks to Eisner's successor, Robert Iger.[107]

Another studio, DreamWorks, also emerged in the field of animation, headed by a former leading executive at Disney, Jeffrey Katzenberg. After making films with moderate success such as *Antz* (1998) and *Chicken Run* (2000), the *Shrek* series (2001, 2004, 2007, 2010 and 2011) proved to be a global franchise with a total box office of $3.5 billion.[108] DreamWorks became renowned worldwide by making fun of Disney-style old fairy tales.[109] By making ogres into heroes, it reversed the traditional perception of characters. Strategically, it was regarded as the antithesis of the Disney formula with the introduction of the 'wacky' factor. Thus the antagonism between Eisner and Katzenberg (Disney versus DreamWorks) resulted in economic and cultural clashes.[110]

Disney executives missed the coming of digital technology and did not realise how much the Disney style had aged. Like Steve Hulett, many criticised the heads of studios such as Tom Schumacher, Peter Schneider and David Stainton who were very educated and intelligent but lacked creativity in animation.[111] Disney also suffered from a haemorrhage of some of its best talent who left Disney for its competitors. For example, Chris Buck left for Sony Pictures Animation. Joe Ranft, Ash Brannon, John Lasseter and Brad Bird all left to work for Pixar. In the same way, Brenda Chapman worked first for Disney, then for DreamWorks and Pixar.[112] However, as Bill Mechanic explains, 'to a certain extent, it is a natural path because it is a funnel. So you are going to lose people. So of course the skill is not to keep the people who want to stay as much as to keep the people who should stay'.[113] Consequently, Disney underwent a brain drain of talent—key people went elsewhere and produced more innovative work with their new employer than they did at their former studio.

In 1984 as in 2005, the successive departures of leading teams proceeded with difficulty and with much uproar. Top managers had established a stronghold on the Board of Directors. Having been in the limelight after so much success, they became arrogant and entrenched in their outdated creative stances and strategy. As a result, company growth slowed down[114] while the studio declined and lost money with the failure of big-budget films like *Pearl Harbor* (2001). The disastrous over-expansion of Disney stores and the ill-considered purchase of the ABC television channel only made matters worse. Lastly, in the Parks and Resorts division, the difficult beginnings of California Adventure and the permanent deficit of Disneyland Paris shook up the Eisner leadership. In the end, all these failures and colossal losses questioned the legitimacy of Disney leaders.[115]

Another factor worsened the fate of the major studio: bureaucratic heaviness. Although Watts has affirmed that the founder Walt Disney battled against it, his firm has been particularly prone to this problem.[116] A trend in contemporary business practices encourages the development of Hollywood sectors into huge industrial conglomerates that are risk-averse. Through inflexible hierarchies they favour standardised work processes and oppose creative enterprise.[117] So a structural contradiction within the organisational logic of studios comes into play. This reminds us of Joseph Schumpeter's analysis on capitalism confronted with the progressive bureaucratisation of the economy. In this logic, existing company structures stifle the entrepreneurial spirit which would call those very structures into question. However, as Schumpeter showed, the class of entrepreneurs makes an effort 'to reform or revolutionize the pattern of production by exploiting an invention or, more generally, an untried technological possibility for producing a new commodity or producing an old one in a new way'.[118] The hierarchical organisation of leisure ensures this structuring, which makes it all the more rigid and difficult to change. Whereas independent companies react quickly and give birth to innovative ideas, entertainment companies, such as Disney, become at times 'a bureaucratic machine dedicated not only to movie production, but also to the various spheres of creation, which slows down, if not prohibits, rapid adaptation'.[119] In addition, the Parks and Resorts division systematically seeks to reproduce outdated methods. For example, many attractions remained rooted in the past. As another executive pointed out, 'it is nonsense for Disney to impose on its subcontractors hundreds of more-than-50-year-old specifications which double the cost of the same attractions'.[120] Although the company is widely recognised for the quality of its entertainment, the price of the latter became excessive. Thus, the Disney corporate culture arguably slowed down the creative processes and the emergence of innovation.

Consequently, although these great companies enabled Hollywood to come up with large-scale attractions and an ever increasing number of products, they also inhibited innovation. They were in the forefront of deploying popular and entertaining leisure to everyone. In addition, these bureaucratic structures formed the necessary framework for worldwide entertainment enterprises. Many stigmatise the logic at play in these cultural activities which would globally diffuse the principles of 'efficiency, calculability, predictability and control'. This would lead to a 'McDonaldisation' of the world. Such a rationalisation process would cause the imprisonment of individuals in what Max Weber termed the 'iron cage'.[121] Disney represents a firm of 180,000 employees based in audio-visual and non-audio-visual creation. Its subsidiary, Disneyland Paris employs 15,000 people.[122] Between 1992 and 2012, Disney invested more than $7.6 billion and created value added of $54 billion while attracting 250 million visitors.[123] As an executive, who preferred to remain anonymous, stated: 'Disney is organized in a matricial way, it is a very heavy, complicated and expensive maelstrom. This structure looks like the reversed Mexican army: lots of managers and very few soldiers'.[124]

More than any other activity, the organisation of theme parks and spectacles requires discipline and drastic supervision. Indeed, the strict co-ordination between all divisions, the professionalism of workers and the global organisation of the Imagineering department have maintained the enchanting aspect of Disney activities. In this respect, one can point out the meticulous shaping of spaces. The constant concern for detail and the ceaseless search for perfection result in the magic of Disneyland parks.[125] As part of this approach, the Disney Company selects employees according to their physical characteristics. In each park, the talent casting department deals with the recruitment of those who look physically like the Disney characters they might impersonate. Moreover, all the employees have to respect specific rules regarding their appearance, be it the size of their earrings, the length and colour of their nails or even the length of their hair. In addition to the function they occupy in the company, each employee is asked to work on his or her emotions. What is presented as 'the act of expressing socially desired emotions' supposes an effort of the employee to 'actively and more or less consciously manage his/her emotions'.[126] This framing manifests in the interaction with visitors. Employees must be available and cordial, without being too kind and casual. Such apparently harmless behaviour in fact presupposes an incessant demand on each employee and great rigour in his or her behaviour given that the aim is to cause emotion and empathy among visitors. Although this kind of work can be fulfilling, it can trigger phenomena of emotional discord, which can bring about 'a clash between personal values and role requirements' and an 'estrangement between felt and expressed emotions'.[127] Indeed, this can frustrate and exhaust people nervously, since many of their roles require intense acting to perform successfully.

The special vocabulary of theatrical shows is at work in the parks. To this aim, Disney operates a rephrasing which contributes to the parks' enchantment. So, employees are called 'cast members'; they wear costumes, not uniforms. They host guests rather than visitors. Parks are split between 'backstages' and 'onstages'. This systematic naming reflects the ambition to create a merry and magical atmosphere and to transfigure reality. On this subject, some interviewed guests shared their admiration,[128] while others, on the contrary, regarded the practices as the totalitarian dimension of a company which formats the feelings and emotions of a captive consumer.[129] As for Alan Bryman, these activities mirror a societal evolution that he describes as 'Disneyisation'. This concept encapsulates the processes of merchandising, thematisation, emotional work and the dedifferentiation of consumption.[130] Admittedly, a visit to one of these parks entices people into a dream-related universe. This artificial world can only exist, however, under the influence of the decor and the co-ordinated efforts of the employees.

The Adjustment of Major Studios to Sociocultural Changes

Symbolic attributes constrain cultural capitalists which must increase their production, widen their audiences and adapt to social change. The structures of symbols appear at the same time to be fragile, requiring constant attention of the studios, and difficult to adapt to societal evolution. On this subject, Disney has acquired a strong position in children's entertainment which its label embodies. However, its competitive advantage is periodically transformed into a straightjacket in which the firm finds itself locked up, trying to reproduce old successes indefinitely. Even Walt Disney himself complained about the constraints of the label.[131] In this respect, the first successors of Walt showed particular concern about remaining rigidly faithful to the brand without searching for creative renewal. The inertia brought on by such a policy appeared all the more absurd as major cultural transformations had been taking place since the 1970s.

After Eisner came to head the studios in the 1980s, the release of PG (Parental Guidance) and PG-13 (Parental Guidance for children under 13 years old) films became more general practice, thus showing the willingness of studios to produce films appropriate not only for children but also for teenagers and parents. Expanding the boundaries of the Walt Disney Pictures label was essential to attract new categories of the public to its cinemas, television shows, parks and stores. In this respect, there has always been a fragile compromise to reach between keeping the interest of adults and producing content for children. A Vice President of production wishing to remain anonymous declared that he watched *Pirates of the Caribbean* with his five- and-seven-year-old children: 'All went well during the movie until their sleep. In the middle of the night, they woke up in tears and finished in our bed.' Beyond its anecdotal character, this story reveals the conflict between contradictory requirements, inherent in Disney films.

The firm focuses on a genuine policy of prestige, which associates all its key activities with the name of its founder. It tries to hide from the general public its involvement in ordinary creations. For example, the Touchstone Pictures studio (owned by Disney) allowed the Eisner team to thrive in the movie business. The first R-classified (Restricted) films were launched under this label with *Off Beat* (1986) and *Outrageous Fortune* (1987). Several former executives at Disney, such as Charlie Nelson, explained that Touchstone was created as a different entity to protect the Disney brand. Nelson released the criteria which determined the label for each film: 'filmmakers, a big cast, language and violence'.[132] Similarly, for animated films, Igor Khait argued that Disney management closely watched the language, cast characterisation and the attractiveness of the storyline, concluding that 'it has to fall in a certain Disney formula'.[133] However, despite the merger of the two entities, Walt Disney Pictures and Touchstone Pictures, this policy of labelling continues even today.[134]In order to complete its audio-visual line-up, the Disney Company purchased an entity specialising in niche audiences. On 30 June 1993, Disney acquired Miramax for $80 million, a company that was founded by the Weinstein brothers in New York City. Since their buyout, Miramax has distributed *The Piano* (1993), *Trainspotting* (1996) and produced *The English Patient* (1996),

Pulp Fiction (1994) and *Gangs of New York* (2002). Having produced 550 films between 1979 and 2004, the company was then worth $2 billion.[135]

However, the integration of Disney in the tumultuous world of Hollywood turned out to be detrimental to its image. As stated before, Disney wanted to become an influential studio and was determined to widen its audience in the process. To do so, Disney immersed itself in the movie business and recruited Hollywood talents. But it faced their eccentricity and their extravagance. Illustratively, the most polemical of Miramax films, *Kundun* (1997) and *Fahrenheit 9/11* (2004), have thwarted Disney in its lobbying both in Beijing and in Washington DC. Particularly the documentary *Fahrenheit 9/11*, which showed the close relations between the Bush and the Al Saud families, interfered with Disney's negotiations for cable licenses. Although Eisner had refused any involvement in such films, the Miramax entity continued to finance them but gave distribution to another company. As a result, Disney came under crossfire. For conservatives, the firm was a left-leaning company, while for liberals it appeared as a censor preventing freedom of speech.[136] In fact, such a wide-ranging production of movies exposed the Disney Company to all sorts of polemics common in the Hollywood milieu.

The image of an impeccable company—patiently built and carefully preserved before the Eisner period—suffered from scandals. The latter resulted in aligning the Disney Company with other Hollywood firms. Nevertheless, the firm always searched to escape from such an alignment. It claims to be different from the rest of the Hollywood milieu. In this respect, Claudine Reynes, a former executive at Disney, recalls the terminological precision whereby 'in the Disney Company, we never said "I'm going to Los Angeles", we would rather say "I'm going to Burbank"'.[137] What counts is that for decades Disney built an image based on innocence and sentimentality in films intended for children, which Charlie Nelson, in charge of advertising at Disney, expresses in this way: 'Disney is the only true brand in Hollywood [...] When a film is released under the Disney label, people can immediately identify it'.[138] Nevertheless, many cases have since tainted the Disney image. For example, the litigations about Michael Ovitz as well as the departure of Jeffrey Katzenberg made public the colossal wages and the doubtful behaviour of Disney management.[139] In addition, a long judiciary battle also took place between Disney and the Slesinger family on the ownership of the character Winnie the Pooh.[140]

As Stanley Gold has asserted,

> Walt Disney represents the family and good values. When they [audiences] saw people like Eisner making so much money and fighting so hard to keep his job […] I think it has tarnished the brand. It makes the managers look like they are selfish, piggish […] they look like spoiled brats.[141]

The coming of the current Disney CEO, Robert Iger, has brought change to Disney's strategy. He re-centred the activity of the group around the Walt Disney brand, confirming this as the core asset of the firm. The dismissals in the summer of 2006, the reshuffling of the leading executive team and the identity redefinition of the company with the rebranding of Buena Vista under the Walt Disney Studios name, have all led to a focusing of its activities—in particular of its creations—on the very spirit of its founder. The major studio zeroed in on what formed its distinctive core value. As Dick Cook maintains, 'We have a real brand name known around the world […] The top 80 movies [of all time] could be Disney, if you take out a word or two or modify a scene'. The movie slate has been reduced to the production of ten films under the Walt Disney label and only two or three other films under the Touchstone label.[142] In other words, the company has finally refocused on its core activity after a cycle of overall expansion through entertainment.

In addition, the Disney Company is also confronted with adapting to major changes in society. Indeed, not only does the firm have to find the right inspiration and the key concept which will make a film successful, but it also has to adapt to social transformations. As Eisner, the former head of Disney, has affirmed: 'Kids are ageing'.[143] Such a joke underlined that current younger generations were more mature in audio-visual matters than previous ones. This change has limited the influence of the Disney label to a decreasing number of younger children. In this respect, one of the interviewees confided to us that, 'I enjoy Pixar films with the *Incredibles* and *Toy Story* more than Disney films. Disney studio productions look old fashioned compared to the creativity of Pixar'.[144] Concerning the parks, Gérard Couturier underscored the current issue confronting the major studio:

> Thirty years ago, when American students graduated from high-school, they would celebrate with their family at Disneyland. Today, very few young people go to a park for graduation and, even if they do, they go without their families and they seek to take full advantage of the attractions, which implies fewer purchases during their visits.[145]

Other indicators have also shown the loss of appeal of the brand. Disney products have been purchased for increasingly younger children. In the analysis based on a questionnaire, family expenses for Disney products fall as soon as children reach the age of six. Then, they sharply diminish after children reach the age of 11. More than 80 % of the responding parents, who had children under the age of ten, recently bought Disney products, while only 56 % of the responding parents who had 11- to 15-year-old children did so.

During the fieldwork for this study, mothers often affirmed that 'their children were too old for this type of branded product since they were over the age of seven'.[146] In the same sense, many respondents were embarrassed to recognise that older children were buying such products.[147] That people actually ceased buying such goods or that they did not dare acknowledge that they were actually doing so points to a strong relation between Disney and early youth. Thus, the undeniable competitive advantage this major studio has always profited from also proves to be a handicap, all the more so as the firm has endeavoured for some years to attract 'empty-nesters, senior citizens, honeymooners and post-college single people'.[148] The difficulties of attracting teenagers have led Disney to acquire Marvel and Lucasfilm.[149]

Disney managers worry about any loss of brand loyalty. As Charlie Nelson has affirmed, 'we have the obligation to protect the Disney brand but we also have to keep it contemporary [...] So we have to expand the boundaries of Walt Disney Pictures'.[150] In fact, Disney needs to adapt to current societies without betraying the confidence which parents grant it. The difficulties this implies are not easy to resolve because Disney's inoffensive universe and reassuring innocence are confronted with sociocultural changes in new generations. Its products can appear tedious and old-fashioned for contemporary children and teenagers. However, the concern of renewing universes by adopting a shifted tone appears very delicate to implement insofar as it can puzzle the audiences of these narrations. On this subject, the firm remains divided on which policy to adopt. Roy E. Disney, the guardian of his uncle's legacy, castigated consumer products such as a t-shirt on which Snow White appeared with the caption '[she] hangs out with seven small men'. In the face of such criticism, Andrew Mooney, head of the Consumer Products department, quickly withdrew this line of clothing.[151]

Regarded as the epitome of children's culture, Disney is torn between conservative tendencies—which rebuff any contemporary transformations—and liberal tendencies which view the firm as old-fashioned, even anachronistic. The expansion of the company into cinema and entertainment has triggered many negative campaigns from conservative associations. If their economic impact remains limited, they have nonetheless contributed to tarnishing the Disney image. For example, Evangelist and Catholic associations organised a boycott on Disney products from 1996 to 2005. In fact, the firm's recognition of homosexuality shocked them. According to the associations, Disney has been promoting gay culture by organising Gay Days at Disney World since 1991.[153]

Moreover, certain Miramax films *Priest* (1994), *Pulp Fiction* (1994), *Dogma* (1999) and *Kids* (1995) sparked the anger of right-wing extremists.[154] However, the latter stopped their protest after the dismissal of the Weinstein brothers and the production of the Christian-inspired film, *Chronicles of Narnia: The Lion, the Witch and the Wardrobe* (2005).[155] Actually, Michael Eisner's policy starting in the 1980s was the focus of particularly harsh criticism, even if it did lead to the expansion and renewal of the studio. All this underlines the extent to which Disney must take into account contemporary mutations occurring in society.

Unlike this supposed excess of liberalism, liberals have regarded the Disney Company as conveying stereotypes and preserving old-fashioned values. As outlined in a number of gender studies, Disney narratives portray women as passive beings—as Jasmine in *Aladdin* (1992) and Beauty in *Beauty and the Beast* (1991) illustrate.[156] Moreover, liberal activists reproached the studio for being prejudiced against minorities. They took the example of the supposedly degrading way Disney represented Africans, Jews or Arabs in *Aladdin*.[157] As for Afro-Americans and Hispanics, they appeared as hyenas in *The Lion King*. Disney fought back against the criticism with the production of the film about the Indian Pocahontas. In 2009, it released *The Princess and the Frog* (2009), a full-length film in which the main role was held by a young Afro-American girl. Finally, these questions appear all the more topical as Disney wants to expand abroad.[158] Obviously, the conquest of new markets demands that Disney products stop caricaturing the lifestyles and culture of the people that they want to attract.

At the end of the Eisner period, the firm had lost any ability to anticipate profit opportunities for films and for new technologies. It missed many occasions to produce hits such as the adaptation of the novel *Lord of the Rings* as advocated by Harvey Weinstein. It partly disengaged from the successful Disney film, *The Sixth Sense* (1999), while it fully produced projects such as *Pearl Harbor* (2001) and *Armageddon* (1998) which were disappointing financially.[159]

In addition, the declining company failed to enter the Internet sphere effectively. Its Go.com portal turned out to be an unsuitable format for this new media even though it benefited from massive investments. After heavy losses, the studio ended up closing the site and laying off 400 employees.[160] In fact, when Disney decided it wanted to develop its in-house activities, it arrived late on the market, whereas others, such as Michael Ovitz, at the time President of the Walt Disney Company, proposed to acquire shares in the search engine Yahoo! as early as 1997.[161] As Stanley Gold acknowledged,

> Michael Eisner did not understand the digital revolution. He wanted to try [and] Disney spent nearly a billion dollars on the Internet portal called Go.com. They quit and closed it the same month than the two boys [Larry Page and Sergey Brin] started Google which today makes zillions of dollars [...] The same month, the big old company Disney quit this business and two guys who didn't even know what was a sports coat or a tie [created their hugely successful business].[162]

Let us recognise however that these disappointments proved to be commonplace among established moguls in the image of Time Warner. The fusion of the latter with AOL in 2001 turned out to be a financial disaster. It seems imperative for companies to arrive first on emerging markets. They are thus in a better position to adapt from the start to any changes in sociocultural and consumer behaviour.[161] Each company then engages in a tough battle during which 'as new technologies arrive, the studio tries fitting them into whatever business model is most favourable from an accounting point of view, just as they did with DVDs and home video'.[163] Intertwined spheres and community-driven networks of the Internet and the digital age have transformed audio-visual consumption, which Hollywood has trouble in addressing.

Notes

1. L. Klady (1999) 'Hollywood's Holidaze', *Variety*, 376 (3), 5 September, 7.
2. J. Dumazedier (1962) *Vers la civilisation des loisirs* (Paris: Seuil), p. 29. My translation.

3. Dumazedier, *Vers la civilisation*, pp. 17–21. My translation.
4. Dumazedier, *Vers la civilisation*, pp. 21–2. My translation.
5. PricewaterhouseCoopers (2015) *Global Entertainment and Media Outlook 2015–2019*, available at http://www.pwc.com.
6. The School of Birmingham initiated a number of research programmes in cultural studies in the 1960s. It concentrated on sociological studies and reception of mass culture. See R. Hoggart (2009/1957) *The Uses of Literacy: Aspects of Working-Class Life* (London: Penguin); S. Hall, D. Hobson, A. Lowe and P. Willis (1980) (eds.) *Culture, Media, Language* (London: Hutchinson).
7. N. Élias (1993) *La Société de cour* (Paris: Flammarion); T. Veblen (1979) *Théorie de la classe de loisir* (Paris: Gallimard).
8. On consumption analysis, see P. Du Gay (1996) *Consumption and Identity at Work* (London: Sage); A. Warde (2015) 'The Sociology of Consumption: Its Recent Development', *Annual Review of Sociology*, (41), April, 117–34.
9. J. O'Shaughnessy and N. J. O'Shaughnessy (2003) *The Marketing Power of Emotion* (New York: Oxford University Press); S. Robinette, C. Brand and V. Lenz (2001) *Emotion Marketing: The Hallmark Way of Winning Customers for Life* (New York: McGraw-Hill).
10. F. Braudel (1987) *Grammaire des civilisations* (Paris: Arthaud-Flammarion).
11. See S. Siwek (2014) *Copyright Industries in the U.S. Economy: The 2013 Report*, available at http://www.iipa.com, p. 5.
12. S. Tripathi and A. Rimmer (2012) *Profitable Growth Strategies for the Global Emerging Middle. Learning from the 'Next 4 Billion' markets*, PricewaterhouseCoopers, available at http://www.pwc.com; H. Kharas (2010) *The Emerging Middle Class in Developing Countries, OECD Development Working Papers*, January, available at http://www.oecd.org.
13. J. Walters and Y. Kuo (2015) *A Tale of Two Chinese Consumers*, Boston Consulting Group, available at http://www.bcg.com.cn, p. 2.
14. M. Yui (2015) 'Uniqlo Chief Says China Slowdown 'No Impact' on Growth Plans', *Bloomberg Business*, 26 September 2015.
15. On this subject, T. Lisanti (2015) 'The 150 Global Licensors, Global License!', *Top 150 Global Licensors Report*, 18 (2), May, http://www.licensemag.com/license-global/top-150-global-licensors-1.
16. F. Braudel (1985) *La Dynamique du capitalisme* (Paris: Arthaud), pp. 64–5. My translation.
17. Braudel, *La Dynamique*. My translation.
18. See S. Watts (1997) *The Magic Kingdom: Walt Disney and the American Way of Life* (Boston: Houghton Mifflin), p. 33.
19. B. Schmitt (2010) 'Experience Marketing: Concepts, Frameworks and Consumer Insights', *Foundations and Trends in Marketing*, 5 (2), 55–112.

20. L. Percy (2014) *Strategic Integrated Marketing Communications* (Abingdon: Routledge).
21. M. McLuhan (1964) *Understanding Media. The Extensions of Man* (London: Routledge & Kegan Paul), p. 22.
22. McLuhan, *Understanding Media*, p. 23.
23. S. G. Davis (1996) 'The Theme Park: Global Industry and Cultural Form', *Media, Culture and Society*, 18 (3), July, 406.
24. Davis, 'The Theme Park', 399–400.
25. É. Durkheim (1985/1912) *Les Formes élémentaires de la religion* (Paris: PUF), pp. 158 *ff.*, 459 *ff.*, 593 *ff.*
26. Interview with H. Richardson, senior executive for distribution at Disney studios, DreamWorks and then Paramount, 11 August 2006. For more information, see Appendix 5. On the immersion created by the entertainment and toy industry, see G. Brougère (2008) (ed.) *La Ronde des jeux et des jouets* (Paris: Autrement); F. Rose (2011) *The Art of Immersion: How the Digital Generation is Remaking Hollywood, Madison Avenue and the Way We Tell Stories* (New York: W.W. Norton).
27. L. Muzellec, T. Lynn and M. Lambkin (2012) 'Branding in fictional and virtual environments: Introducing a new conceptual domain and research agenda', *European Journal of Marketing*, 46 (6), 811–26; D. Edery (2006) 'Reverse Product Placement in Virtual Worlds', *Harvard Business Review*, 84 (12), 24.
28. A. Reading and R. Jenkins (2015) 'Transportation to a World of Fantasy: Consumer Experiences of Fictional Brands Becoming Real', *Journal of Promotional Communications*, 3 (1), 154–73.
29. Information obtained at http://www.licensing.disney.com. See also The Walt Disney Company (2014), *2013 Factbook*, accessed at https://thewaltdisneycompany.com/.
30. Data obtained at https://www.disneyconsumerproducts.com.
31. Quotes from Y.-F. Tuan cited by M. Utsler (1989) 'Owning a Private Piece of the Public Disney Rock: Consumer Response and the Main Street Electrical Parade Light Bulb', *Journal of American Culture*, 22 (2), summer, 19.
32. A. De Vany (2003) *Hollywood Economics. How Extreme Uncertainty Shapes the Film Industry?* (London: Routledge), pp. 2, 4.
33. H. Vogel (2014) *Entertainment Industry Economics. A Guide for Financial Analysis* (New York: Cambridge University Press), p. 145. Also De Vany, *Hollywood Economics*, pp. 8, 12.
34. See the trend of the decreasing share of the Studio Entertainment division in the revenues of the company since the mid-1990s, in Appendix 4, Graph 1.

35. The Walt Disney Company (2015) *2014 Annual Report*, available at http://www.thewaltdisneycompany.com, p. 36.
36. J. Wasko (2004) 'Show Me the Money. Challenging Hollywood Economics' in A. Calabrese and C. Sparks (eds.) *Toward a Political Economy of Culture: Capitalism and Communication in the Twenty-First Century* (Lanham/Oxford: Rowman & Littlefield), p. 134.
37. Walt Disney Company (2007) *Annual Report 2006*, accessed at http://www.thewaltdisneycompany.com. See also Appendix 4.
38. D. Smith (1998) *Disney A to Z. The Updated Official Encyclopedia*, 2nd edn. (New York: Hyperion), p. 423.
39. Watts, *The Magic Kingdom*, pp. 148–9.
40. Smith, *Disney A to Z.*
41. Smith, *Disney A to Z*, pp. 362–3.
42. Watts, *The Magic Kingdom*, pp. 146–9.
43. In parallel with the outstanding expansion of the studio, Disney stores opened in shopping malls and global city centres. Between 1987 and 1997, more than 600 stores opened in 11 countries. In 1999, a total of 747 stores welcomed 250 million customers per year. After some restructuring in the 2000s, there would be 200 Disney stores in North America, 40 in Japan and 100 in Europe according to the company's corporate website. The two priorities for Disney are developing online sales globally and retail sales in China. On this point, see J. Goldsmith (2004) 'Mouse Cashes Out of Retail', *Variety*, 396 (10), 25 October, 5 (1); K. Rapoza (2012) 'Guess where Disney Plans to Open 40 Stores', *Forbes*, 18 January.
44. Data obtained at http://www.boxofficemojo.com.
45. Theme Entertainment Association/AECOM, *2014 Theme Index & Museum Index: The Global Attractions Attendance Report*, 2015, available at http://www.aecom.com.
46. Interview with H. Richardson.
47. Euro Disney S.C.A., *Résultats de l'exercice 2014*, accessed at http://corporate.disneylandparis.fr.
48. A. Feitz (1992) 'Euro Disney: Dissection d'un lancement', *Médias*, (327), April, 24-31; A. James (2005) 'Euro-Mickey Braces for Wild Ride: Popular But Debt-ridden Paris Park Pulls Out the Stops to Pack in Patrons', *Variety*, 399 (11), 8 August, 22 (2); F. Bostnavaron (2007) 'Parcs de loisirs. Nouveau départ pour Disney', *Le Monde*, 18 April, 25.
49. See P. Lambert (2006) 'Biographies' in B. Girveau (ed.) *Il était une fois Walt Disney aux sources de l'art des studios Disney* (Paris: Éditions de la Réunion des Musées Nationaux), pp. 294–318.
50. For a study on emotions and connections provoked by 'reverse product placement', see Reading and Jenkins, 'Transportation to a World of Fantasy'.

51. D. Groves (2002) 'Made-for-Video Toons Cash in Across Globe', *Variety*, 388 (3), 2 September, 18 (1); M. Graser (2004) 'H'wood's Direct Hits: DVD Preems Boffo, But Biz Frets Over Sequel-Mania', *Variety*, 396 (4), 13 September, 1 (3).
52. Interview with J. Holder, animator and former executive at Hanna Barbera, 8 August 2006. For more information, see Appendix 5.
53. On the collaboration of Disney with prestigious companies such as Christofle and Baccarat, see the interview with C. Reynes, former Vice President Merchandising at Disneyland Paris, 6 June 2006. For more information, see Appendix 5.
54. D. Bloom (2002) 'Are Disney Characters Ready for Rough Ride?', *Variety*, 388 (5), 16 September, 7 (1); On the intersection between video games and animated films, see G. Papazian and J. M. Sommers (2013) *Game on, Hollywood! Essays on the Intersection of Video Games and Cinema* (Jefferson, N. C.: McFarland).
55. These data come from a questionnaire answered by one thousand people. See Appendix 3.
56. See Appendix 4, Graph 3.
57. 'The Lion King' musical breaks box office record with $6.2 billion worldwide', *The Associated Press*, 22 September 2014, available on New York Daily News website, http://www.nydailynews.com.
58. On the revamping of the 42nd West of New York, see M. Eliot (2001), *Down 42nd Street. Sex, Money, Culture and Politics at the Crossroads of the World* (New York: Warner Books).
59. W. Baumol and W. Bowen (1966) *Performing Arts: The Economic Dilemma; a Study of Problems Common to Theater, Opera, Music and Dance* (New York: 20th Century Fund).
60. Interview with J. Holder.
61. See G. Brougère, D. Buckingham and J. Goldstein (2005) (eds.) *Toys, Games and Media* (Mahwah: Lawrence Erlbaum Associates).
62. The Walt Disney Company (2014), *2013 Factbook*, accessed on the corporate website at https://thewaltdisneycompany.com/, p. 14.
63. Smith, *Disney A to Z*, pp. 93, 146; 'Ferries and Cruiselines', *Duty-Free News International*, (66), January 2005.
64. B. Macdonald (2015) 'What to Expect at China's Universal Studios Beijing', *Los Angeles Times*, 23 February.
65. S. Davis (1996) 'The Theme Park: Global Industry and Cultural Form', *Media, Culture and Society*, 18 (3), July, 406.
66. Davis, 'The Theme Park', 403.
67. Davis, 'The Theme Park', 403.
68. B. Stiegler (2004) 'Le désir asphyxié, ou comment l'industrie culturelle détruit l'individu', *Le Monde Diplomatique*, July.

69. M. Horkheimer and T. W. Adorno (2002) *Dialectic of Enlightenment. Philosophical Fragments* (Stanford: Stanford University Press), p. 136.
70. Horkheimer and Adorno, *Dialectic of Enlightenment*, p. 169.
71. E. Panofsky (1966/1934) 'Style and Medium in the Motion Pictures' in D. Talbot (ed.) *Film: An Anthology* (Berkeley: University of California Press), p. 16.
72. J. Schumpeter (1939) *Business Cycles. With Theoretical, Historical and Statistical Analysis of the Capitalist Process* (New York/London: McGraw-Hill Books), p. 84.
73. Schumpeter, *Business Cycles*, p. 88.
74. First-mover firms have a specific form of competitive advantage which comes from being the first one to enter a market segment or use a technology. Consequently, they benefit from a temporary monopoly-like position, higher brand recognition and better profitability. Hence the phrase 'first-mover takes all'. Cf. M. B. Lieberman and D. B. Montgomery (1998) 'First-Mover (Dis)Advantages: Retrospective and Link with the Resource-Based View', *Strategic Management Journal*, 19 (12), December, 1111–25.
75. Schumpeter, *Business Cycles*, p. 137.
76. J. Schumpeter (2003/1943) *Capitalism, Socialism and Democracy* (London/New York: Routledge), p. 83.
77. Schumpeter, *Capitalism*, p. 84.
78. Schumpeter, *Business Cycles*, p. 137.
79. C. Baudelaire (1980) 'Salon de 1859' in C. Baudelaire, *Œuvres Complètes* (Paris: Éditions Robert Laffont), p. 751. My translation.
80. See The Walt Disney Company, *Annual Report*, 2000–2010, accessed at http://corporate.disney.go.com. In addition, the decreasing share of the Studio Entertainment division can be observed in the split of revenues and operating income in Appendix 4.
81. See Appendix 4, Graph 2.
82. See The Walt Disney Company (2006) *2005 Fourth Quarter Report* (Burbank, Walt Disney Company), pp. 20, 26; M. Marr (2005) 'Disney Expects Its Movie Studio To Post Big Loss', *The Wall Street Journal*, 15 September, B3.
83. See The Walt Disney Company (2009) *2008 Annual Report*, accessed at http://corporate.disney.go.com, p. 1.
84. D. Gomery (2005) *The Coming of Sound: a History* (New York/Abingdon: Routledge).
85. McLuhan, *Understanding media*, p. 285.
86. Interview with H. Richardson.
87. As early as 2000, revenues coming from home video have outperformed national box office in the United States. Turnover from video formats

amounted to $11.6 billion and from rentals $8.3 billion compared with a box office of $7.5 billion. On this point, see S. Hettrick (2001) 'Tarzan Puts Grinch in Vidlock', *Variety*, 381 (7), 8 January, 1.

88. PricewaterhouseCoopers, *Outlook 2014–2018.*
89. Interview with D. Kornblum, Vice President Distribution at Buena Vista, 24 August 2006.
90. J. Stewart (2005) *Disney War* (New York: Simon & Schuster), pp. 438–9.
91. Interview with a former Senior Vice President at Disney studios who has since become a producer, 5 January 2007. For more information, see Appendices 3 and 5.
92. See C. Eller (2006) 'Picture This: Warner Bros. Having a Rare Down Year', *Los Angeles Times*, 18 August, C1 (C2).
93. Interview with C. Nelson, 19 August 2006. For more information, see Appendix 5.
94. Stewart, *Disney War*, p. 23; B. Génin (2006) (ed.) *Special Issue: Disney au Grand Palais. Les influences européennes, Télérama*, September.
95. Watts, *The Magic Kingdom*, p. 64.
96. Stewart, *Disney War*; Smith, *Disney A to Z*, p. 309; B. Guénin (2006) 'Walt Disney. Portrait d'un génie de la féérie' in Génin, *Disney au Grand Palais*, p. 15. On the technologies used by the Disney firm, see J. P. Telotte (2008) *The Mouse Machine. Disney and Technology* (Illinois: University of Illinois Press); N. Lee and K. Madej (2012) *Disney Stories: Getting to Digital* (New York: Springer).
97. B. Girveau (2006) 'Disney au Musée?' in Girveau, *Il était une fois Walt Disney*, p. 28. My translation.
98. Girveau, 'Disney au Musée?', p. 34. My translation.
99. Stewart, *Disney War*, p. 104, 108.
100. J. Rayport, C.-I. Knoop and C. Reavis (1998) 'Disney's 'The Lion King' (A): The $2 Billion Movie', *Harvard Business School Cases.* Brighton, MA: Harvard Business Publishing.
101. Interview with I. Khait, producer and production manager at the Walt Disney Studios, 6 September 2006. For more information, see Appendix 5.
102. Quotes from B. Fritz (2006) 'Change is Big Draw at Mouse', *Variety*, 402 (3), 6 March, 3 (1).
103. The worldwide box office of the movie *Chicken Little* reached $314 million. It only earned $40 million during the first weekend; its production budget was estimated at $150 million.
104. T. McCarthy (2005) 'Chicken Little', *Variety*, 400 (12), 7 November, 22 (1).
105. Stewart, *Disney War*, p. 86.
106. Stewart, *Disney War*, p. 411. C. DiOrio (2001) ''Potter' Plangs WB on Top of Market', *Variety*, 385 (6), 24 December, 12 (1); R. La Franco

(2006) 'Creative Drive—Pixar at 20', *The Hollywood Reporter*, 9–11 June, 43–6.

107. L. Holson (2007) 'He Runs That Mickey Mouse Outfit', *The New York Times*, 4 March.
108. J. Young (2005) 'Jeffrey's Wild Kingdom', *Variety*, 398 (13), 16 May, S60 (5).
109. On the Pixar and DreamWorks studios, see M. Mallory (2004) 'Cel Research', *Variety*, 396 (13), 15 November, A2 (2). See also A. Bohas (2010) 'DreamWorks Animation SKG or the Global Triumph of the Anti-Disney Position', *Inaglobal*, November, available at http://www.inaglobal.fr.
110. Y. Puig (2004) 'Toon Rivalry Gets Animated', *Variety*, 396 (12), 8 November, 5 (1).
111. Peter Schneider and Tom Schumacher come from the live-theatre sector while David Stainton graduated from Harvard and began his career at Disney in the Strategic Planning department. See the interview with S. Hulett, former animator at Disney and Business Representative of the Animation Guild, 1 July 2006, Appendix 5.
112. See also B. Fritz (2007) 'Poach Approach: D'works Takes Top Disney Talent', *Variety*, 294 (63), 28 March, 1 (2).
113. Interview with B. Mechanic, former leading executive at Buena Vista and then Fox, 4 August 2006. For more information, see Appendix 5.
114. J. Wasko (2001) *Understanding Disney: the Manufacture of Fantasy* (Cambridge: Blackwell), p. 40. In 1997, Disney's Board of Directors was named the worst board in America in *Business Week*'s annual analysis of the state of corporate governance. For a breakdown of Disney's annual revenues, see Appendix 4, Graphs 1 and 2.
115. R. Smith (1999) 'Wedded Bliss Eludes TV Marriages', *Variety*, 376 (8), 11 October, 10; N. D. Beaulieu and A. M. G. Zimmerman (2005) 'Saving Disney', *Harvard Business School Cases*. Brighton, MA: Harvard Business Publishing.
116. Watts, *The Magic Kingdom*, p. 171.
117. A. Bryman (1995) *Disney and His Worlds* (London: Routledge), p. 51.
118. Schumpeter, *Capitalism, Socialism and* [illegible]
119. Interview with [illegible]
120. Interview with Gérard Couturier, former leading executive in the Imagineering department of Disney, 29 May 2006. Separately from the interview, Couturier optimistically said that 'a new President will rejuvenate the company and Disney will continue to be the world leader of family entertainment. Disney has always been able to go through difficult times and adjust and adapt to a changing world.' For more information, see Appendix 5.

121. G. Ritzer (1993) *The McDonaldization of Society: An investigation Into the Changing Character of Contemporary Social Life* (Newbury: Pine Forge Press), p. 33.
122. M. Robert (2007) 'Disney renforce son impact sur l'économie de l'Ile-de-France', *Les Échos*, 9–10 February, 5; F. Bostnavaron (2007) 'Parcs de loisirs. Nouveau départ pour Disney', *Le Monde*, 18 April, 25.
123. Délégation interministérielle au projet Euro Disney, Disneyland Paris (2012) *Étude de contribution économique et sociale*, Press file, 12 March, available at http://www.corporate.disneylandparis.fr, pp. 2, 4, 5.
124. Interview with a senior manager at Disney's Imagineering department in France, 10 June 2006.
125. Carine Fenot remembers that 'when [she] was working within Disneyland's Santa Fe Hotel, a tag had been printed out of the computer to notify the dish offered by the restaurant. [...] The tag needed to respect the theme of the hotel, its colours, its fonts and its letters, which correspond to the Mexican universe and its symbols such as cactus'. On this occasion, she had forgotten to request the intervention of the Show Quality Support Team which was in charge of studying such requests and proposing solutions. Interview with C. Fenot, former manager at Disneyland Paris, 20 November 2006 (for more information, see Appendix 5). On Disney as a model for the customer experience relationship, see B. Loeffler and B. T. Church (2015) *The Experience: The 5 Principles of Disney Service and Relationship Excellence* (Hoboken, N.J.: John Wiley & Sons).
126. B. Ashforth and R. Humphrey (1993) 'Emotional Labor in Service Roles: The Influence of Identity', *The Academy of Management Review*, 18 (1), January, 88, 94.
127. A. Rafaeli and R. Sutton (1987) 'Expression of Emotion As Part of the Work Role', *The Academy of Management Review*, 12 (1), January, 32.
128. Interview with Marie-France F.
129. Interview with Emmanuelle M.
130. See A. Bryman (2004) *The Disneyization of Society* (London: Sage).
131. Stewart, *Disney War*, pp. 45–46. According to Ron Miller, Walt Disney's son-in-law, Walt declared: 'I wish I could make movies like that [*To Kill a Mockingbird* (1962)]. I've worked my whole life to create the image of what "Walt Disney" is. It's not me. I smoke, and I drink, and all the things that we don't want the public to think about.'
132. Interview with C. Nelson.
133. Interview with I. Khait.
134. In this respect, some have mentioned Michael Eisner's anger when Diane Sawyer, famous presenter of CBS' *60 Minutes* broadcast, revealed during an interview that the Walt Disney Company owned the Touchstone label. After the programme, Eisner told her: 'Thanks Diane, now all America

knows that we own Touchstone'. Sawyer had exposed the business links that Disney executives had tried to hide, undermining the company strategy of compartmentalising the two studios. See the interview with I. Khait.

135. 'A Mouse Minus Miramax? Pic partners ponder prospects as Eisner, Weinstein haggle', *Variety*, 18 July 2004.
136. Stewart, *Disney War*, p. 429 *ff.*, 520.
137. Interview with Claudine Reynes, former Vice President Consumer Products at Disneyland Paris, 6 June 2006. For more information, see Appendix 5.
138. Interview with C. Nelson.
139. Stewart, *Disney War*, pp. 321–322; J. Goldsmith (2004) 'Shifts Across the Board?', *Variety*, 397 (5), 20 December, 7 (2).
140. See 'Pooh Honey Battle Grows Stickier', *Variety*, 388 (13), 11 November 2002, 2 (1).
141. Interview with Stanley Gold, President and CEO of Shamrock Holdings, Roy E. Disney's private investment company, 16 August 2006. For more information, see Appendix 5.
142. See A. Thompson (2006) 'Risky Business', *The Hollywood Reporter*, 21 July.
143. Interview with G. Couturier.
144. Interview with Clémence L., mother of three children, 9 November 2006.
145. Interview with G. Couturier.
146. Quote collected during the questionnaire. See Appendix 3.
147. On this question, see also E. Meehan, M. Philips and J. Wasko (2006) (eds.) *Dazzled by Disney? The Global Disney Audiences Project* (Leicester: Leicester University Press), pp. 41, 43–4.
148. T. L. Stanley (1995) 'Disney Pitch: 'Not Just Mickey Mouse'', *Brandweek*, 13 February, 18.
149. M. Garrahan (2015) 'Disney: Let It Grow', *Financial Times*, 22 May.
150. Interview with C. Nelson.
151. Stewart, *Disney War*, p. 355.
152. For more information, see http://www.christianaction.org.
153. R. Ostman (1996) 'Disney and Its Conservative Critics: Images Versus Realities', *Journal of Popular Film & Television*, 2 (24), summer, 82–9.
154. A. Johnson (2005) 'Southern Baptists End 8-Year Disney Boycott', MSNBC, 22 June.
155. On the supposed sexism of Disney animation, see B. Ayers (2003) (ed.) *The Emperor's Old Groove: Decolonizing Disney's Magic Kingdom* (New York: Peter Lang); A. M. Davis (2007) *Good Girls and Wicked Witches: Women in Disney's Feature Animation* (New Barnet, U.K.: John Libbey).
156. J. Cheu (2013) *Diversity in Disney Films: Critical Essays on Race, Ethnicity, Gender, Sexuality and Disability* (Jefferson, N.C.: McFarland); M. A. Towbin, S. A. Haddock, T. S. Zimmerman, L. K. Lund and L. R. Tanner (2004) 'Images of Gender, Race, Age, and Sexual Orientation in

Disney Feature-Length Animated Films', *Journal of Feminist Family Therapy*, 15 (4), 19–44; J. Sperb (2012) *Disney's Most Notorious Film: Race, Convergence, and the Hidden Histories of Song of the South* (Austin: University of Texas Press).

157. A. Sprauve (1992) 'Out of the Closet', *The Hollywood Reporter 62nd Anniversary Issue*, 36; S. Chagollan (1994) 'Attitude Adjustment', *The Hollywood Reporter 64th Anniversary Issue*, 22.
158. See Stewart, *Disney War*.
159. M. Graser (2001) 'Traditional Rules', *Variety*, 382 (2), 26 February, S4.
160. Stewart, *Disney War*, p. 335; M. Graser (1999) 'TV Webs Power Up Portal Perspectives', *Variety*, 377 (2), 22 November, 22.
161. Interview with S. Gold.
162. G. Szalai (2006) 'PwC: Net to Fuel Industry', *The Hollywood Reporter*, 21 June, 1 (27).
163. Quotes from Larry Stein, entertainment litigator, in J. Hiestand (2006) 'Profit Anticipation', *The Hollywood Reporter*, 6–12 June, 22.

CHAPTER 5

A Shallow Structuration of Hollywood Narratives

The Uneven Diffusion of Entertainment Universes

Attractive Symbols in a Mass-Production Economy

The global supremacy of Hollywood companies derives from the deep integration of their brand names and symbols into the daily lives of people across the world. Associated companies can profit from these narratives and symbols which confer a distinct cultural competitive advantage and postpone consumerist disillusions. However, this integration has not happened in a uniform way, accounting for substantial variations in product consumption and knowledge. Indeed, the latter vary in function of socio-economic configurations and of actors' strategies. National imagined communities and practices also interfere in people's reception and adoption of these entertainment universes. Disney's market penetration is variously affected by all of these issues.

On this point, an analysis of the reception of Disney's influence mirrors concerns of international business theorists over the need for a unified message across all media (cross-channel communication). This perspective also represents another way to study consumer experience, namely the 'cumulative experiences across multiple touchpoints and in multiple channels over time'[1] between the brand, the company and customers. Focused on customer perceptions in all their diversity, it corresponds to what companies are looking for: 'the internal and subjective

A. Bohas, *The Political Economy of Disney*, International Political Economy Series, DOI 10.1057/978-1-137-56238-8_5

response customers have to any direct or indirect contact with a company'.[2] When it is strongly positive and seamless, long-term success, effectiveness and loyalty are assured, leading consumers from one purchase to another. In addition, a supposed 'purchasing path' is assumed, beginning with movies and gathering momentum with consumer products and parks. All these elements deserve examination in the light of the findings of this research.

Hollywood symbols and narratives confer an appeal on products, which enables them to dominate competitive markets. By giving products emotional and sociocultural dimensions, consumerism is redefined as a pleasurable act. Sales of by-products, spin-off merchandise and also associated products gain a real commercial advantage with these extra dimensions. Interweaving the rational, cultural and emotional is an important strategy in the firm-customer relationship, showing that the classical notion of the market overshadows the combinations of 'communautarisation' and 'societisation'.[3] In addition, companies can reach an increasingly transitory audience by inserting Hollywood narrations into their product lines.[4]

On this subject, companies endeavour to transform advertising into branded entertainment, recognising that there is an opportunity to extend the recognition and global reach of their product brands by strategic placements in films.[5] This can imply the need for increasingly demanding modifications of scenarios, so companies ask for a 'meaningful integration with the story'.[6] Christy Grosz and Dan Bronson have added that 'branded entertainment moves into the realm of narrative and character'.[7] With such a step, promotion becomes dissimulated—even subliminal—while it amalgamates the targeted products with the action of the film.

Overabundant markets have led companies to use cinema narratives and imageries in order to distinguish themselves from their competitors. This differentiation based on culture allows these corporations to prevail. Postmodernists react to the considerable reinforcement of culture in socio-economic relations, in particular through images and media. Some researchers—such as Frederic Jameson or Jean Baudrillard—have spoken of simulation replacing reality.[8] According to them, the era of the *hyper-real* obliterates the difference between actuality and appearance. Symbols would structure existence without referring any longer to real facts. Although these scholars may appear excessive in arguing that signs are detached from reality, and that this constitutes a fundamental change, they underline 'the aestheticization of everyday life'.[9]

This distinction by culture and emotions corresponds to a search for economic advantage in consumption. Narratively-themed goods are irreducible to their functional use because creations engender multiple emotional and irrational bonds between narratives and spectators.[10] Also, cinematic symbols orient audiences, whose implicit loyalty is crucial for business. As a result, businesses structure the sphere of knowledge central for the conquest of power. Pascal evokes it in these terms: 'What but this faculty of imagination dispenses reputation, awards respect and veneration to persons, works, laws, and the great? How insufficient are all the riches of the earth without her consent!'[11] We need to take into account symbolic references since 'a conceptual system of beliefs, rules, and values [...] lies behind different ways of behaving [...] Such vivid "transporting" experiences characterise all forms of media consumption [...] it [the media world] seems vividly real'.[12]

In recent decades, we have observed the generalisation of goods-symbols combinations on markets. Engaging fully in marketing, designing and distribution strategies, they have become crucial stages in world commodity chains.[13] Consequently, these developments are obvious in general consumption, in particular in the sectors dedicated to children. For instance, the toy industry has adopted this cultural resource to a large extent, even financing new audio-visual creations integrating pre-existing toys, as discussed previously.[14] As a result, the economy does nothing more than use symbolic supremacy and compelling narratives created and sustained by cultural companies.

In addition, many deplore that Disney's animated films covertly employ commercial strategies such as product placements, commercial partnerships or cross-advertising campaigns. According to cinema specialists, these mercantile associations would sully movie productions. Strongly inspired by the Frankfurt School, they only understand the multiple commodifications of films in commercial terms. Mass culture, which has resulted from these productions, would threaten individuality and creativity. Walter Benjamin even feared the disappearance of artistic aura during the 'age of reproducibility'.[15] Nevertheless, these studies overlook that the value of these sectors comes precisely from their artistic production and from their capacity to produce this aura. In other words, they live from creative innovation. Consequently, instead of regretting such exploitation, it is vital to explain and to understand the reasons which have led the rest of the economy to ally themselves with these firms.

In fact, they are imbued with a sacred nature, the demonstration 'of a reality of another type quite apart from "natural" realities'[16] found in ordinary goods, which are stripped of any cultural reference. By evoking the imageries of a film or an attraction, for example, goods mean more than their materiality. In other words, they are irreducible to the product itself. Their presence must always exceed their appearance; otherwise the 6–12 % revenue taken for licensing royalties would not be justified.[17] In this respect, we can identify this apparently mysterious sacralisation of these goods due to the meaning consumers place on them.[18] The acquisition is different from a simple exchange.

Besides, the mythical dimension of movies' narratives and imageries, their ability to bring people together across generations and social classes and their capacity to speak to primary human urges make such products unique in increasingly fragmented societies.[19] This is why corporations acquire for colossal sums the imageries which will imbue their goods with this quasi-religious aspect. Indeed, they wish the latter to represent not only one purely functional object but also a culturally, emotionally and aesthetically appealing one by its unique design and its reference to narratives. Thus companies intend to cause an emotional attachment with regard to a simple artefact. In other words, commodification is too simplified a concept to account for the commercial use of entertainment.

By their strategy of branded promotion, major studios build a proximity and impose the supremacy of their products on others in the market. Little by little, their symbols and narratives penetrate the daily reality of individuals whose 'social stock of knowledge differentiates reality by degrees of familiarity', according to Peter Berger and Thomas Luckmann.[20] The two authors add that this 'state leaves the totality of that world opaque [...] the reality of everyday life always appears as a zone of lucidity behind which there is a background of darkness'.[21] Disney animated films have remained the benchmark for generations, due to the quality of the offering as much as to the policy of keeping narratives alive and widespread. In other words, companies use merchandising, publicity and media to build one socially-constructed everyday world which integrates their symbols and imageries posing as socio-economic referents.

Moreover, imageries and narratives develop in a transnational configuration where national referents are significantly blurred and reduced. Indeed, identities appear more than ever heterogeneous. They meddle with new values and images, indicating that globalisation multiplies the identities rather than threatens them.[22] The abundance of commercial offerings makes world markets obscure and unclear. However, firms institute their economic and cultural imageries and symbols as reliable referents in an uncertain global environment. Trust relations consequently develop among social groups and transnational firms in the context of a 'disembedded modernity' characterised by abstract capacities and engagements without real face-to-face communication.[23] In spite of criticism, people easily grant credit to these referents, while at the same time reports regularly question their quality and reliability.[24]

In addition, consumers-spectators' emotional attachment to cinema narratives and imageries should be fully taken into account. Indeed, the industry brings to life real personal bonds between an audience and fictional characters. The resulting emotions are deeply integrated into the collective imaginaries which bind consumers-spectators to symbols and narrative universes. Although Disney's animated films may seem puerile and rather superficial to adults, they cause extreme excitement among children. For example, one interviewee mentioned that his son 'cries each time he watches the death of Simba's father in *The Lion King* [1994]'.[25] Another person remembers having felt much sorrow in her childhood by looking at the film *The Fox and the Hound* (1981).[26] On this point, several studies carried out amongst children confirm the identification and adoption processes engendered by Disney's activities.[27] Using the same logic, attractions generate much excitement among youngsters. A mother remembers that 'one of her children was terrified during the Pinocchio attraction [consisting of a theme ride during which phantoms appear in the darkness], he screamed when the whale opened its mouth'.[28] Certain adults were also fascinated by 'the creativity and the abundance of objects. There was something fairy-like [...] it was stunning'.[29]

The firm intends to impose a consensual conception of family entertainment in all developed societies.[30] In these markets, the Disney Company wants to appear central, foundational and inescapable, revealing an endeavour of a hegemonic kind. As Hal Richardson asserted, 'Disney created this family-friendly approach'.[31] In this respect, the phrase 'Disney classics', repeatedly mentioned during interviews, reveals that Disney's early works are unavoidable and take on a truly artistic authority. Indeed the recurrence of this terminology shows the presence of a consensus on their cultural value, hence their marketing power. In addition, the company contributed to creating a clearly identified social group—children—by the promotion of a whole way of life through full-length films and their by-products for youngsters. Thus the company created and opened up new markets. However, from the very beginning it has avoided traditional fractioning in terms of social groups.[32] The Disney studio has also avoided politicisation and affiliation with any political party. It seeks consensus in order to gain the goodwill of all parents, claiming to be involved only in entertainment. In spite of the cyclical decline of its productions and the emergence of other labels, the studio remains central and imposes its brand as a cultural reference, supplanting its competitors. In other words, it still profits from the notoriety and recognition owed to continual innovation, its first-moving to children's markets and then decades of quasi-monopoly on children's entertainment.

Unlike traditional analyses that portray Disney as conservative, Douglas Brode argues that Disney films deal with pacifism, anti-authoritarianism, feminism and racial integration, the same values which characterised the sixties counterculture. According to Brode, Disney contributed to the rise of youth culture which resulted in rock 'n' roll, the Woodstock festival and the hippies.[33] As a result, the emergence of social groups with specific practices and values confirms that, in addition to contents, 'the media is [also] the message'.[34]

The structuring of symbols and narrative universes carried out by the Disney firm shows that all the markets are embedded in a whole set of different relations. As a result, it is necessary to accept 'the contingent nature of economic action with respect to cognition, culture, social structure and political institutions'.[35] In this sense, the companies are keen on developing multiple relations with studios. They seek to benefit from the Hollywood stronghold on practical knowledge because 'when you get it right and match up a film property that has current cultural significance with a product that has brand equities that relate to that property, as a general matter, you get increased presence in stores and see increased volume'.[36]

The appeal of Hollywood productions also comes from their ability to delay the disappointment of consumers. In this respect, Albert Hirschman observes in modern societies the 'shifting involvements' between public action and private interest.[37] While great satisfaction and pleasant surprise accompany the passage from one activity to another, disappointments encourage giving up one activity and moving on to the other. For example, corruption, the cost of political engagement and the complexity of public affairs incite social actors to change from public action to the private sphere. However, in Hirschman's view, private activity can also appear disappointing because the pleasure coming from the passage of material discomfort to comfort reduces with time.[38] As material accumulation becomes an end in itself, it no longer brings the self-fulfilment it once did at the beginning. Nevertheless, societies remain very much attached to private happiness however temporary it may be. People are putting off their investment in the political field all the more so as consumption practices prove to be fundamental in constructing their identity.

According to Hirschman, the type of consumption can exert an impact on the disappointing effect of material abundance. Its irregular use and ephemeral aspect can mitigate the degree of disappointment. Major studios propose goods which are used temporarily or irregularly. Some are instantaneously and individually consumed and destroyed after their purchase—for example, going to cinemas, parks and themed restaurants. Others belong to sustainable goods while they are used in a discontinuous way. These types of goods, such as DVDs, clothing and toys, can give way to a rediscovery when they are used again.

Cinema companies renew their by-products each time a film is launched. By doing so, they are able to put off—if not slow down—the disappointment referred to above by Hirschman. While traditional industries manufacture similar artefacts over several years, cultural capitalists cyclically modify narrative universes. They use new imageries and symbols for similar types of product figurines, clothing and toys. Hollywood products and entertainment present a similar dynamic. Even attractions in theme parks are periodically renewed. Nevertheless, although film sequels do not make original and new imageries, they deepen the storyline with new plots, which feed cycles of products. Always new, films and various attractions lead people to buy in quantity, which brings comfort to those already withdrawn in their private space. In other words, fictional worlds attenuate—even occult—the impression of reiteration.

The productions of cultural companies prove to be plainly entertaining in Blaise Pascal's sense. Although Pascal fitted into a Jansenist perspective, his notion of diversion captured the function of entertainment when he wrote: 'take away diversion, and you will see them dried up with weariness. They feel then their nothingness without knowing it; for it is indeed to be unhappy to be in insufferable sadness as soon as we are reduced to thinking of the self, and have no diversion'.[39] For the philosopher of the seventeenth century, entertainment would keep us from any metaphysical reflection. In a contemporary sense, cultural goods would divert people from being involved in the political sphere. People would confine themselves exclusively to the search for happiness in the private sector. In this respect, for different reasons, conservatives and liberals have criticised the withdrawal of individuals from the public sphere. The former are afraid of the social upheavals that this tendency could cause while the latter regard them as a factor aggravating socio-economic inequalities.[40] Although the infantilising aspect of entertainment can be pointed out, one can stress that new material inventions are 'unable to change in any way the tragic and frightening characteristics of the human predicament [...] the time during which any one object can truly amuse us is strictly limited'.[41]

Pascal considers that 'the only thing which consoles us from our miseries is diversion, and yet this is the greatest of our miseries [...] diversion amuses us, and leads us unconsciously to death'.[42] If in fact he thought especially of religion, his remarks on diversion remain relevant to account for the withdrawal of citizens from politics. This falls under a postmodern context wherein market societies are saturated with signs. Indeed, postmodernity values self-fulfilment as key. It takes place through consumption in multiplex cinemas and shopping malls. The massive diffusion of imageries responds to the colossal offer of goods whose sales depend on how entertaining they are. Consequently, entertainment consumption replaces the way of acquiring during the Fordist age, which alters even the act of consumption.[43] Thus, consumption transforms into entertainment, which Henry Giroux called the 'dissimulation' of the Disney Company. Giroux uses this term to denounce the pure and innocent image of Disney. This company would be a greedy institution that excessively commodifies its symbols and surreptitiously propagates consumerism.[44] Although this analysis appears excessive, it underlines the multiple issues at stake at the heart of commercial culture.

Culture companies need constant novelty. The production of innovative films and activities is very important for commercial culture since it delays the loss of meaning coming from consumption. Major studios also play a structural role in maintaining consumerist economies. The latter are based on people's search for private happiness through consumption. In this respect, this injunction for new entertainment is essential for all Hollywood attractions. This is especially true for theme parks about which Susan Davis has observed that 'parks need regular, even annual infusions of new attractions, whether these be rides, character shows, parades, performances or short films'.[45] Indeed, parks as well as films permanently aim at innovating to construct 'the event' since they encourage audiences to visit and to visit again often. Concerning the visitors of the park, one parent confided to this study that 'during our second visit, the attraction was much more limited, there was no longer the surprise effect and the sense of amazement we felt the first time. We did not feel the same amount of pleasure'.[46] Thus we can note with Hirschman that imageries and narratives do nothing but put off 'disappointment in the search for happiness through private consumption'.[47] On this subject, as previously discussed, the lack of renewal at the Disney Company remains the main cause of economic failure at the end of the Eisner years.

The profitability of cultural companies is closely related to the ability to entertain. Although Hollywood attraction is often castigated for its mercantile entertainment, it still needs to be taken into account. As already mentioned, many Weber-inspired analysts drew up models of transnational and rationalised firms which have decisively transformed societies. Ritzer underlined this process of McDonaldisation which aims at effectiveness, calculability, predictability and control. As for Bryman, he coined the Disneyisation term which includes the thematisation, merchandising, emotional work and dedifferentiation of consumption. These analyses identify considerable changes in contemporary society.[48] However, they still adopt too external a perspective on such activities, which prevents them from considering the emotional attachment of spectators and visitors to these rational organisations. In fact, they do not consider the reasons why people enjoy going there so much, standing in line for long hours and buying expensive by-products.[49] Furthermore, the research misses the randomness of these productions since it leaves only little room for the emotions provoked by entertainment and their artistic dimension. It does not devote enough attention to the strategic role major studios play in the world economy, in particular their function of enchantment. In addition, the studies insufficiently take into account innovative cycles and the special role of creative content in the boom-and-bust economy of entertainment.

In fact, Hollywood productions are connected with fashion. Adoption of trends is characterised by consumer frenzy and after the fad passes there is a huge reduction in audience. The logic of diffusion in a consumer society corresponds to the avant-garde model rather than to the elite-population model.[50] Companies need to renew product lines quickly and to impose themselves permanently as cultural referents. Cultural capitalists have invested in these sectors of fads and fashions, and the creative aspect of their content and its attendant popularity have contributed to sustaining their dominant imageries.

However, the loss of impetus proper to the creation cycle triggers disappointment amongst spectators. In particular, as Gérard Couturier has posited, tension coming from the merchandising 'exists between the relatively-expensive "branding" compared to the consumer's purchasing power and this mass production. Branding cannot explain a price ten times higher than the real cost'.[51] In times of strong creativity, this anomaly is reduced since the marvellous aspect of movies justifies the high cost of its by-products. In times of decelerating innovation, this aberration becomes blatantly apparent. The mercantile attitude of the company is exposed in all its crudeness. Under these conditions, the branding price is no longer assured because according to Susan Davis it presupposes 'creating a solid base of recognition for companies and characters, as well as associating the company with "high quality" merchandise and an upscale shopping experience'.[52] In the early 2000s, the Global Disney Audience Research Project observed this disaffection and disillusionment with Disney.[53]

An Unequal Recognition of Hollywood Symbols

Despite intense promotion, the narrative universes and symbolic systems of Hollywood are diversely received by audiences, whose knowledge varies widely according to their sociocultural background, leading to a reconsideration of the relations maintained between consumers-spectators and commercial imageries. Indeed, this study shows significantly dissimilar interpretations, schemes and perceptions in one particular country. Cultural specifics remain, exerting a crucial impact on the integration of global cultural universes and imageries.[54] After reviewing the various meanings and realities of Disney productions, these blurred symbolic attributes will be examined.

People are engaged in their day-to-day actions with these narratives and imageries, which has far-reaching implications. They maintain various relationships to commercial cultures whose scope is global, but collective representations remain strongly marked by existing local environments. The latter modify the acceptance and the interpretation of the narrative universes coming from entertainment companies. Consequently, far from being mechanical, this transmission is distorted. In fact, as Stuart Hall has plainly stated, consumers-spectators interpret cultural flows and adopt them according to differentiated social uses.[55] As a result, it is necessary to take into account discursive and material specificities and their attendant distortions. In this case, these elements condition the reception of cultural companies which, by definition, implies a cognitive dimension.

Defined as a 'respatialisation of social life',[59] leading to an uneven 'reordering of economic, political, and socio-cultural differences and complementarities across different scales, places, and networks',[57] globalisation transforms deeply not only political contexts but also cultural and economic ones. In audio-visual domains, over the last two decades, this process has resulted in the global dissemination of American narratives and imageries. Indeed, the density of relations thus created contributes to the diffusion of a living standard in which major studios take part. Diffused by non-state actors, these goods-symbols continue to be regarded financially and economically within the framework of relations between nongovernmental organisations, firms and states. However, their impact must also be analysed at the micro-political scale.[58] Social actors live on a daily basis among the transnational flows that they interpret, adopt more or less consciously, or fear. For this reason, one must focus on apprehending social actors involved in a plurality of roles and in a direct grip of the media giants of the business world. From this standpoint, globalisation appears as a reconfiguration of the relations between actors as much as a major transformation marked by the rise of societies in international relations.

The study of this book has observed judgements regarding the Disney Company in France—a country often portrayed as rather anti-American. Indeed, the qualifying adjectives which the respondents to the questionnaire associate the most with the Disney label are a small group of positive terms. Six of the fifteen words chosen account for 80 % of the answers and evoke a brand which is 'entertaining', 'marvellous' and 'family-oriented'. Notwithstanding, the image of Disney is also associated with the term 'commercial' (12 %).[59] Consequently, the company faces some criticism although it is perceived overall in a very positive way. As Janet Wasko noticed, consumers-spectators are 'able to compartmentalize their approach to Disney as business versus Disney as entertainment. While certain aspects of Disney as business were reported to be objectionable, Disney as entertainment was still considered to be wholesome, safe, and, most of all, fun'.[60] In addition, the most pejorative terms are under-representative. Indeed, words such as 'invading', 'superficial' and 'tedious' accounted each for less than 3 % of the answers. Another research carried out in 18 countries has also shown a convergence around the ideals diffused by Disney. This label is associated with fun (95 %), fantasy (93 %)

and happiness (88 %). Negative qualifiers such as racist are only occasionally evoked (19 %).[61]

The introduction of the criteria of 'place' or of 'social and economic category' reproduces the same polarisation in favour of the major studio. However, there are differences among social categories and regions. Identified variations draw less homogeneous and coherent profiles than those openly claimed by the firm. The penetration and the adoption of American goods-symbols are diverse.[62] Thus one can isolate a 'thick globalization'[63] whose range globally affects social life; another 'diffuse', which combines various processes with a weaker result and lastly a 'fine globalisation', where the growth of flows remains inconsequential.

Disney productions take on diverse meanings according to the social groups the consumers belong to but also according to the regions they live in. On this point, one can distinguish between four models which cover the configurations of populations' top-of-mind awareness. Two basic variables prove discriminatory: the first reflects the knowledge acquired through audio-visual formats. It includes home video as well as the cinema, which represent a mode of socialisation to the symbols mainly based on audio-visual media. As for the second variable, it attests to the level of familiarisation with other products—including parks—which belong to non-audio-visual domains. Although by-products appeared very early, these activities have been considerably developed in recent decades. So, four ideal typical profiles can be established (Graph 5.1).

First of all, the classical pattern of knowledge about Disney is made up of film content. It constitutes a profile referring to a very positive yet outdated image of the Disney studio. According to the questionnaire, it is most

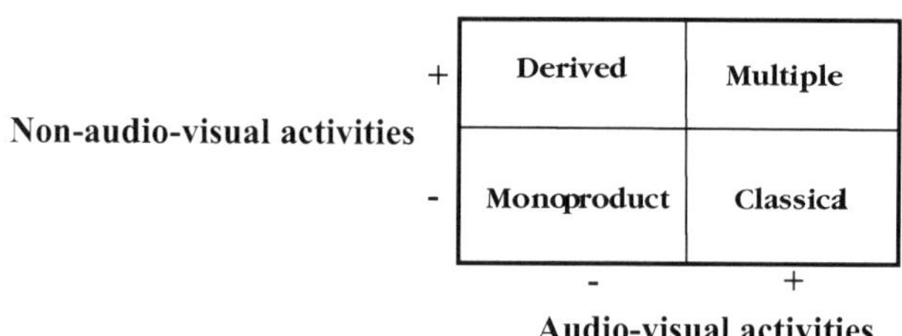

Graph 5.1 The types of Disney knowledge

present among people living in the provinces of France such as the town of Saint-Claude in the Jura Mountain, where a third of the people interviewed there mention only feature films. This mono-product association with Disney increases with the age of the respondents: 21 % of under 25-year-olds; 33 % of over 56-year-olds. This behaviour also follows socio-economic lines: 40 % of workers only quote films, while few of them mention other kinds of products. Concerning feelings inspired by Disney, Saint-Claudians distinctively chose the term 'marvellous' and were less critical about the company. This model refers to the company at its beginnings during the 1930s. When leading the way in innovation and creation in animated films, the firm may have appeared magical despite its commercial merchandising facets.

This model of consumption does not take into account the construction of Disneyland Paris and the launching of Disney stores. It refers to a socialisation of the company before its transformation into an entertainment firm strongly involved in global merchandising. The inhabitants of Saint-Claude have relatively limited access to the recent development stages of the Disney Company, since they are an hour and half's drive away from the closest Disney store in Lyon and four and a half hours from Disneyland Paris, which is quite far by French standards. In addition, this ideal type questions cultural synergies on which the prosperity of Disney relies. In fact, largely familiar with the Disney universe through its films, this public knows very little about the additional products and activities of the firm, which calls into question Disney's marketing strategy. Consumption cycles resulting from films and attraction to by-products and other productions do not occur. Consequently, as Richard Hoggart posited, media firms have only a limited stranglehold on popular practices and conceptions.[64] Sociocultural subcultures and configurations diminish the impact of transnational companies.

On the other hand, the multiproduct model of consumption includes respondents with an acute awareness and a large knowledge of Disney merchandise. While their audio-visual knowledge remains significant, film familiarity is connected to a large number of other products of the company. Not only do people remember films, but they also mention many by-products along with Disneyland parks. Obviously they are aware and familiar with all the activities, even if they do not necessarily appreciate every one of them. This phenomenon is observed in particular among young people. Among the latter, associations of several types of Disney products represent 62 % of the responses, whereas they account for only 44 % among those over 56 years old. Moreover, concerning the familiarity of the brand according to age, knowledge of the three main types of available purchases (movies, parks and consumer products) drops with the age of the respondents.

This category of consumer is mostly present among the upper and middle classes as well as employees, whose associations of several kinds of goods account for approximately 60 % of the responses compared to only 28 % among the working class. Moreover, this profile is concentrated in the wealthy districts of Paris: whether it be Saint-Michel, Edgar Quinet station or Passy, films on their own only represent 20–30 % of the responses whereas their association with additional goods exceeds 49 % of the responses. Of those who are aware of all three Disney products (movies, parks and consumer goods), the highest percentage is among the middle class (12 %). As may be expected, these categories are more prone to evoking some of the negative aspects of Disney, even if the percentages remain small. In terms of the company's phases of development, this corresponds to the boom of the studio as a fully fledged entertainment company under the Eisner administration (1984–2005): hundreds of Disney stores opened, several resorts and parks were launched around the world, and successful animated films gave rise to multimedia globalised merchandising and franchising platforms.[64] By comparison, awareness of the three product lines amongst the lower classes amount to only 4 %.

To these two models, one can add a third which grants a considerable place to non-audio-visual activities. Surprisingly, many respondents to the questionnaire do not refer to Disney films. The greatest number of these respondents comes from middle- and working-class groups, representing nearly 24 % for technicians and associate professionals, 31 % for employees and 37 % for the working class. This knowledge about Disney appears more abundant in poor districts such as the market of Barbès Rochechouart (Paris) and Villeneuve-le-Roi (a suburb of Paris) where respectively 47 % and 33 % of the respondents only remember consumer products. These results remind us of the importance of the Disney phenomenon outside the film sector. In Disney's annual report, the Consumer Products and Parks and Resorts divisions account for 39 % of turnover and 31 % of operating income for the 2014 fiscal year.[66] These results are also related to a tendency of the firm to over-expand recurrently in by-products all the while reducing film productions. In the 1970s, the company almost closed its animation studios while developing parks in the USA and abroad. As a result, the overdevelopment of the firm in by-products can be found in the collective representations of people. All non-audio-visual entertainment—which acquired substantial autonomy—shows the maintenance of deeply-rooted imageries independent from any film. Consumer products are goods-symbols which disseminate imageries and narratives and encapsulate emotions and values.

It also seems crucial to underline the influence of the theme park. As evidenced in the study for France, it has become recognised as a true brand medium in the hands of the mass media. On this subject, Gérard Couturier underlines the park experience as 'an influence impossible to quantify for the company, the brand and the characters'.[67] Indeed, it should be pointed out that even in an area as geographically isolated as the Jura, 31 % of the respondents thought of the park when the words Walt Disney were mentioned.

In many cases, respondents were unable to name specific products, showing a weak vision of the Disney universe. In the end, the ability of the company to trigger the impetus to consume remains limited. For example, 72 % of workers answered by giving only one type of product despite repeated follow-up questions such as 'what else?' and 'anything else?' This type of information was limited to 44 % for employees and 40 % for upper and middle classes.[68] Thus, the self-promotion carried out by Disney goods—often decried by researchers—appears ineffective. This fourth model of consumption reminds us that globalisation is an uneven phenomenon which differs according to spheres, activities and interactions.[69] As a consequence, transnational goods-symbols are diversely adopted not only at the national level but also at the subnational level. In a well-established nation-state, fluctuations can be highly differentiated in their scope and impact.

Furthermore, this variation sheds light on the limited ability of brand content, marketing and customer experience managers. The latter fail to frame awareness and knowledge of the firm in a clear and homogeneous way.[70] More importantly, this questions cultural synergies and the cross-channel spiral of consumption on which the prosperity of Disney relies and which the firm has been forcefully pursuing for decades. In other words, the vast promotion campaigns which intend to encourage multiple-product consumption, that is the acquisition of one product calling for the purchase of another one, have not proved to be fully successful.

The weakness of information relating to Disney entertainment also appeared during the course of this study in an inability of people to name clearly any type of Disney product or knowledge about the firm in general. Although it is impossible to distinguish between people who did not want to answer and those who really do not know the company, some respondents explicitly recognised that they were unable to think of a precise reference. During in-depth interviews, many individuals found themselves in similar situations, in particular if they had grown up without television in the countryside. In these cases, the opportunity to become familiar with Disney products never occurred.[71] In addition, responses from some parents were inaccurate. Confusion among films characterised the remarks of some of them: 'I mix them all up. For me any [American and animated] film is a Disney film'.[72] This decreases the specificity of the label brand, while attesting at the same time to its hegemonic position in the collective imagination. In other words, approximate and limited knowledge about Disney productions reveals an 'oblique'[73] attention towards the cinematographic universe and casual consumption with regard to advertising messages.

This fragmentation of Disney imageries, references and consumption underlines the inertia of the knowledge structure which the author has expanded upon elsewhere.[74] The different interpretations and understandings of what Disney really stands for come from the company's phases of development, successively marked by creativity and over-commercialisation. These stages remain present, many generations later, in the strata of the collective imagination as well as in markets. Furthermore, this corresponds to Bourdieu's hysteresis effect which he defined as 'inertia of habitus which has a spontaneous tendency to perpetuate structures corresponding to their conditions of production [...] dispositions out of line with the field and with the "collective expectations" which are constitutive of normality'.[75] Once the structure of knowledge has been deeply shaped around symbols, imageries and behaviour, it orients practices and determines knowledge for years. It favours such symbols all the while disfavouring others. It leads interviewees to associate any Hollywood animated film with Disney, since the latter created the first animated film and maintained a monopolistic position over the genre for decades. This absence of discrimination among content shows that the hegemonic strength of a brand does not always benefit the owner of the very same brand.

This lack of knowledge establishes the real frontiers of the Hollywood global economy which does not conform to any official national border. These 'neutral zones'[76] are spaces where acquisition of these products and familiarisation with Disney grow blurred. They include areas escaping from the dominant order within the world-economy. Braudel defined them as 'backward zones [which] riddle central areas themselves of multiple regional spaces [...] all the advanced economies are thus perforated by innumerable wells, outside of the time of the world'.[77] A uniform penetration of a dominant universe of meaning would entail a deep modification of sociocultural practices through a long process of socialisation, which Hollywood studios, including the Disney Company, are not looking for.

Moreover, the presence of geo-cultural variations results from disparities already evoked in its time by Dumazedier in connection with leisure. On the subject, a certain underdevelopment characterised the 'workers who inhabited the isolated cities or the suburbs in which social segregation and inadequate collective infrastructures [and] areas in the countryside persisted'.[78] These inequalities slow down—and even considerably limit—the expansion of leisure activities in society. This is why major studios clearly prefer countries where creation centres still exist. Without the latter, the cinema economy is underdeveloped, which reduces the profit potential by just as much. If the networks of cinematographic theatres are weak, a source of symbolic diffusion and profitability disappears. In fact, entertainment firms thrive in the areas where substantial markets already constitute enormous outlets.

The development of the Disney Company and sociocultural configurations shape patterns of Disney knowledge which, in turn, give rise to differences in perception and habitus.[79] For example, the inhabitants of Saint-Claude, who had been less confronted with the invading and omnipresent merchandising of Disney, referred the most to the marvellous and entertaining sides of Disney. Conversely, technicians and associate professionals, who mentioned the most the three types of Disney products with 12 % of the respondents, underlined the most the commercial dimensions of these activities: the excess of consumerism reducing de facto their magical character.

Through their products, narratives and imageries, the universes of commercial culture depend on globalisation. Disney has attained world recognition, in Western countries as well as in developing areas. Company officials underline the global dimension of the business, hence the famous saying 'It is a Small World After All'.[80] As already evoked, the company conveys family values, happy feelings and childhood memories.[81] But Disney embodies a symbol referring to different practices that attracts massive audiences. Other studios have also been mentioned, which can be explained by the diversification of the Disney offering and the loss of Disney's monopolistic position in animated films.[82] People refer to some of the characters. Thus, 10 % of their first responses to the questionnaire were 'Mickey'. According to interviewees, *Shrek* by DreamWorks would be more aimed at the adult population whereas *Nemo*, *Cars* and *Toy Story* by Pixar would be rather intended for the whole family. In fact, not only does the Disney label refer to various realities but it also appears to be attached to vague symbols with a reduced density of meaning. In many instances, it only represents a simple logo of commercial culture, remaining in the collective consciousness because of its deep integration. In addition to sociocultural configurations, this loss in the intensity of meaning also results from the overall expansion and exceptional diversification of the Disney label; as an example, in the movie sector it includes such disparate titles as *Frozen* (2013) and *Star Wars: The Force Awakens* (2015).

Spectators perceive each type of children's films in vague and rudimentary ways. The productions that parents allow their children to watch are broadly based on preconceived ideas stemming from their national origin. In interviews, three categories were generally considered. First, interviewees were mistrustful about Japanese cartoons since they regard them as violent. Consequently parents were reluctant to buy such cartoons. One mother even mentioned that she 'had hidden Japanese videos that had been offered to her children in a cupboard'.[83] In addition, Japanese animation is seen as less qualitative. They are wrongly considered as rough: 'their colours too sharp, their special effects not credible, their graphics not elaborated'.[84] It is worth mentioning that very few of the parents had recently watched any Japanese animated film.

Second, domestic (French) animated films, such as *Azur and Asmar: The Prince's Quest* (2006), *Kirikou and the Sorceress* (1998) and *Kirikou and the Wild Beasts* (2005), were appreciated[85] when interviewees had seen them. However, there too, prejudice undermines these creations—one interviewee commented that audiences were 'not finding them as good as American movies since they remained too realistic and their decorations were not studied enough'.[86] A lawyer in the wealthy district of Paris (Passy) explained that he had never bought any French films because he suspected them of being ideologically biased whereas he said 'with Disney, I [am] sure of the message transmitted by the film'.[87]

Third, American productions received the overall approval of audiences although interviewees criticised commercial exploitation by the companies and in particular their consumer product activities. American animation benefits from the trust of parents, which plays a considerable role on the market.[88] A study led in 18 countries revealed that 'the great majority of respondents indicated that they would introduce their children to the Disney universe partly because they estimated that these offers were safe'.[89] As a mother said, 'if it is a Disney film, I trust it. I consider that unlike TV broadcasting the content of the film was previously worked over'.[90] When reminded of scenes showing the heroes confronted with painful events, the same interviewee added, 'rather than hiding them [children] from such events, I prefer letting them watch so that they can discover little by little certain dimensions of life. It's a good way to tackle serious subjects and to diffuse interesting messages'. In other words, when an American film can shock youth by its intrigue or violence, it opportunely reveals the cruel aspects of life; when a film of a different origin makes the same point, it ratifies negative prejudice. As a result, spectators perceive similar contents differently according to their nationality, which confirms the weight of preconceived ideas and encourages the purchasing of such products. So, in the choice of animation one may observe the importance of predominant opinions. From a business perspective it implies that favourable perceptions of consumers need to be shaped along the consumer path but also even before consumers enter the market.

A Random Appropriation of the American Way of Life

The Multiple Strata of Re/Decoding

Hollywood studios' culture diversely disseminates across societies due to pre-existing ways of living and sociocultural references which remain widespread even in global markets. Hollywood productions and other commercial activities also undergo subnational appropriations and segmentations which reveal the extent to which they are socially grounded. Hollywood shapes social practices but remains dependent on pre-existing culture to which it needs to adapt. These practices develop over time through a process of socialisation out of which grows an emotional and cultural attachment to brands, characters and narratives. Used in repetitive promotional messages, they draw collective attention towards specific products lines. Moreover, Hollywood studios have an effect on the media. As Marshall McLuhan has shown,

> the medium is the message [...] the personal and social consequences of any medium—that is, of any extension of ourselves—result from the new scale that is introduced into our affairs by each extension of ourselves, or by any new technology [...] For the 'message' of any medium or technology is the change of scale or pace or pattern that it introduces into human affairs.[91]

In the case of Disney, its appeal leads individuals to consume goods and to visit theme parks. Consumers-spectators interpret cultural flows and adopt them according to differentiated social uses. The appropriation of films and products sold by the studios can appreciably attenuate their use and their message. Being situated between Disney narratives and consumers, the social, cognitive and material institutions intervene either as a buffer which distances them from one another or as a bond which brings them together. In fact, Disney's attraction and its influence on foreign societies depend on a configuration of many sociocultural layers: first, the domestic environment; second, subnational codes; third, social contexts; and fourth, people's perception of and strategy for dealing with Disney.

First, the domestic environment strongly marks collective representations and practices.[92] It modifies the acceptance and the interpretation of narrative universes coming from cinematographic companies. Although transnational firms diffuse values and symbols, every national culture keeps its own autonomy. It remains an imagined community whose specificity remains within the context of globalisation. Institutions and societies assert their particularism, contributing to the differentiated integration in local and national contexts. Research has shown the influence of mass media on the collective imagination in the wake of Anderson's foundational book.[93] Indeed, the mass media introduce, within the nation-state, differences into cultural development, values and lifestyles. Following Katz and Liebes' analysis of the *Dallas* TV series, films have dissimilar significance and attraction depending on the countries they are seen in. Whereas the series enjoyed enormous notoriety at the world level—except in Japan—this soap opera underwent various readings which resulted in debate over its homogenising aspect.[94] In fact, the ideological decoding of the media product exerted different influences depending on the culture of the audience. In addition, if the message diffuses stereotypes regarding style or class, denunciation can occur, as Marc Doucet has shown.[95]

For this reason, although former Disney executive Bill Mechanic is in favour of the direct and global management of the films of major studios, he advocates a partnership with national distributors in Japan and France since these countries

> are the most unique markets in the world in terms of how films are watched and of the sensitivity to the local market. There are more similarities between the US and Germany than between the US and France where it is easy for films to be given the cold shoulder and ignored. France and Japan are also very difficult markets for Disney because they have their own good animation industry.[96]

In these countries, the Disney firm endures harsh competition in movie theatres as it does in home video segments. Illustratively, in Japan, *Porco Rosso* (1992) by Studio Ghibli arrived ahead of Disney's *Beauty and the Beast* (1991) while video sales of the *Neon Genesis Evanglion* series outperformed that of *Pocahontas* (1995) and *Toy Story* (1995).[97]

In France, the diffusion process appears particularly delicate, which justified alliances between Buena Vista and Gaumont from 1993 to 2004 and between UGC and Fox from 1995 to 2005. Indeed, French audiences approach films according to artistic and aesthetic criteria. This approach differs from American audiences, the majority of whom allegedly perceive films according to their entertainment criteria. Thus, interviewees typically expressed some artistic considerations. They often opposed manga to American cartoons to justify their preference for the latter. Like real aesthetes, they claimed graphic research on 'the smoothness of characters, the artistic side and the bucolic landscapes'. As noted previously, they described Japanese productions as 'rough'.[98] They mentioned 'the enjoyment of the moment'[99] to explain why they were mixing up various animated films. Some interviewees mentioned the French animated film *The King and the Mockingbird* (1980) by Paul Grimault (with Jacques Prévert writing the screenplay). They put forward its poetic and literary dimensions.[100] Many mentioned Disney's early productions such as *Fantasia* (1940), the least popular but the most artistic of its first animated films.[101]

In addition, people often minimised their purchases and the role played by Disney in their daily lives, which recalls the comments collected by

Ien Ang on the series *Dallas* or by Dominique Pasquier on the French soap opera *Hélène et les garçons*.[102] Often the sentences occulting such knowledge result in remarks such as 'I did not grow up with the Disney culture'.[103] Some people went so far as to regret the 'uniformization of culture' exemplified by the 'same American attractions controlled in Paris, Tokyo or in California'.[104] Despite these critical comments, nobody refused to buy Disney products for their children. When visiting his son's room, a father recognised 'the Disney poster on the wall, two toys from *Toy Story* and *Monsters, Inc.* and a large Mickey teddy bear'[105] before asserting that 'Disney is not omnipresent [...] it should not be excessive in the home'. On the contrary, one parent thoroughly enjoyed Disney imageries and was much less critical of the company's film output. He mentioned that he had already bought for his nineteen-month-old daughter 'stickers, toys, a walking Winnie the Pooh, the Winnie's car [...] four Disney teddy bears and some clothes'.[106] And he declared afterwards, 'we do not buy only Disney products, just some of them. We are not narrow-minded.' Consequently, all the interviewed parents refused to be called Disney consumers, even if they contributed in different degrees to the prosperity of the firm. In this regard, the commercial culture of Hollywood requires neither explicit adhesion from their customers, nor full awareness of their acts, but only a tacit assent orienting their daily purchases.

Second, the presence of subnational codes largely affects the appropriation and the use of Hollywood commercialism. Although the globalisation of markets brings cultures and lifestyles closer together, this does not imply a better knowledge of those elements because fragmentation, heterogenisation and hybridisation are at work in what may be called the 'fragmegration'[107] process, which distorts knowledge and messages. As previously discussed, what is understood by the Disney label will be interpreted in various ways by different social groups because sociocultural configurations intervene in the approach that each one takes. Furthermore, globally distributed identical product lines and marketing material will be received differently, influenced by national identities and cultural differences.[108] Indeed, populations maintain ambivalent relations with the world of cinema.

The links that the studios maintain with their public are looser than one might think at first sight. On this subject a parallel can be drawn between theorists who noticed hybrid phenomena in the world sphere on the one hand and the authors of cultural studies who observed local resistance and autnomous categories among populations in their relationship with the media on the other. All academic approaches to this subject have underlined the complexity of changes that are irreducible to one simple global integration.

The success of Disney products also depends greatly on sub national lifestyles. In this context, remarks from some interviewees became somewhat critical with regard to Disney: 'I am against all the merchandising that has nothing to do with the film'.[109] One teacher even said that she was upset by 'the omnipresence of Disney [...] with Mickey forks, Mickey food ...'.[110] Indeed, toys as well as licensed artefacts were severely criticised. In the meantime, relatives as well as friends of the family were often brought up to justify the acquisition of a product. This is why one mother explained that 'the grandparents bought a whole assortment of goods: a helmet with Mickey's ears which light up, a mermaid which turns itself on automatically etc'.[111]

By contrast, newspapers and Disney books were valued among most interviewees, arising from the specific social value this medium enjoys in France. Disney publishing has been very successful among French youngsters. *Le Journal de Mickey* was first published as early as October 1934, followed by *Mickey Parade* (March 1966), *Picsou Magazine* (February 1972) and *Mickey Poche* (April 1974).[112] Despite its status as by-product material in this format is as highly thought of as films. On this subject, the statements of a father interviewed were revealing: 'books that make them [his sons] read history again are interesting. Although one can classify them as by-products, I do not regard them as such. They are different'.[113] Although books demand artistic work, they often remain, from an analytical viewpoint, spin-offs of cinema narratives, showing once again that the commercial/artistic dichotomy remains unsatisfactory. Disney publishing belongs to 'a culture that everyone knows',[114] as if these imageries were more legitimate in this form. This particular status is not new since a retired person remembers that, 'During the holidays we spent near the seaside in the '50s, my mother used to buy comic strips for each one of us. As there were four of us, we would choose different albums, one of which was an album of Mickey Mouse'.[115]

It seems risky to rely on the adoption of cultural material by foreign countries to develop a successful business, and while compelling imageries can attract consumers in huge numbers, the road to profitability can be long and hazardous. If box-office blockbusters can be integrated easily into the audio-visual sector, other activities appear difficult to promote. For example, theme parks require a huge infrastructural commitment which supposes considerable sales to reach a break-even point. In Europe, visitors go in massive numbers to Disneyland Paris, but they do not spend as much money as American tourists. The financial losses of this park have resulted from underutilisation of the resort and overestimates of sales forecasts.[116] Hence the economic disaster which has worsened an initial over-investment. Furthermore, the same difficulties have also plagued other initiatives of the US major studios in the same sector.[117]

Interview comments about Disneyland were rather negative: 'there was too much waiting time. We waited in line for 45 minutes for just 30 seconds of pleasure'.[118] The toys sold in the parks were judged too expensive. These reasons help to explain ambivalent attitudes with regard to the attractions. European visitors are less willing to remain in luxurious Disney hotels, attend shows and buy many souvenirs.[119] As Claudine Reynes declared, 'the challenge was to integrate a US culture in Europe [...] But, European consumers do not have the same behaviour as American visitors'.[120] Moreover, the same former executive at the Disney merchandising department added that substantial mistakes in forecasts were made about potential customers. She remembered that 'according to studies, the target was the upper-middle classes [...] In the first months after the opening, we saw lower-class young couples wearing poor quality t-shirts and flip-flops [...] with a picnic in their bags'.

In addition, Disneyland is generally regarded as a place for children's entertainment. Although it attracts many European tourists, its magic for European parents is confined to their kids.[121] Another person having many negative prejudices and who would never 'have gone there without [his kids]'[122] declared that 'it was pleasurable for them [his kids]'. It was his way of saying that the theme park was only designed for children. Visitors are usually children accompanied by one or two adults, which is due to 'the merry-go-round tradition. But one would never go there alone for fear of being judged by the others'.[123] Finally, according to interviewees, the Disney Park would be more appropriate for the 5–15-year-old age group, whereas the French Astérix Park would be more appropriate for the 10–20-year-old age group as well as adults. Consequently, the commercial potential of Disneyland is all the more limited. Impassioned by Disney, an interviewee reported the differences in behaviour adopted by Europeans and Americans in these terms: '[the latter] take part fully, go voluntarily and play; the former are much more restrained. They need to justify their visit by specifying that they "took along their children"'.[124] Also, although the attractions, rides and activities in theme parks attract a wide spectrum of public in North America just as in Europe and in Japan, visitors to them adopt different entertainment practices according to their cultural backgrounds and perceptions. As a result, there are many uncertainty factors determining the success or failure of the huge investments undertaken by cultural capitalists.

Third, these productions are integrated in social contexts marked by a will of self-assertion and social distinction.[125] They are adopted and/or dismissed according to the dynamics of social positioning. In this respect, Dominique Pasquier showed how the symbols produced by cultural industries constituted signs of social marking and distancing for teenagers.[126] Indeed, popular groups use these symbols to assert themselves, whereas people from the middle and upper classes would rather seek to distance themselves from them. Generally, the latter groups were more wary regarding the questions posed to them about their consumption of Disney products. They deliberately undervalued the purchases of these goods by stating at first that 'I have not bought any of these products for a long time'.[127] Then the interview revealed that, after evoking recent memories and practices, they acquired some Disney merchandise on several occasions.[128] Such reactions could be qualified as symbolic dissimulation driven by social distinction. Several interviews with a few mothers appeared very poor because they refused to disclose their actual consumption, using their lack of knowledge as a pretext: 'we are not big Disney consumers, I can tell you frankly [...] I am not a good example'.[129]

On the other hand, lower-class groups adopted a radically different attitude towards their Disney purchases which are used as a way to assert their belonging to the upper classes. This appears close to practices of conspicuous consumption or *consommation d'apparat*.[130] These groups openly admitted to purchasing these by-products and took great care to detail all the Disney-branded items they bought: 'the bowl, the plates, paperboard and bib'. They also claimed to have gone several times to Disneyland and found it pleasurable.

Fourth, parents conduct a subtle game of distancing their children from Disney. If their offspring's proximity towards the company's products increased, they became worried about preserving them from intrusive merchandising. Thus, the great majority of people were concerned about their children being too 'immersed in the Disney culture',[131] showing definite hostility towards by-products. In fact, families were very selective regarding their Disney purchases.[132] The consumerist spiral, often described as alienating by detractors of the company, appeared more dubious and loose. If the consumption of one product includes the promotion of another, individual behaviour is not reduced to the simple acceptance of what is being advertised. The commercial dimension only constitutes an underlying discourse which is clearly perceived by the public and which diminishes the attraction and the magic of the product. A mother vehemently specified, 'it is fraud: toys are very expensive because they have the Disney brand'.[133] Consequently, all these tactics, these micro-strategies and the refusal to follow the logic encouraged by the firm represent barriers to its prosperity.[134]

Underlining the commercialism of the Disney studio amounts to tarnishing its image and discouraging the appeal of its purchases. In fact, this type of criticism decreases the special dimension and the magic of the brand and only emphasises the small intrinsic value of the product against its high retail cost, reducing its capacity to seduce and to enchant. The study and questionnaire showed a definite denunciation of the commercial perspective relating to familiar items and images that people have become accustomed to. The result is that the buying public is not a passive consumer, but engages in 'active negotiations' with Disney's product presentation.[135]

The Transnational Fragmegration[136] of Demand

Entertainment markets have diversified considerably under the effects of revised company strategies and demands of consumers-spectators. Firms follow as much as they contribute to this process of national disaggregation and transnational aggregation. They target specific groups through their labels and promotion policies in accordance to the dynamics of the contemporary economy which seem to be 'more concerned with cultural preferences and niche marketing' than nation-states.[137] But in the last instance the objective always remains to reach a maximum of diverse households and not an allegedly homogeneous population unit. As Arjun Appadurai observed, 'the emergent postnational order proves not to be a system of homogeneous units (as with the current system of nation-states) but a system based on relations between heterogeneous units'.[138] At a time of content overabundance, deterritorialised television audiences would induce instability. Indeed, all the major studios are concerned with the volatility of audiences, as Dick Cook, former head of the Disney studios, declared: 'with more than 100 channels [only in the United States] and a very fragmented demand [...] it is difficult nowadays to address the mass public'.[139]

One can trace this fragmentation back to Salzman's successes, whose live-action films, such as *Rock Around the Clock* (1956), were the first steps of

Hollywood's engagement with youth culture. Later, another segment, the 'tween', emerged for children not old enough for the full-length films dedicated to teenagers. This segment split up once again with the 'pre-tween'. On this point, these neologisms increasingly mirror segmented markets often discovered through unexpected successes. All the companies gradually accepted and targeted these segments, adopting the imprecise wording. For example, Disney became particularly innovative in the 9–14-year-old age group, and remains the leader in this sector with the Disney Channel. Within its studios, it was responsible for the emergence of genuine stars such as Raven-Symone through the series *That's So Raven*, the most popular programme in the United States for the 6–14-year-old age group, which exceeded 100 episodes. It has also been broadcast in 100 countries, which has represented for Disney a considerable merchandising platform.[140]

The company launched sets of goods-symbols for each age group and gender. The main characters are the traditional figures of Mickey Mouse and Winnie the Pooh, the latter being intended specifically for young people (toddlers and pre-schoolers). According to *Forbes* magazine, in 2003 they earned respectively $5.8 and $5.6 billion for Disney, ranking first and second in the classification of top-earning fictional characters.[141] For young girls, the *Disney Princess* franchise has represented a big platform since its launch in 1999. In addition, movies are released regularly (under the Walt Disney Pictures label), which target these audiences. They often depict women confronted with unexpected events such as *The Princess Diaries* (2001), *Ice Princess* (2005) or *Maleficent* (2014). It goes without saying that such audience segmentation is present in all activities of the company, including clothing, films, DVDs, musical albums as well as ice shows.[142]

The fragmentation of target audiences has made the penetration of these markets easier for other major studios. Disney must consequently compete with other actors in every segment, which Charlie Nelson expresses very well in these terms: 'In the past, it was not as targeted. It used to be one size fits all, with one message [...] Today there is a much more significant targeting by age, which facilitates the competition for Disney on the multiple markets of childhood'.[143] This phenomenon results from a change in configuration where multiple offers targeting every age group exacerbate competition as customers become more demanding. Nowadays, films and associated product lines are entirely dedicated to certain age groups. Consumer frenzies and fashions are also apparent amongst young people, which has led media companies to develop material dedicated solely for them. As an example, Disney faces intense competition in the cartoon genre aimed at early childhood segments where Nickelodeon and its characters Dora the Explorer and SpongeBob SquarePants are well established.[144] In response, Disney has dedicated a channel to the 3–8-year-old segment entitled Playhouse Disney and then Disney Junior.[145]

In addition to specialisation of creations and parks, the fragmentation of entertainment is also reflected in the advertising campaigns of full-length films. Major studios follow the global combination of sociocultural sets whose structuring goes beyond nations-states. For several years, they have all adapted the marketing of their films to various audiences. For a typical film, Charlie Nelson asserts that '[studios] design one TV spot for Americans, Hispanics, boys, girls, moms, adult males, adult female and parents [...] we place them in the right markets'.[146] Therefore it is less a question of announcing a film than of 'sending the right message at the right moment to the right people', which corresponds to the *raison d'être* of marketing and advertising.[147]

Cinema firms endeavour to attract subnational minorities which, rather than being integrated in national societies, remain autonomously organised communities. Different types of behaviour and languages characterise these people who are concentrated in certain areas. For example, Latin American minorities have kept their linguistic specificity in the United States. Hollywood companies increasingly buy advertising spots on Spanish-speaking channels, Univision and Telemundo.[148] In addition, they produce advertising clips and Spanish films to conquer these niche markets.

Studios resort to their foreign subsidiaries to launch their films abroad. The foreign subsidiaries of studios are carefully listened to avoid 'running up against anything which is controversial or not PC [politically correct]'.[149] Consequently, according to the regions targeted, major studios modify many of the film's characteristics such as the format, spots, names, colour pallet, poster and sometimes even the cut. For instance, Disney removed entire scenes from the film *Aladdin* (1992) for the video release after the dissatisfaction caused by awkward dialogues.[150] Consequently, one understands how crucial it is 'to seize the energy of a film and to adapt promotion consequently'.[151] In this respect Charlie Nelson recalled the differences in strategy which are adopted sometimes, taking as an example *Signs* (2002), a full-length film directed by M. Night Shyamalan:

> for *Signs*, we did not use the face of the big star Mel Gibson in the promotion campaigns in the United States [...] We felt that selling Shyamalan's

> creepy scary story and the unknown around it, would have much more impact. Overseas we did use Mel Gibson because a well-known actor would attract international audiences, in particular in Asian territories.[152]

For American studios, the launching of a film abroad is always delicate because each country has diverse cultural, social and juridical approaches. For example, TV commercials are strictly regulated in Europe, whereas this mode of advertising faces fewer restrictions in the United States. However, the most significant barriers remain cultural. American comedies have had a hard time being successful in Japan because US humour is often inappropriate for Japanese audiences. Also, *The Chronicles of Riddick* (2004) was not distributed in Islamic countries because the presence of a religious character called Imam was likely to create tensions. Moreover, many films require some knowledge of the content to be able to appreciate fully the storyline. For instance, *Invincible* (2006) and *The Game Plan* (2007) relate to American football and baseball whose rules seem at first sight very obscure to foreign audiences. How can such full-length films still be appealing when they deal with a sport unknown to the audience?

The Disney Company has also been confronted with cultural challenges in emerging countries which, as mentioned above, have a high concentration of the new middle classes and potential for future growth. As these social groups remain distinctive from Western middle-income families, Disney has appeared at odds with them culturally, requiring major adjustments. In this respect, the first years of Hong Kong Disneyland are a case in point. In fact, Disney's first commercial campaigns awkwardly represented couples with two children, which was at the time prohibited by the Chinese government under the one-baby policy. Also, Disney expounded the opportunities for family entertainment in a hierarchical country that valued the hard work ethic.[153] More seriously, the company ran up against the limits of its own influence. Indeed, few Chinese adults recognised Disney characters because they were unfamiliar with them. However, the company endeavoured to adapt its activities, even using Feng Shui philosophy.[154]

Finally, the cultural gap remains most alarming because it concerns socialisation and the emotional attachment of the public to Disney. The company is confronted with these issues with the opening of its theme park in Shanghai in June 2016.[155] Although the resorts in Paris and Tokyo also had to face serious issues of adaptation, they never had to cope with lack of knowledge of the Disney narratives.[156] One can appreciate the sociocultural depth necessary for the success of the major studios as well as the eminently cultural character of their activities.[157] Consequently, it is no surprise that Disney had problems attracting a Chinese audience.[158] Furthermore, Disney, as with any Hollywood company, is confronted with the limited number of film releases authorised by the government in China. As a result, it has used other media such as parks and consumer products to make Chinese people more sensitive to its narratives.[159] The Disney group has employed various strategies in its attempt to accelerate the dissemination of its narratives and imageries in the inland regions of China.

Notes

1. A. Rawson, E. Duncan and C. Jones (2013) 'The Truth About Customer Experience', *Harvard Business Review*, September, 90–114. B. Schmitt (2010) 'Experience Marketing: Concepts, Frameworks and Consumer Insights', *Foundations and Trends in Marketing*, 5 (2), 55–112.
2. C. Meyer and A. Schwager (2007) 'Understanding Customer Experience', *Harvard Business Review*, February, 116–28.
3. M. Weber (1971) *Économie et société* (Paris: Plon), p. 41. See M. Löwy and H. Wismann (2004) 'Max Weber, la religion et la construction du social', *Archives de sciences sociales des religions*, (127), July–September, 5–7.
4. C. Grosz and D. Bronson (2003) 'When Worlds Collide. Consumer Brands and Hollywood Are Uniting in an Effort to Reach a Broader Audience', *The Hollywood Reporter*, 28 April, S2; see J.-M. Lehu (2007) (ed.) *Branded Entertainment: Product Placement and Brand Strategy in the Entertainment Business* (London/Philadelphia: Kogan Page).
5. Grosz and Bronson, 'When Worlds Collide', S2.
6. Grosz and Bronson, 'When Worlds Collide', S4.
7. Grosz and Bronson, 'When Worlds Collide', S8.
8. F. Jameson (1991) *Postmodernism: Or, the Cultural Logic of Late Capitalism* (London: Verso). On the parallel between the rise of postmodern culture and the change in the capitalist accumulation mode, see D. Harvey (1989) *The Condition of Postmodernity* (Oxford/Cambridge: Blackwell).
9. M. Featherstone (2007) *Consumer Culture & Postmodernism* (London: Sage), p. 64 *ff.* On the relations between art and current capitalism, see G. Lipovetsky and J. Serroy (2013) *L'Esthétisation du Monde. Vivre à l'âge du capitalisme artiste* (Paris: Gallimard). On symbolical consumption, see W. Dolfsma (2007) (ed.) *Consuming Symbolic Goods: Identity and Commitment, Values and Economics* (London: Routledge).
10. P. Du Gay and M. Pryke (eds) (2002) *Cultural Economy: Cultural Analysis and Commercial Life* (London: Sage).
11. B. Pascal (1958/1670) *Pascal's Pensées* (New York: E. P. Dutton & Co.), pp. 24–5.

12. J. L. Caughey (1984) *Imaginary Social Worlds. A Cultural Approach* (Lincoln/London: University of Nebraska Press), p. 9, 34, 35.
13. M. Korzeniewicz (1994) 'Commodity Chains and Marketing Strategies: Nike and the Global Athletic Footwear Industry' in G. Gereffi and M. Korzeniewicz (eds.) *Commodity Chains and Global Capitalism* (Westport: Praeger), pp. 247–61. The author analyses the strategies of the Nike Company in terms of national marketing and global production.
14. G. Brougère, D. Buckingham and J. Goldstein (2005) *Toys, Games and Media* (Mahwah, N.J.: Lawrence Erlbaum Associates).
15. W. Benjamin (2000/1935) 'L'Œuvre d'art à l'ère de sa reproductibilité technique' in W. Benjamin, *Œuvres*, t. III (Paris: Gallimard), pp. 68–143.
16. M. Éliade (1965) *Le Sacré et le profane* (Paris: Gallimard), p. 14. My translation.
17. Interview with L. Besson, former executive at the French toy company, Smoby, 27 January 2007 (for more information, see Appendix 5); J. Wasko (2001) *Understanding Disney: the Manufacture of Fantasy* (Cambridge: Blackwell), pp. 222–4. In 2015, the royalty rate of licensed products regarding the new *Star Wars* movie would have reached 20 %. See M. Garrahan (2015) 'Star Wars: May the Franchise Be with You', *Financial Times*, 11 December.
18. T. O'Guinn and R. Belk (1989) 'Heaven on Earth: Consumption at Heritage Village, USA', *The Journal of Consumer Research*, 16 (2), September, 227–38; A. Reading and R. Jenkins (2015) 'Transportation to a World of Fantasy: Consumer Experiences of Fictional Brands Becoming Real', *Journal of Promotional Communications*, 3 (1), 154–73.
19. On the 'monomyth' structure, see J. Campbell (2004) *The Hero With a Thousand Faces* (Princeton : Princeton University Press). On the artistic and popular appeal of movies, see E. Panofsky (1966/1934) 'Style and Medium in the Motion Pictures' in D. Talbot (ed.) *Film: An Anthology* (Berkeley: University of California Press), pp. 15–32. In the context of the release of the seventh *Star Wars* movie, see 'Star Wars, Disney and myth-making', *The Economist*, 19 December 2015; 'The Force is strong in this firm', *The Economist*, 19 December 2015.
20. P. L. Berger and T. Luckmann (1971) *The Social Construction of Reality. A Treatise in the Sociology of Knowledge* (London: Penguin Books), p. 57.
21. Berger and Luckmann, *The Social Construction*, p. 59.
22. J. Tomlinson (1999) *Globalization and Culture* (Chicago: Chicago University Press).
23. A. Giddens (1991) *Consequences of Modernity* (Paris: Polity Press), p. 108. Anthony Giddens sees 'three great dynamic forces of modernity—the separation of time and space, disembedding mechanisms, and institutional reflexivity'.

24. As with other companies, Disney has experienced safety and defective issues with faulty products. See United States Consumer Product Safety Commission (2015) 'Disney Store Recalls Pencil Cases Due to Ingestion Hazard (Recall Alert)', 5 August, available at <http://www.cpsc.gov/>.
25. Interview with Gérald C., father of two children, 9 November 2006; see the same remark on the hunters for *Bambi* (1942), W. Hastings (1996) 'Bambi and the Hunting Ethos—Walt Disney Co. Character', *Journal of Popular Film & Television*, summer, 24 (2), 53–9.
26. Interview with Élodie C., mother of two sons, 9 November 2006.
27. S. Thiroux (2003) *Étude des processus identificatoires chez les enfants et les adolescents âgés de trois à seize ans et demi dans le cadre du visionnage de longs métrages d'animation de Walt Disney*, PhD defended by Pascale Planche at the University of Bretagne Occidentale; D. Buckingham (2005) *The Media Literacy of Children and Young People. A review of the research literature on behalf of ofcom*, available at <http://www.eprints.ioe.ac.uk>.
28. Interview with Clémence L., mother of three children, 9 November 2006.
29. Interview with Marie-France F., mother of two daughters, 3 February 2007.
30. On the case of Greece and Australia, see E. Meehan, M. Philips and J. Wasko (2006) (eds.) *Dazzled by Disney? The Global Disney Audiences Project* (Leicester: Leicester University Press), pp. 65–87 and 135–59.
31. Interview with H. Richardson, senior executive for distribution at Disney studios, DreamWorks and then Paramount, 11 August 2006. For more information, see Appendix 5.
32. See D. Kalifa (2001) *La Culture de masse en France 1860–1930*, t. 1 (Paris: La Découverte).
33. D. Brode (2004) *From Walt to Woodstock: How Disney Created the Counterculture* (Austin: University of Texas Press).
34. M. McLuhan (1964) *Understanding Media. The Extensions of Man* (London: Routledge & Kegan Paul), p. 7.
35. S. Zukin and P. DiMaggio (1990) *Structures of Capital. The Social Organization of the Economy* (Cambridge: Cambridge University Press), p. 15.
36. Quote from Frank Cooper, PepsiCo's Vice President Promotions, Interactive and Entertainment Marketing, in G. Schiller (2005) 'Warfare', *The Hollywood Reporter*, 10–16 May, S4.
37. A. O. Hirschman (2002) *Shifting Involvements: Private Interest and Public Action* (Princeton: Princeton University Press).
38. Hirschman, *Shifting Involvements.*
39. Pascal, *Pensées*, p. 48.
40. Hirschman, *Shifting Involvements*, pp. 55–7.
41. Hirschman, *Shifting Involvements*, p. 57.
42. Pascal, *Pensées*, p. 49.

43. J. Goss (1993) 'The 'Magic of the Mall': An Analysis of Form, Function, and Meaning in the Contemporary Retail Built Environment', *Annals of the Association of American Geographers*, 83 (1), March, 18–47.
44. H. Giroux (1999) *The Mouse that Roared: Disney and the End of Innocence* (Lanham: Rowman & Littlefield).
45. S. Davis (1996) 'The Theme Park: Global Industry and Cultural Form', *Media, Culture and Society*, 18 (3), July, 407.
46. Interview with Marie-France F.
47. Hirschman, *Shifting Involvements*, p. 80.
48. A. Bryman (2004) *The Disneyization of Society* (London: Sage).
49. See B. Smart (1999) (ed.) *Resisting McDonaldization* (London: Sage).
50. E. Katz and R. Meyersohn (1957) 'Notes on a Natural History of Fads', *The American Journal of Sociology*, 62 (6), May, 594–601.
51. Interview with Gérard Couturier, former leading executive in the Imagineering department of Disney, 29 May 2006 (for more information, see Appendix 5). Branding can be defined as the technique of valuing an item by the combined use of brand, imageries and narratives.
52. Davis, 'The Theme Park', p. 408.
53. Meehan et al., *Dazzled by Disney?*
54. A. Smith (1990) 'Towards a Global Culture?', *Theory, Culture and Society*, 7 (2), June, 171–91. The author is sceptical regarding the thesis of national identities being replaced by other identities. On the last point, the most stimulating argument is Inglehart's in-depth analyses based on intergenerational change concerning global identities, the United Nations Organization and English (R. Inglehart (1997) *Modernization and Postmodernization. Cultural, Economic and Political Change in 43 Societies* (Princeton: Princeton University Press)).
55. S. Hall, D. Hobson, A. Lowe and P. Willis (1980) (eds.) *Culture, Media, Language* (London: Hutchinson).
56. J. A. Scholte (2005) *Globalization: a critical introduction* (Basingstoke: Palgrave Macmillan), p. 84.
57. B. Jessop (2013) 'Dynamics of Regionalism and Globalism: A Critical Political Economy Perspective', *Ritsumeikan Social Science Review*, 5, 5.
58. On the Everyday International Political Economy, see J. Hobson and L. Seabrook (2007) (eds.) *Everyday Politics of the World Economy* (Cambridge: Cambridge University Press).
59. Data obtained from a questionnaire completed by 1,000 people in the context of this author's PhD thesis. See Appendix 3. See also Meehan, et al., *Dazzled by Disney?*, p. 49.
60. J. Wasko (2001) *Understanding Disney: the Manufacture of Fantasy* (Cambridge: Blackwell), p. 192.
61. See Meehan et al., *Dazzled by Disney*, p. 44.

62. Other researchers have highlighted hybridisation phenomena between Disney productions and non-Western cultures. See B. Weinbaum (1997) 'Disney-Mediated Images Emerging in Cross-Cultural Expression on Isla Mujeres, Mexico', *Journal of American & Comparative Cultures*, 20 (2), summer, 19–29.
63. D. Held, A. G. McGrew, D. Goldblatt and J. Perraton (1999) *Global Transformations: Politics, Economics and Culture* (Cambridge: Polity Press), pp. 21–3.
64. R. Hoggart (2009/1957) *The Uses of Literacy: Aspects of Working-Class Life* (London: Penguin).
65. J. F. Rayport, C.-I. Knoop and C. Reavis (1998) 'Disney's 'The Lion King' (A): The $2 Billion Movie', *Harvard Business School Cases*, Brighton, MA: Harvard Business Publishing.
66. See Appendix 4.
67. Interview with G. Couturier.
68. See Appendix 3.
69. See B. Jessop, 'Dynamics of Regionalism and Globalism'; Scholte, *Globalization*.
70. See B. J. Pine and J. H. Gilmore (1999) *The Experience Economy. Work is Theater & Every Business a Stage* (Boston: Harvard Business Review Press); Schmitt, 'Experience Marketing'.
71. Interviews with Nelly C., 15 November 2006; Colette C., 2 August 2007 and Maria M., 14 November 2006. All three senior people have had children who are now adults.
72. Interview with Élodie C.
73. R. Hoggart (1958) *The Uses of Literacy: Aspects of Working-Class Life* (London: Penguin), p. 239
74. A. Bohas (2015) 'Transnational Firms and the Knowledge Structure: The Case of the Walt Disney Company', *Global Society*, 29 (1), 23–41.
75. P. Bourdieu (2000) *Pascalian Meditations* (Stanford, CA: Stanford University Press), p. 160.
76. F. Braudel (1993) *Civilisation matérielle, économie et capitalisme XV–XVIIIème siècle, vol. 3. Le temps du monde* (Paris: Armand Colin), p. 39.
77. Braudel, *Civilisation matérielle*, pp. 38–39. My translation.
78. J. Dumazedier (1962) *Vers la civilisation des loisirs* (Paris: Seuil), p. 23. My translation.
79. P. Bourdieu (1972) *Esquisse d'une théorie de la pratique* (Paris/Genève: Droz), p. 178.
80. See the study led in Mexico, in S. Molina Y Vedia (1998) 'Disney en México: observaciones sobre la integración de objetos de la cultura global en la vida cotidiana', *Revista Mexicana de Ciencias Politicas y Sociales*, (171), January–March, 97–126.

81. See Meehan et al., *Dazzled by Disney*, p. 44.
82. Interview with Virginie S., 2 February 2007.
83. Interview with Élodie C.
84. Interview with Gérald C.
85. Interview with Clémence L.
86. Interview with Clémence L.
87. Quote collected during the questionnaire. See Appendix 3.
88. For an overview of the different dimensions of trust, see P. Sztompka (1999) *Trust: A Sociological Theory* (Cambridge: Cambridge University Press).
89. Meehan et al., *Dazzled by Disney*, p. 49.
90. Interview with Élodie C.
91. M. McLuhan (1964) *Understanding Media. The Extensions of Man* (London: Routledge & Kegan Paul), pp. 7–8.
92. T. Risse-Kappen (1995) (ed.) *Bringing Transnational Relations Back In. Non-State Actors, Domestic Structures and International Institutions* (Cambridge: Cambridge University Press); A. P. Cortell and J. W. Davis Jr (2000) 'Understanding the Domestic Impact of International Norms: A Research Agenda', *International Studies Review*, 2 (1), 65–87; J. T. Checkel (1997) 'International Norms and Domestic Politics: Bridging the Rationalist–Constructivist Divide', *European Journal of International Relations*, 3 (4), 473–95. On the importance of ideas, domestic politics and transnational relations, see T. Risse-Kappen (1994) 'Ideas do not Float Freely: Transnational Coalitions, Domestic Structures and the End of the Cold War', *International Organization*, 48 (2), 185–214.
93. B. Anderson (1983) *Imagined Communities. Reflections on the Origin and Spread of Nationalism* (London: Verso).
94. T. Liebes and E. Katz (1990) *The Export of Meaning: Cross-cultural Readings of Dallas* (New York: Oxford University Press; I. Ang (1985) *Watching Dallas: Soap Opera and the Melodramatic Imagination* (London/New York: Methuen).
95. M. Doucet (2005) 'Child's Play: The Political Imaginary of International Relations and Contemporary Popular Children's Films', *Global Society*, 19 (3), July, 289–306.
96. Interview with B. Mechanic
97. D. Hughes and J. Clements (1997) 'Arts: Manga Goes to Hollywood', *The Guardian*, 14 April. See <http://www.nausicaa.net> on the Disney-Tokuma deal.
98. Interview with Gérald C.
99. Interview with Nelly C.
100. Interview with Gérald C.
101. Interview with Nicole M., a retired person with no children, 26 November 2006.

102. Ang, *Watching Dallas*, p. 89 *ff*. In this book, the author shows the ability of people to watch and enjoy a soap opera while rejecting all of its ideological dimensions and taking a critical position.
103. Interview with Emmanuelle M., mother of three, 6 December 2006.
104. Interview with Benjamin P., father of a son, 4 December 2006.
105. Interview with Benjamin P.
106. Interview with Frédéric F., father of a daughter, 28 November 2006.
107. J. N. Rosenau (1990) *Turbulence in World Politics: A Theory of Change and Continuity* (Princeton, NJ: Princeton University Press).
108. M. Abélès (2008) *Anthropologie de la globalisation* (Paris: Payot); J. N. Pieterse (2005) 'Globalization as Hybridization' in M. Featherstone, S. Lash and R. Robertson (eds.) *Global Modernities* (London: Sage), pp. 45–68.
109. Interview with Clémence L.
110. Interview with Emmanuelle M.
111. Interview with Élodie C.
112. J. Guyot, 'France: Disney in the Land of Cultural Exception' in Meehan et al., *Dazzled by Disney*, p. 121.
113. Interview with Gérald C.
114. Interview with Gérald C.
115. Interview with Nicole M.
116. J. Alison (2005) 'Euro-Mickey Braces for Wild Ride', *Variety*, 8 August, 399 (11), 22 (2).
117. D. S. Cohen (2005) 'Asia Locales Offer Scary Upside', *Variety*, 8 August, 399 (11), 22 (1).
118. Interview with Gérald C.
119. J. Stewart (2005) *Disney War* (New York: Simon & Schuster), p. 129.
120. Interview with C. Reynes.
121. Interview with Benjamin P.
122. Interview with Gérald C.
123. Interview with Frédéric F.
124. Interview with Frédéric F.
125. P. Bourdieu (1979) *La Distinction. Critique sociale du jugement* (Paris: Éditions de minuit).
126. D. Pasquier (2005) *Cultures lycéennes. La tyrannie de la majorité* (Paris: Éditions Autrement).
127. Interview with Emmanuelle M.
128. France was the country where the consumption of merchandising was the lowest. See Meehan et al., *Dazzled by Disney*, p. 43.
129. Interview with Carole D., mother of two children, 6 May 2007.
130. See T. Veblen (1978/1899) *Théorie de la classe de loisir* (Paris: Gallimard); N. Élias (1985/1933) *La Société de cour* (Paris: Flammarion).
131. Interview with Clémence L.

132. Hoggart, *The Uses of Literacy*, p. 295.
133. Interview with Élodie C.
134. M. de Certeau (1990) *L'Invention du quotidien 1. Arts de faire* (Paris: Gallimard).
135. T. Liebes and E. Katz (1992) 'Six interprétations de la série 'Dallas' in D. Dayan (ed.) *À la recherche du public. Réception, télévision, médias, Hermès*, (11–12), 125.
136. J. N. Rosenau (1990) *Turbulence in World Politics: A Theory of Change and Continuity* (Princeton, NJ: Princeton University Press).
137. J. Staiger (1997) 'Le commerce international du cinéma et les flux culturels mondiaux: une approche néomarxiste' in P.-J. Benghozi and C. Delage (eds.) *Une Histoire économique du cinéma francais (1895–1995). Regards croisés franco-americains* (Paris: L'Harmattan), p. 362.
138. A. Appadurai (2001) *Modernity at Large. Cultural Dimensions of Globalization* (Minneapolis, U.S.: University of Minnesota), p. 23.
139. N. Laporte (2004) 'Navigating Change', *Variety*, 23 February.
140. K. Nordyke (2006) 'Disney Channel a Youth Market Creative Force', *The Hollywood Reporter*, 1–7 August, 1 (23).
141. The top ten fictional characters jointly earned $25 billion in revenue in 2003. See V. Gisquet and L. Rose (2004) 'Top Characters Gross $25B', *Forbes*, 19 October.
142. J. Goldsmith, 'Disney Fairies Aim to Capture Princess Magic', *Variety*, 405 (13), 12 February 2007, , 16 (2).
143. Interview with C. Nelson, former Vice President for advertising at Disney, 19 August 2006. For more information, see Appendix 5.
144. 'Global Television Broadcasting Companies Ranked by Number of Half-Hour Episodes of Children's Animated Television Series as of November 2005', *Screen Digest*, (383), December 2005.
145. J. Dempsey (2001) 'Disney Preps Channel for the Preschool Set', *Variety*, 383 (6), 25 June, 18.
146. Interview with C. Nelson.
147. P. Minju (2005) 'Target Practice', *The Hollywood Reporter*, 14 March, S6 (8).
148. C. Gardner (2006) 'Marketing to Hispanics', *Variety*, 30 July.
149. Interview with C. Nelson
150. L. B. Stammer (2004) 'Digging for the Deeper Meaning in Disney Movies', *Los Angeles Times*, 21 August, B2.
151. Interview with C. Nelson.
152. Interview with C. Nelson.
153. M. Marr and G. A. Fowler (2006) 'Hong Kong Disneyland Tries to Bridge Gap', *The Wall Street Journal*, 14 June.
154. L. Holson (2005) 'Disney Bows to Feng Shui', *The New York Times*, 25 April.

155. On the adaptation of Disney to Chinese specifics, see C. Palmeri (2015) 'Shanghai Disneyland Is Customized for the Chinese Family', *Bloomberg Businessweek*, 20 July; E. Smith and J. Areddy (2009) 'Shanghai Disney Project Includes Hotels, Shopping', *The Wall Street Journal*, 5 November; M. Zuo (2015) 'Shanghai Disney theme park to conjure string of firsts', *South China Morning Post*, 16 July.
156. On the adaptation of Disneyland in Tokyo, see A. Raz (2000) 'Domesticating Disney: Onstage Strategies of Adaptation in Tokyo Disneyland', *Journal of Popular Culture*, 33 (4), spring, 77–99.
157. M. Stokes and R. Maltby (2005) *Hollywood Abroad: Audiences and Cultural Exchange* (London: BFI Publishing), pp. 21–34 and 99–120.
158. W. Foreman (2006) 'Hong Kong Park Misses Visitor Goal', *Orlando Sentinel*, 6 September.
159. On the acceleration of Disney penetration in China, see C. Simons (2007) 'Bringing Disney to China Seems as Tough as Shark Fin Soup', *TheLedger.com*, 11 February; E. Pfanner and P. Landers (2015) 'Uniqlo Aims for Bigger China Gains With New Disney Deal', *Dow Jones Institutional News*, 2 August; 'The Walt Disney Company & Shanghai Media Group Expand Strategic Entertainment Alliance in China', *Dow Jones institutional News*, 14 April 2014.

CHAPTER 6

Conclusion

This book has analysed the interwoven spheres of culture, the economy and politics while taking a broad perspective on the Disney phenomenon, including the company, its products, imageries and audiences. It has also fended off artificial disciplinary barriers, widespread prejudices and common misconceptions about the Disney Company. In this respect, it has demonstrated all the advantages of introducing cultural studies (in this instance the differential integration of symbols in societies and their random appropriation by individuals) into International Political Economy (IPE). Through this global perspective, the study has highlighted the specifics of the Disney phenomenon, its strengths and its weaknesses. Categorising Disney an ideal type of cultural capitalism, this book has also brought to light new findings about the Hollywood industry, its contribution to American power and the study of IPE.

The Cultural Capitalism of Hollywood

Cultural capitalism is an economy based on accumulating and renewing imageries and narratives through creative processes to promote and distribute vast ranges of products and types of activity. Branded products are valued because they convey an emotional, cognitive and cultural attraction. Although historically founded on films, cultural capitalism expanded beyond audio-visual fields throughout the twentieth century. Its

A. Bohas, *The Political Economy of Disney*, International Political Economy Series, DOI 10.1057/978-1-137-56238-8_6

development has been based on the power of its narratives and their global diffusion. Remaining the only studio still independent from other conglomerates, the Disney firm is the closest major studio to this ideal type. The artistic and financial successes of Disney have resulted from a capitalist accumulation resulting from its production programmes and their related activities. Its themed attractions are completely successful while the Disney name and brand enjoy unparalleled and durable recognition. Its artistic works amaze and fascinate audiences, creating a considerable demand for its spin-offs. During prosperous periods, the growth of the studio can appear endless, with opportunities for exceptional expansion. Each of its new creations triggers unlimited and unrivalled economic possibilities for by-products, which bring about a significant increase in sales.

However, Disney is periodically confronted with creative crises. Suddenly, its revenues dwindle, the talent of its artists is regarded as dull and its leading executives are no longer innovative. The latter have a hard time adapting to social transformations and conforming to the changing tastes of audiences. The economic growth of the firm comes to an end. Its new productions bring about moderate profits or heavy losses. Its merchandising becomes mundane, which provokes disappointment among its audiences. The company's creations are viewed as tedious, resulting in financial losses while their new symbols are not attractive enough to maintain durably. No longer fascinating, the studio lets slip its mercantile and unattractive company face to the world. As it no longer anticipates market trends, new competitors emerge, breaking its monopoly in popular animation. Consequently, the Disney Company no longer generates revenue, lacks creativity and loses support. In this light, the search for creativity and inspiration explains the buyouts of Pixar, Marvel and Lucasfilm.

True accumulation of cinematographic capital distinguishes Hollywood from other creative centres. Benefiting from a specific ethos and considerable distribution capacities, the industry takes advantage of its previous successful franchises, and maximises profits for every new creation. Artistic denial, the search for a rigorous production process and control over creative talent provoke specific practices and attitudes towards films that foster capital accumulation. Moreover, Hollywood is also in 'elective affinities' with other business sectors, which creates a high level of confidence and favours economic relations. However, this rationalist ethos is continuously jeopardised by uncertainties unique to the movie industry. Indeed, success has always resulted from commercial and distribution processes subject to the whims of its (non-)receptive audience.

This imperceptible dimension is too often ignored even though it causes creative destruction within the sector.

In addition, complex rivalries affect Hollywood's major studios—on the one hand their solidarity ensures a global commercial position; on the other they compete ferociously for new business opportunities. Since the end of the traditional studio system, their relations have become more competitive and production is nowadays often contracted to smaller companies, leaving the larger studios to concentrate on financing and distribution. Technicians and actors are recruited today based on personal relationships, skills and abilities, and previous production profitability—there has been a transformation in the structure of business relationships from mechanical to organic, including the rise of outsourcing, which has made the Hollywood sector more unstable. Nevertheless, decisive stages in pre-production and post-production remain centralised in Los Angeles where large studios locate their headquarters.

Hollywood is also integrated into the rest of the economy in multiple ways. At a global level, cultural capitalists are at the centre of the world-economy in the entertainment sphere, investing in international networks, audio-visual programmes and leisure activities. Today, they are expanding their presence into the domains of sport, culture and outdoor games. All cultural capitalists belong to immense conglomerates. They produce new worlds, imageries and texts, giving a civilisational dimension to all their products and activities. All these productions contribute to a durable integration of symbols, imageries and narratives that complements an original film in innovative and entertaining ways.

In many sectors of the economy, their imageries are associated with numerous product lines because Hollywood-branded goods and characters offer a competitive advantage. The attractiveness of Hollywood productions has increased with market saturation and the blossoming of postmodernity. Their imageries have been diversely used through promotional campaigns. Financially, Hollywood companies depend on the rules of profitability and undergo the same pressure from shareholders as does any other company. Their works are assessed by the yardstick of their financial results and not by the yardstick of aesthetic criteria. At the individual level, according to the close examination of this research, a wide gap amongst executives continues to exist. On the one hand, those in charge of promotion and distribution come from various legal and economic sectors, having little to do with film creation. As they maintain no special artistic affinities with the Hollywood milieu, they rigorously control the production process. In other words, they impose the constraints of profitability. On the other hand, executives in production and producers themselves appear sensitive to the risks of movie failures. Their career paths are marked by back-and-forth movements between major studios and small production companies. Integrated in the Hollywood milieu, they experience the unpredictability inherent in their field just as much as directors and actors do.

Entertainment firms also have to contend with economic and cultural constraints. Economically it is vital to maintain and strengthen the prominence of major studios' narratives and imageries whose value depends on continuous renewal and innovation. So, a company's commercial worth is maintained by powerful communication, broad distribution and creative research in line with social and technological changes. However, commercialisation sometimes only helps to accelerate the depreciation of creative content and the boredom of Hollywood audiences, and at times the vast organisation of these economic behemoths encourages the simple replication of movies according to ready-made formulas.

In addition, major studios are continuously attempting to expand their presence in the global economy by searching for new audiences and markets. They invest in emerging economies, such as China and India, which are the fastest developing nations and possess the highest concentration of affluent middle classes. Yet, they are faced with cultural obstacles—people unfamiliar with Hollywood narratives and consumer practices. Consequently, before achieving any potentially lucrative presence, they must adapt their productions to these audiences, all the while launching a strategic socialisation process to familiarise the population with its Western narratives and imageries.

Hollywood, American Power and the Ideational Sphere

Cultural capitalists hold transnational power in a world-economy that does not respect official borders. Their 'geography' corresponds to the level of sociocultural integration of their symbolic systems into societies. At the politico-legal level, the Motion Picture Association, which represents the major studios, takes care of the access to markets and the maintenance of legal systems favourable to its member-companies which are always in search of new outlets. But their preponderance is also based on a transnational and socio-economic framework which enables them to introduce consumer practices, produce films and build parks. They diffuse symbols massively in national economies. The symbols they promote and the behaviour they inspire exert a considerable impact on economies, lifestyles and collective representations in many countries abroad. Often they more or less implicitly impose essential references in the everyday lives of people. The supremacy of the Hollywood cluster is based on successful familiarisation and artistic experiences which a successful Porter-type combination of distribution and production capacities in entertainment makes possible. Their subsidiaries occupy a crucial place in this process because they must adapt to identity specifics. In the same way, the success of their parks and their merchandise depends on their level of integration in foreign societies while reinforcing the embedding of symbolic systems into the routines of everyday life.

The globalisation of Hollywood differs widely from one region to another depending on situated individuals. It varies along socio-professional trajectories and geo-cultural contexts which limit or increase the proximity to Hollywood narrations. As has been previously pointed out about Disney, the preponderance of these companies erodes as soon as one changes the focus away from great city centres and middle-class families with young children. The presence of Hollywood imageries and goods weakens in less receptive zones. People experience Hollywood civilisation more restrictively; their access to and their knowledge of Hollywood culture are clearly reduced. This represents real limitations to the entertainment world-economy and customer experience management. In other words, the competitive advantage given by the differentiation of Hollywood symbols depends on the shaping of collective imagination. All the same, the knowledge of the publics in less receptive zones proves to be blurry and even weak. Confusion in their minds exists among films or characters. Indeed, despite recognition of the Disney label, they barely manage to associate such-and-such a film with such-and-such a studio, more especially as the animation offer has greatly diversified. A variable appropriation of the American way of life can also be noted, which is considered and lived through national or subnational prisms. The Disney label does not replace pre-existing identities, which implies ceaseless encoding and decoding. It is only integrated gradually and partially into collective practical knowledge. Adaptation to these audiences accompanies the transnational fragmentation of supply and demand.

The study goes beyond the assessment of the differentiated reception given the socio-economic and geo-cultural specifics of consumers-spectators.

Based on these profiles, three processes of ideational structuration have been identified: first, a gradual and repetitive socialisation introduces specific narratives and imageries into the imagination, memory and consciousness. They are present early on in the daily routines of every individual. Second, these specific narratives and imageries may serve individual strategies in different social contexts where they are valued. Third, external shocks can appear decisive for the imposition of predominance on collective representations. In this respect, being immersed in a theme park and watching a film form highly emotional experiences which remain for years in the memory of children who then become adults.

This study encourages one to envisage the varied origins of American power as stemming transnationally from its societies and its non-state actors rather than from its government. Hollywood productions constitute the only set of transterritorial commercial goods-symbols in the Western world. By dominating the economic audio-visual and entertainment markets, major studios structurally reinforce their competitive advantage, obliterate the primacy of national identities and diffuse the American way of life. Relying on leisure preponderance, they contribute to American power by conferring upon it an implicit sociocultural basis in foreign countries. The studios take part in determining what is to be produced and of what one may take for granted. Like many other dominant corporations, they structure the daily lives of people. In other words, they take part in the globalisation of habitus,[1] which depends on a multitude of transnational symbols. Although all these firms are transnational, they continue to be based in the United States. Consequently, they carry and propagate American power. The illusion of universality, which their symbolic systems give, comes from their integration into collective representations, which in the end only represents the ultimate recognition of these symbols. Major studios clearly exert economic and cultural power on the markets, and in so doing just as much on the broader aspirations of people and their futures. This preponderance of America is maintained through knowledge and practices integrated in many different countries. Its influence has been variable at times, or intermittent and periodically fleeting according to the context. In addition, it is not based on any kind of ideological agreement but rather on preferences and emotional relations. Tacitly accepted and rooted in people's practical consciousness, this preponderance is all the more stable.

In addition, the Disney case provides key findings about the ideational sphere and the reliance of power on it. Although this last domain is intertwined with material ones, it substantially distinguishes itself from them.

Imagery and narrative universes make up the ideational domain which they polarise to different degrees. Each one of them concentrates valued meanings and attractive symbolic configurations. As a result, they constitute poles of meanings, resulting from highly emotional experiences and constructed affinity. The preponderant symbolic and narrative universe has the most intense level of polarisation, appearing as referential and central in the domain. Once established, the ideational configuration lastingly weighs on the material worlds since it remains autonomous and slow to change. As in the case of Disney, it has an inherent inertia.[2] On the one hand, the rising ideational sphere establishes itself deeply and slowly through cultural sensitivity, lasting memories and behavioural routinisation; on the other hand, once established, it reproduces lastingly in individuals' behaviour and practices even when the material–ideational combination that led to this ideational crystallisation has disappeared. This explains that material and ideational worlds can diverge substantially, impeding the power of predominant actors. When simultaneity of preponderance in ideational and material worlds occurs, they reinforce one another, forming a greater civilisational strength, with sets of material and ideational elements which transnationally diffuse to peoples, override sectors and crosscut state territories. They create cultural and emotional closeness between their symbolic attributes and people, which encourages specific behaviour, practices and media and consequently frames people's daily lives.

Multinational Corporations, Individuals and IPE Research

The renewed view on the specifics of Hollywood studios and their contribution to American power is possible through methods, notions and tools coming from international business analyses and cultural studies. This twofold perspective on consumers and the company also highlights the institutional arrangements of the Disney phenomenon. It renews the traditional views of the market by bridging the gap between company analyses and reception studies. First, the Disney phenomenon is constituted by the creation, innovation and hard work of Disney employees on the one side, and by the interpretation, behaviour and purchasing of consumers on the other. Both have an impact on this institutional setting. This perspective throws new light on the top-down approach (which stresses the strength of companies) and on the bottom-up approach of reception studies (which minimises the stranglehold held by commercial companies).

Second, the interrelation between the Disney Company and its audiences is socially and culturally constructed by filters and layers which, acting on perceptions, knowledge and behaviour, exert a significant effect on the Disney phenomenon and in turn on both the firm and the audience. They impact the intensity and the closeness of consumers to Disney while shaping the way the Disney Company produces its narratives. This also moulds the terms of market demands, supplies and prices. Third, the interrelationship between Disney employees and its audiences is the crux of the Disney phenomenon and is responsible for the appeal, the profitability and the success of Disney. In other words, what is most interesting is the constant renewal of Disney's products, the steady adaptation to social transformations and the innovative spirit of the Disney staff. The latter should be analysed in parallel with consumers-spectators' willingness or reluctance to pay for goods or services. Is the Disney consumer ready to adopt Disney narratives and symbols? Does he/she construe Disney products favourably? The answers to these two questions would reveal the depth of connection between the company and its audience and the latter's level of attachment to Disney narratives and imageries. Fourth, this institutional setting provides resources and constraints for Disney employees and their customers. For the former, it impacts their work at every level: their creative work, their marketing and sales programmes and their production policies. For the latter, it weighs in on their behaviour depending upon their social strategies and class structure.

This study corresponds to a willingness on the author's part to bring International Relations' analysts closer to the individuals concerned with world phenomena in order to escape the risk of adopting 'too lofty a view' of International Relations.[3] Cultural Political Economy focuses on the cultural dimension of international politics and economy which is inherent in every social relation, phenomenon and structure. It implies also a study of collective and individual practices and beliefs. In this respect, studies of reception and appropriation about goods, imageries and values, at work and in daily life, are most useful.

In this research, the cultural capitalism of Hollywood has been explained by means of cross-examining senior management and customers; in other words, a study of Disney from above and from below. Light has been shed on the extent of the individual dimension of American power by taking into account individuals' behaviour, perceptions and discourse about cultural goods. This led to a reconsideration of power which may not always appear as strong as is commonly presumed—this allowed a better analysis of international actors since it envisioned their strengths and weaknesses from multiple levels. Finally, this approach is all the more necessary in today's context of globalisation, one evidenced by a shrinking globe and erosion of state borders. Individuals, whether by aggregation or collectively organised, have an impact on the global sphere and this should be systematically taken into account in future research.

Notes

1. P. Bourdieu (1972) *Esquisse d'une théorie de la pratique* (Paris/Genève: Droz), p. 178.
2. On the inertia of the ideational configuration, see A. Bohas (2015) 'Transnational Firms and the Knowledge Structure: The Case of the Walt Disney Company', *Global Society*, 29 (1), 23–41.
3. A. Smith (1998), "Espace public européen': une vision (trop) aérienne', *Critique internationale*, (2), Winter, 169–80.

Appendix 1

Profile of the Walt Disney Company

Based in Burbank, California, the Disney Company forms a vast international media conglomerate. It was founded in 1923 by Walter Elias Disney. Shortly thereafter, with the help of Ub Iwerks, Walt created Mickey Mouse, an emblematic character that has remained synonymous with fun, laughter and magic for generations of children and adults. Nowadays, it employs 180,000 full-time staff and recorded a turnover of $49 billion in 2014. Its principal activities comprise four main business sectors: Studio Entertainment (15 % of turnover), Disney Media Networks (44 %), Walt Disney Parks and Resorts (31 %) and Disney Consumer Products (8 %).

The Studio division consists mainly of powerful production entities (Walt Disney Motion Pictures, Walt Disney Animation, Disneytoon, Touchstone Pictures, Pixar Animation, Marvel and Lucasfilm). In addition, it owns a major distribution network, Walt Disney Studios (originally Buena Vista) which forms one of the largest international distribution networks in theatre and home video. Despite their specialisation in films, these entities are also involved in television and live theatrical and musical spheres.

The Media Networks division is an umbrella organisation of domestic and international television channels such as ABC network, ESPN, Disney Channel, ABC Family (now Freeform), Disney XD and Soapnet. Production and international distribution of TV content is carried out under the double banner of ABC and Disney.

A. Bohas, *The Political Economy of Disney*, International Political Economy Series, DOI 10.1057/978-1-137-56238-8

Finally, the Parks and Resorts and Consumer Products businesses contribute jointly to yearly profits (30 % of operating income). The former is responsible for the management of 11 theme parks and their resorts worldwide. The latter, comprising Disney Worldwide Publishing and Disney retail stores oversees sales of all Disney-branded product lines, including product licensing.

Appendix 2

Timeline of the Walt Disney Company

The company

16 October 1923 Foundation of Walt Disney Productions
1953 Launch of Buena Vista
15 December 1966 Death of Walt E. Disney
1983 Launch of the Disney Channel
1984 Launch of Touchstone Pictures
22 September 1984 Nomination of Michael Eisner as CEO
1990 Launch of Hollywood Pictures
1993 Acquisition of Miramax; launch of Buena Vista International
1994 Death of Frank Wells; resignation of Jeffrey Katzenberg
1996 Buyout of the ABC network
2001 Acquisition of Fox Family
1 October 2005 Nomination of Robert Iger as CEO
2006 Purchase of Pixar
2009 Acquisition of Marvel
2012 Purchase of Lucasfilm

A. Bohas, *The Political Economy of Disney*, International Political Economy Series, DOI 10.1057/978-1-137-56238-8

Non-film activities

1929 Creation of the Mickey Mouse Club
1932 Arrival of Kay Kamen at the head of Consumer Products division
1934 Launch of *Le Journal de Mickey*
17 July 1955 Opening of Disneyland Park in Anaheim
1971 Opening of Walt Disney World in Florida
1982 Opening of EPCOT (Experimental Prototype Community of Tomorrow) in Florida
1983 Opening of Tokyo Disneyland in Japan
1987 Launch of the first Disney Store
12 April 1992 Opening of Euro Disney (now Disneyland Paris) in France
1998 First cruise of the Disney Magic liner
2005 Opening of Hong Kong Disneyland
2016 Opening of Shanghai Disney Resort in China

Selected film releases

1928 *Steamboat Willie*
21 December 1937 *Snow White and the Seven Dwarfs*
1940 *Pinocchio; Fantasia*
1950 *Cinderella*
1955 *Davy Crockett, King of the Wild Frontier; Lady and the Tramp*
1970 *The Aristocats*
1987 *Three Men and a Baby*
1989 *The Little Mermaid*
1990 *Pretty Woman*
1994 *The Lion King*
1995 *Pocahontas; Toy Story*
1998 *Armageddon*
2001 *Pearl Harbor*
2003 *Finding Nemo; Pirates of the Caribbean: The Curse of the Black Pearl*
2006 *Cars*
2012 *The Avengers*
2013 *Frozen*
2015 *Star Wars: The Force Awakens*

Appendix 3

Empirical Research on the Disney Phenomenon

I undertook four types of research into the Disney phenomenon. Firstly, I studied the production configurations adopted by the Disney studio within the Hollywood sector as a whole. With the analysis of the trade press, mainly *Variety* and *The Hollywood Reporter*, I examined the number of production and distribution deals the Disney Company concluded with smaller business entities. This list was also put together thanks to editions of the *Hollywood Creative Directory* and to information provided by the Margaret Herrick Library, Beverly Hills, Los Angeles. In addition, I reviewed the firm's annual reports from 1974 to 2014. In particular, I looked into contributions of the main divisions to revenues and operating incomes of the Disney Company (see Appendix 4). I focused on the trends of revenues and operating profits for each division using pro-format annual data when possible. Such data were valuable relating to the success of productions inside and outside the film industry. Consequently, I was able to draw conclusions about the way the studio functions and its interaction with other studios.

Secondly, thanks also to the trade press, I analysed the professional trajectories of Disney executives and their rotation within the media industry. I was interested in studying how intertwined and open the Hollywood milieu was. I was also concerned with the relations between creative and non-creative executives within studios. I studied the executives from Walt Disney Studios—their backgrounds, their functions, their stint at Disney and their career paths. Based on the *Hollywood Creative Directory* and the

A. Bohas, *The Political Economy of Disney*, International Political Economy Series, DOI 10.1057/978-1-137-56238-8

International Motion Picture Almanac, I collected all the names of 'senior vice presidents', 'executive vice presidents' and 'presidents' of the company (E. S. Quigley (2006) (ed.) *International Motion Picture Almanac* (New York: Quigley); Hollywood Creative Directory (2006) *Hollywood Creative Directory*, 57th edn. (Los Angeles: Hollywood Creative Directory). Further information about them was also available at Margaret Herrick's Library of Academy of Motion Picture Arts and Sciences. I did not succeed in finding information on everybody I wanted to. Details on some heads of studios who figured less in the media limelight than others remained impossible to find. Aware of these missing elements, I only took deep tendencies into account. Besides, I concentrated on research between 1986 and 2006, the period when the Disney Company fully developed into a major studio. From the close examination of Disney professionals and talented individuals, I was able to draw a typology of careers and profiles which gave a better grasp of the dynamics and influence of Hollywood on the US economy.

Thirdly, this book includes information about executives and consumers-spectators from 2005 to 2008. As I researched the functioning of the Disney studio and its particular place in the Hollywood sector, I carried out 30 interviews with American and French executives who have had business relations with Disney or who have worked for them (see Appendix 5). Above all I wanted to determine two things—the working practices of the company (to assess synergies and employee standards) and the knowledge base and creative talent of Disney executives and partners. In Los Angeles, obtaining an interview was a challenge since executives were mistrustful of both journalists and fans, and careful over industrial espionage. In addition, in a sector which is based on trust, motion picture managers see no point in giving interviews which could alter their reputation. Furthermore, the Disney Company, which is wary of its reputation, is especially prompt in suing anyone for any publication without its consent. This explains why some interviewees wanted to remain anonymous.

Fourthly, I performed two kinds of research amongst consumers-spectators. The questionnaire (below) was completed by some one thousand participants. They came from nearby grocery stores and malls in several regions of France—the centre of Paris and its suburbs as well as the Jura region, located near Switzerland. The goal was to capture the extent of people's knowledge of Disney, and their consumer-based practices regarding Disney product, while also gathering data on their socio-economic background and their geo-cultural situation. Also, fifteen in-depth interviews were conducted with French people to understand consumer behaviour and perception towards Disney. The individuals, all of whom had partaken in the three ways of experiencing Disney (purchasing retail product, watching films and visiting theme parks), were interviewed about their practices and their understanding of Disney. In so doing, my aim was to get a better grasp of the way they and their children avoided having too much contact with the company. How did they interpret Disney narratives? How did they assimilate Disney products in their lives?

Questionnaire about Disney Knowledge and Purchases

1. What comes to your mind when I say the words Walt Disney? Could you tell me about any productions and or products with the Walt Disney label? Which ones?
2. Encircle the three adjectives which you associate the most with the Walt Disney label.

Invading	Family-oriented	Simplistic
Childlish	Ordinary	Mundane
Entertaining	Fun	Commercial
Superficial	Universal	Agreeable
American	Boring	Marvellous

3. Have you purchased any kind of production and or product with this label over the last 3 years?
4. If yes, which one? For whom?
5. Have you got any children or grandchildren? If so, how old are they?

Age:
Profession:
Gender:
Thank you.

Appendix 4

Financial Analysis of the Walt Disney Company, 1974–2014

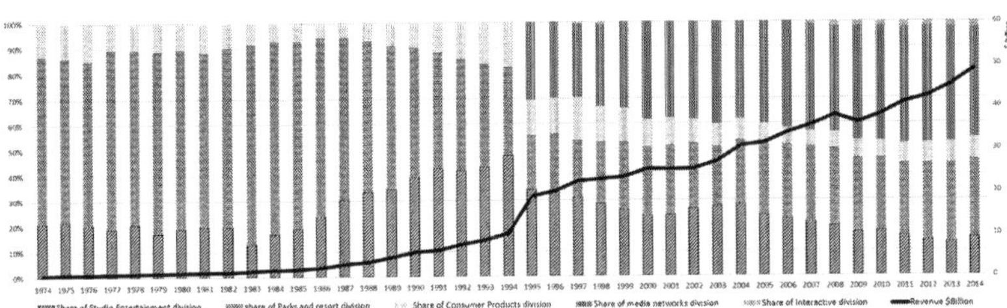

Graph 1 Split of the Disney Company revenues by business division
Source: The Walt Disney Company, *1974–2014 Annual Reports*, available at <www.thewaltdisneycompany.com> and <www.sec.gov>.

A. Bohas, *The Political Economy of Disney*, International Political Economy Series, DOI 10.1057/978-1-137-56238-8

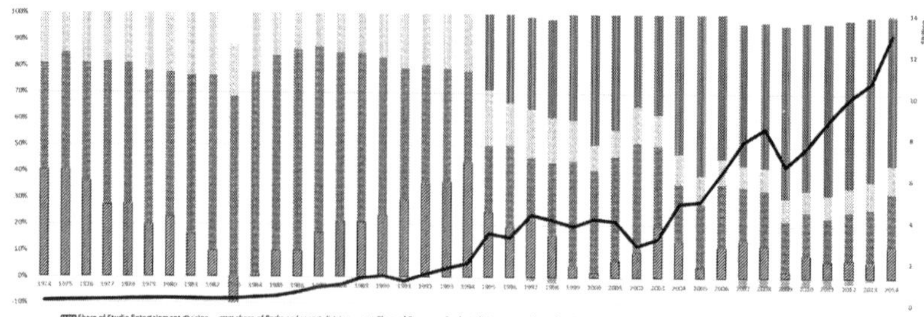

Graph 2 Split of the Disney Company operating incomes by business division
Source: The Walt Disney Company, *1974–2014 Annual Reports*, available at <www.thewaltdisneycompany.com> and <www.sec.gov>.

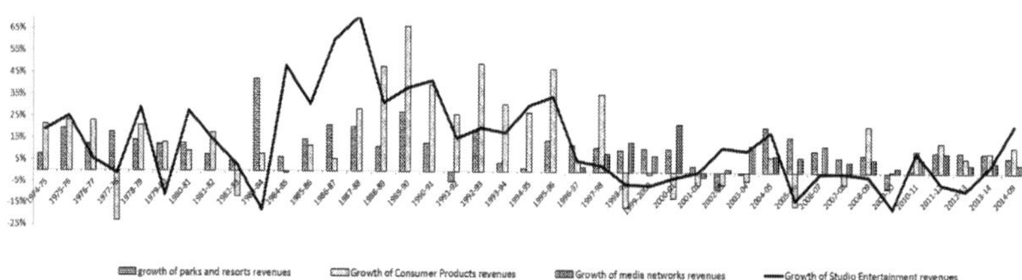

Graph 3 Annual growth rate of the Disney Company revenues by business division
Source: The Walt Disney Company, *1974–2014 Annual Reports*, available at <www.thewaltdisneycompany.com> and <www.sec.gov>.

Appendix 5

List of Interviewed Hollywood Executives

Lucie Besson

27 January 2007, 1hr. 27m.
Previously at the toy company Smoby, Lucie Besson was in charge of negotiating licensing contracts with key film studios such as the Walt Disney Company.

René Bonnell

8 June 2006, 53m.
René Bonnell held a number of senior positions in the French media industry. In particular, he was President of cinema in the pay TV Canal+ Group. He is also a renowned specialist of media studies who has published several books such as *La Vingt-cinquième image: une économie de l'audiovisuel* (Paris: Gallimard, 2001).

Robert Cort

10 August 2006, 1hr. 3m.
In the 1980s, as head of the film company Interscope, Robert Cort produced many films with Touchstone Pictures, notably the American remake *Three Men and a Baby* (1987). During his career, he successively

A. Bohas, *The Political Economy of Disney*, International Political Economy Series, DOI 10.1057/978 1-137-56238-8

occupied several positions with independent producers. He was Vice President of production at several major studios.

Gérard Couturier

29 May 2006, 1hr. 20m.
Executive Vice President at the Imagineering department of Disneyland Paris. Gérard Couturier supervised special projects and contributed to the building of Disneyland in Hong Kong. Since the interview, he has left the company.

Carine Fenot

20 November 2006, 1hr. 5m.
Carine Fenot worked twice at the Disneyland Paris resort between 1999 and 2005 as a cost controller and as a team leader. She was 'ambassador' at the Park in 2001.

Stanley Gold

16 August 2006, 40m.
As President of Roy E. Disney's private investment company, Shamrock Holdings, Stanley Gold was on the Board of Directors at the Walt Disney Company in the 1980s and 1990s. He played a key role in the change of Disney's leading executives in 1984 and in 2005.

Jeff Holder

8 August 2006, 1hr. 8m.
Jeff Holder is a senior executive in the animation business, specialising in media development and production. He worked for ABC TV as a Director of children's programmes from 1987 to 1991. He moved to Hanna Barbera as Vice President for development until 1995 and then to Sony Wonder as Vice President for creative affairs until 2001.

Steve Hulett

1 July 2006, 1hr. 6m.
Previously an animator at Disney in the 1970s, Steve Hulett became the Business Representative of the Animation Guild.

Igor Khait

6 September 2006, 49m.
Igor Khait was employed as an associate producer and became production manager for the Walt Disney Feature Animation studio. He was involved in several Disney films, notably *Atlantis: The Lost Empire* (2001), *Brother Bear* (2003) and *Leroy & Stitch* (2006).

David Kornblum

24 August 2006, 30m.
Arriving at Buena Vista in 1989, David Kornblum held many positions in the distribution department of the Walt Disney Studios before becoming Executive Director of International Theatrical Sales in 1998 and then Vice President of Theatrical Sales & Distribution in 1999.

Adam Leipzig

19 September 2006, 33m.
After holding several positions in live arts, Adam Leipzig was Vice President of production at Touchstone Pictures from 1987 to 1993. Since then, he has moved on as an independent producer and as Production Director at Interscope and National Geographic.

Jean-François Lepetit

1 June 2006, 56m.
President of the production company Flach Film, Jean-François Lepetit maintained close relations with the Disney studio, especially for the remake *Three Men and a Baby* (1987). He also led the French producer representative association, la Chambre syndicale des Producteurs de Films

Bill Mechanic

4 August 2006, 46m.
Bill Mechanic started working at Disney in 1984. He initiated the sell-through consumer home video business and then launched Buena Vista International. He became the leading executive at Fox from 1993 to 2000, where he considerably developed the production slate. He formed four entities: 20th Century Fox, Fox 2000, Fox Searchlight Pictures and

Fox Family Films. In 2001, he became producer and then created his own production society, Pandemonium Films.

Charlie Nelson

19 August 2006, 1hr. 7m.
After an internship at Disney, Charlie Nelson was recruited in 1989 for positions in marketing and advertising. He became Vice President of marketing for Buena Vista Pictures in 1997. He moved on in 2006 to assume other responsibilities in the film industry.

Claudine Reynes

6 June 2006, 48m.
In charge of merchandising at Disneyland Paris between 1990 and 1996, Claudine Reynes played a key role in the opening of the park. Beforehand, she had worked for the clothing industry at Printemps and Habitat (both in France) and Gap. After her stint at Disney, she joined Fila France and then the French Federation for Sport and Leisure.

Hal Richardson

11 August 2006, 1hr. 14m.
After a short period at Showtime and HBO (Home Box Office), Hal Richardson joined Disney as Vice President of pay TV distribution from 1987 to 1997. He left Buena Vista for DreamWorks where he occupied a similar position. Since the buyout of DreamWorks by Paramount, he has become President of international distribution for television.

Jason Squire

19 July 2006, 32m.
While holding diverse positions in the motion picture industry, Jason Squire has been a Professor at the School of Cinematic Arts, University of Southern California. He is the editor of a reference book on Hollywood, *The Movie Business Book* (New York: Simon & Schuster, 2004).

James Stewart

28 August 2006, 44m.
James Stewart is a journalist who won the Pulitzer Prize for his articles on the 1987 stock exchange crisis in *The Wall Street Journal*. He wrote a reference book on the Disney Company under Michael Eisner, *Disney War: The Battle for the Magic Kingdom* (New York: Simon & Schuster, 2005). As a Professor at the University of Columbia, he has written many books including *Flight: In Search of Vision* (Trenton: Africa World Press, 2004) and *Holy Warriors: The Abolitionists and American Slavery* (New York: Farrar, Straus and Giroux, 1976).

Michael Taylor

3 August 2006, 43m.
Independent producer Michael Taylor worked with Touchstone Pictures for the films *Phenomenon* in 1996 and *Instinct* in 1999.

Bibliography

Abdelal, R., M. Blyth, and C. Parsons, eds. 2010. *Constructing the International Economy*, Ithaca, NY: Cornell University Press.

Abélès, M. 2008. *Anthropologie de la globalisation*. Paris: Payot.

Anderson, B. 1983. *Imagined Communities. Reflections on the Origin and Spread of Nationalism*. London: Verso.

Ang, I. 1985. *Watching Dallas: Soap Opera and the Melodramatic Imagination*. London: Methuen.

Appadurai, A. 1996. *Modernity at Large. Cultural Dimensions of Globalization*. Minneapolis: University of Minnesota.

Arquembourg, J., G. Lochard, and A. Mercier, eds. 2007. *Événements mondiaux, regard nationaux. Hermès* 46(Spring).

Ashforth, B., and R. Humphrey. 1993. Emotional Labor in Service Roles: The Influence of Identity. *The Academy of Management Review* 18(1): 88–115.

Ayers, B., ed. 2003. *The Emperor's Old Groove: Decolonizing Disney's Magic Kingdom*. New York: Peter Lang.

Barrier, J.M. 2007. *The Animated Man: A Life of Walt Disney*. Berkeley: University of California Press.

Baudelaire, C. 1980. *Œuvres Complètes*. Paris: Éditions Robert Laffont.

Baumol, W., and W. Bowen. 1966. *Performing Arts: The Economic Dilemma; A Study of Problems Common to Theater, Opera, Music and Dance*. New York: 20th Century Fund.

Baumol, W., J. Panzar, and R.D. Willig. 1982. *Contestable Markets and the Theory of Industry Structure*. New York: Harcourt Brace Jovanovich.

Beaulieu, N.D., and A.M.G. Zimmerman. 2005. Saving Disney. *Harvard Business School Cases*, Brighton, MA: Harvard Business Publishing.

A. Bohas, *The Political Economy of Disney*, International Political Economy Series, DOI 10.1057/978-1-137-56238-8

Bell, E., L. Hass, and L. Sells, eds. 1995. *From Mouse to Mermaid: The Politics of Films, Gender and Culture*. Bloomington: Indiana University Press.

Benghozi, P.-J., and C. Delage, eds. 1997. *Une Histoire économique du cinéma francais (1895–1995). Regards croisés franco-americains*. Paris: L'Harmattan.

Benjamin, W. 2000/1935. L'Œuvre d'art à l'ère de sa reproductibilité technique. In *Œuvres, t. III*, ed. W. Benjamin, 68–143. Paris: Gallimard.

Berger, P.L., and T. Luckmann. 1971. *The Social Construction of Reality. A Treatise in the Sociology of Knowledge*. London: Penguin Books.

Blyth, M., ed. 2009. *Routledge Handbook of International Political Economy (IPE). IPE as a Global Conversation*. Abingdon: Routledge.

Bohas, A. 2006. The Paradox of Anti-Americanism: Reflection on the Shallow Concept of Soft Power. *Global Society* 20(4): 395–414.

———. 2007. La Firme Disney: Analyse du capitalisme culturel d'Hollywood, Ph.D, University of Paris 1 Panthéon-Sorbonne.

———. 2015. Neopluralism and Globalization: The Plural Politics of the Motion Picture Association. *Review of International Political Economy* 22(6): 1188–1216.

———. 2015. Transnational Firms and the Knowledge Structure: The Case of the Walt Disney Company. *Global Society* 29(1): 23–41.

Bonnell, R. 2001. *La Vingt-cinquième image. Une économie de l'audiovisuel*. Paris: Gallimard.

Bordwell, D. 2006. *The Way Hollywood Tells It: Story and Style in Modern Movies*. Berkeley, CA: University of California Press.

Bordwell, D., J. Staiger, and K. Thompson. 1988. *The Classical Hollywood Cinema. Film, Style and Mode of Production to 1960*. 2nd ed. London: Routledge.

Boujut, M., ed. 1992. *Europe-Hollywood et retour. Cinémas sous influences*. Paris: Autrement.

Bourdieu, P. 1972. *Esquisse d'une théorie de la pratique*. Paris: Droz.

———. 1979. *La Distinction. Critique sociale du jugement*. Paris: Éditions de Minuit.

———. 1992. *Les Règles de l'art. Genèse et structure du champ littéraire*. Paris: Seuil.

———. 2000. *Pascalian Meditations*. Stanford, CA: Stanford University Press.

Bourget, J.-L. 1998. *Hollywood. La norme et la marge*. Paris: Armand Colin.

Braudel, F. 1985. *La Dynamique du capitalisme*. Paris: Champs/Flammarion.

———. 1987. *Grammaire des civilisations*. Paris: Arthaud-Flammarion.

———. 1993. *Civilisation matérielle, économie et capitalisme XV–XVIIIème siècle*. Paris: Armand Colin.

Brode, D. 2004. *From Walt to Woodstock: How Disney Created the Counterculture*. Austin: University of Texas Press.

Brougère, G., ed. 2008. *La Ronde des jeux et des jouets*. Paris: Autrement.

Brougère, G., D. Buckingham, and J. Goldstein, eds. 2005. *Toys, Games and Media*. Mahwah, NJ: Lawrence Erlbaum Associates.

Bryman, A. 1995. *Disney and His Worlds*. London: Routledge.

———. 2004. *The Disneyization of Society*. London: Sage.

Buckingham, D. 2005. *The Media Literacy of Children and Young People. A Review of the Research Literature on Behalf of Ofcom*. http://www.eprints.ioe.ac.uk.

Budd M. and M. Kirsch, eds. 2005. *Rethinking Disney: Private Control, Public Dimensions*. Middletown: Wesleyan University Press.

Byrne, E. 1999. *Deconstructing Disney*. London: Pluto Press.

Calabrese, A., and C. Sparks, eds. *Toward a Political Economy of Culture: Capitalism and Communication in the Twenty-First Century*. Lanham, MD: Rowman & Littlefield.

Campbell, D.T. 1969. Variation and Selective Retention in Socio-Cultural Evolution. *General Systems* 14: 69–86.

Campbell, J. 2004. *The Hero with a Thousand Faces*. Princeton, NJ: Princeton University Press.

Casetti, F. 2003. *Les Théories du cinéma depuis 1945*. Paris: Nathan.

Caughey, J.L. 1984. *Imaginary Social Worlds. A Cultural Approach*. Lincoln: University of Nebraska Press.

Cerny, P.G. 2010. *Rethinking World Politics. A Theory of Transnational Pluralism*. New York: Oxford University Press.

Checkel, J.T. 1997. International Norms and Domestic Politics: Bridging the Rationalist–Constructivist Divide. *European Journal of International Relations* 3(4): 473–495.

Cheu, J. 2013. *Diversity in Disney Films: Critical Essays on Race, Ethnicity, Gender, Sexuality and Disability*. Jefferson, NC: McFarland.

CNC. 2015. *Bilan 2014, Les dossiers du CNC*. 332(May). http://www.cnc.fr.

Cooper, C., S. Sedgwick, and S. Mitra. 2014. *California's Film and Television Tax Credit Program: Assessing Its Impact*. Los Angeles County Economic Development Corporation, March. http://www.scag.ca.gov.

Cortell, A.P., and J.W. Davis Jr. 2000. Understanding the Domestic Impact of International Norms: A Research Agenda. *International Studies Review* 2(1): 65–87.

Couldry, N., A. Hepp, and F. Krotz, eds. 2010. *Media Events in a Global Age*. Abingdon: Routledge.

Cox, R., and T. Sinclair, eds. 1996. *Approaches to World Order*. Cambridge: Cambridge University Press.

Créton, L. 1998. *Cinéma et (in)dépendance: Une économie politique*. Paris: Presses de la Sorbonne Nouvelle.

Dale, M. 1997. *The Movie Game. The Film Business in Britain, Europe and America*. London: Cassell.

Darré, Y. 2003. Le cinéma, l'art contre le travail. *Mouvements* 27/28(May–August): 120–125.

Davis, S.G. 1996. The Theme Park: Global Industry and Cultural Form. *Media, Culture and Society* 18(3): 406.

Davis, A.M. 2007. *Good Girls and Wicked Witches: Women in Disney's Feature Animation*. New Barnet: John Libbey.

Dayan, D. 1992. *À la recherche du public. Réception, télévision, médias. Hermès* (11–12).

Dayan, D., and E. Katz. 1992. *Media Events. The Live Broadcasting of History*. Cambridge, MA: Harvard University Press.

de Certeau, M. 1990. *L'Invention du quotidien 1. Arts de faire*. Paris: Gallimard.

de Maussion, C. 1992. L'autre Disney: le studio de production de Hollywood. *Communication & Langages* 92: 49–61.

De Vany, A. 2003. *Hollywood Economics. How Extreme Uncertainty Shapes the Film Industry?* London: Routledge.

DeJean, J. 2006. *The Essence of Style. How the French Invented High Fashion, Fine Food, Smart Coffees, Style, Sophistication, and Glamour*. New York: Free Press.

Délégation interministérielle au projet Euro Disney, Disneyland Paris. 2012. Étude de contribution économique et sociale, Press file, March 12. http://www.corporate.disneylandparis.fr.

Deprez, C. 2010. *Bollywood: Cinéma et mondialisation*. Villeneuve d'Asq: Presses Universitaires du Septentrion.

Dicken, P. 2003. *Global Shift: Transforming the World Economy*. London: Sage.

Doherty, T. 2006. The Wonderful World of Disney Studies. *Chronicle of Higher Education*. 19(July): B10–B11.

Dolfsma, W., ed. 2007. *Consuming symbolic goods: Identity and commitment, values and economics*. London: Routledge.

Dorfman, A., and A. Mattelart. 1976. *Donald l'imposteur ou l'impérialisme raconté aux enfants*. Paris: A. Moreau.

Doucet, M. 2005. Child's Play: The Political Imaginary of International Relations and Contemporary Popular Children's Films. *Global Society* 19(3): 289–306.

Drache, D., and M.D. Froese. 2006. Globalisation, World Trade and the Cultural Commons: Identity, Citizenship and Pluralism. *New Political Economy* 11(3): 361–382.

Du Gay, P. 1996. *Consumption and Identity at Work*. London: Sage.

Du Gay, P. and M. Pryke, eds. 2002. *Cultural Economy: Cultural Analysis and Commercial Life*. London: Sage.

Dumazedier, J. 1962. *Vers la civilisation des loisirs*. Paris: Seuil.

Dunning, J.H., and G. Boyd. 2003. *Alliance Capitalism and Corporate Management: Entrepreneurial Cooperation in Knowledge Based Economies*. Cheltenham: E. Elgar.

Durkheim, E. 1985/1912. *Les Formes élémentaires de la religion*. Paris: PUF.

———. 1998/1893. *De la division du travail social*. Paris: PUF.

EAO. 2014. *Yearbook. Television, Cinema, Video and On-Demand Audiovisual Services in Europe*. Strasbourg: Council of Europe.

Edery, D. 2006. Reverse Product Placement in Virtual Worlds. *Harvard Business Review* 84(12): 24.

Eliade, M. 1965. *Le Sacré et le profane*. Paris: Gallimard.

Elias, N. 1993. *La Société de cour*. Paris: Flammarion.

Eliot, M. 2001. *Down 42nd Street. Sex, Money, Culture and Politics at the Crossroads of the World*. New York: Warner Books.

Elmer, G., and M. Gasher, eds. 2005. *Contracting Out Hollywood: Runaway Productions and Foreign Location Shootings*. Lanham, MD: Rowman & Littlefield.

Euro Disney S.C.A. (2015) Résultats de l'exercice 2014. http://corporate.disneylandparis.fr.

Featherstone, M. 2007. *Consumer Culture & Postmodernism*. London: Sage.

Featherstone, M., S. Lash, and R. Robertson, eds. 2005. *Global Modernities*. London: Sage.

Feitz, A. 1992. Euro Disney: Dissection d'un lancement. *Médias* 327(April): 24–33.

FilmL.A. Research. 2015. 2014 Feature Film Study. http://www.filmla.com.

Forest, C. 2001. *Économie contemporaine du cinéma en Europe. L'improbable industrie*. Paris: CNRS Éditions.

Freeman, G., J. Kyser, N. Sidhu, G. Huang, and M. Montoya. 2005. *What is the Cost of Run-Away Production? Jobs, Wages, Economic Output and State Tax Revenue at Risk When Motion Picture Productions Leave California*. Los Angeles, CA: Los Angeles County Economic Development Corporation.

Gabler, N. 1989. *An Empire of Their Own. How the Jews Invented Hollywood*. New York: 1st Anchor Book Edition.

Gereffi, G., and M. Korzeniewicz, eds. 1994 *Commodity Chains and Global Capitalism*. Westport, CT: Praeger.

Germain, R., ed. 2000. *Globalization and Its Critics, Perspectives from Political Economy*. Basingstoke: Macmillan.

Giddens, A. 1984. *The Constitution of Society: Outline of the Theory of Structuration*. Cambridge: Polity Press.

———. 1991. *Consequences of Modernity*. Paris: Polity Press.

Gill, S., ed. 1993. *Gramsci, Historical Materialism and International Relations*. Cambridge: Cambridge University Press.

Gill, S., and A.C. Cutler. 2014. *New Constitutionalism and World Order*. Cambridge: Cambridge University Press.

Gilpin, R. 1981. *War and Change in World Politics*. Cambridge: Cambridge University Press.

Giroux, H. 1999. *The Mouse that Roared: Disney and the End of Innocence*. Lanham, MD: Rowman & Littlefield.

Girveau, B., ed. 2006. *Il était une fois Walt Disney aux sources de l'art des studios Disney.* Paris: Éditions de la Réunion des Musées Nationaux.

Glickman, L., and M. Rothschild. 2012. Tax Credits and Other Film and TV Incentives: The World Outside Canada and the United States. The American Bar Association Forum on the Entertainment and Sports Industries, Annual Meeting, Las Vegas, NV, October 6.

Goehler, G. 2000. Constitution and Use of Power. In *Power in Contemporary Politics. Theories, Practices, Globalizations*, eds. H. Goverde, P.G. Cerny, M. Haugaard, and H. Lentner, 41–59. London: Sage.

Gomery, D. 2005a. *The Coming of Sound: A History.* New York: Routledge.

———. 2005b. *The Hollywood Studio System: A History.* London: British Film Institute.

Goold, M., and Campbell A. 1998. Desperately Seeking Synergy. *Harvard Business Review* (September–October), 130–43.

Goss, J. 1993. The 'Magic of the Mall': An Analysis of Form, Function, and Meaning in the Contemporary Retail Built Environment. *Annals of the Association of American Geographers* 83(1): 18–47.

Gramsci, A. 1996. *Cahiers de prison 1.* Paris: Gallimard.

Granovetter, M. 1985. Economic Action and Social Structure: The Problem of Embeddedness. *The American Journal of Sociology* 91(3): 481–510.

Grover, R. 1991. *The Disney Touch: Disney, ABC & The Quest for the World's Greatest Media Empire.* Chicago, IL: Irwin Professional Pub.

Hall, S., D. Hobson, A. Lowe, and P. Willis, eds. 1980. *Culture, Media, Language: Working Papers in Cultural Studies, 1972–79.* London: Hutchinson.

Hanssen, A. 2000. The Block Booking of Films Reexamined. *Journal of Law and Economics* 43(2): 395–426.

Harrington S. 2014. *The Disney Fetish.* New Barnet, UK: John Libbey.

Hartley, J., ed. 2005. *Creative Industries.* Oxford: Blackwell.

Hartley, J., W. Wen, and H. Siling. 2015. *Creative Economy and Culture. Challenges, Changes and Futures for the Creative Industries.* London: Sage.

Harvey, D. 1989. *The Condition of Postmodernity.* Oxford: Blackwell.

Hastings, W. 1996. Bambi and the Hunting Ethos—Walt Disney Co. Character. *Journal of Popular Film & Television* 24(2): 53–59.

Held, D., and H.L. Moore, eds. 2008. *Cultural Politics in a Global Age: Uncertainty, Solidarity and Innovation.* Oxford: Oneworld Publications.

Held, D., A.G. McGrew, D. Goldblatt, and J. Perraton. 1999. *Global transformations: Politics, Economics and Culture.* Cambridge: Polity Press.

Hirschman, A.O. 2002. *Shifting Involvements: Private Interest and Public Action.* Princeton, NJ: Princeton University Press.

Hobson, J., and L. Seabrook, eds. 2007. *Everyday Politics of the World Economy.* Cambridge: Cambridge University Press.

Hoggart, R. 2009/1957. *The Uses of Literacy: Aspects of Working-Class Life.* London: Penguin.

Hollywood Creative Directory. 2006. *Hollywood Creative Directory.* 57th ed. Los Angeles, CA: Hollywood Creative Directory.

Holt, J. 2001. In Deregulation We Trust. The Synergy of Politics and Industry in Reagan-era Hollywood. *Quarterly Film* 55(2): 22–39.

Horkheimer, M., and T.W. Adorno. 2002. *Dialectic of Enlightenment. Philosophical Fragments.* Stanford, CA: Stanford University Press.

Inglehart, R. 1997. *Modernization and Postmodernization. Cultural, Economic and Political Change in 43 Societies.* Princeton, NJ: Princeton University Press.

Jameson, F. 1991. *Postmodernism: Or, the Cultural Logic of Late Capitalism.* London: Verso.

Jessop, B. 2013. Dynamics of Regionalism and Globalism: A Critical Political Economy Perspective. *Ritsumeikan Social Science Review* 5: 3–24.

Kalifa, D. 2001. *La Culture de masse en France 1860–1930*, t. 1. Paris: La Découverte.

Katz, E., and R. Meyersohn. 1957. Notes on a Natural History of Fads. *The American Journal of Sociology* 62(6): 594–601.

Keck, M., and K. Sikkink. 1998. *Activists Beyond Borders: Advocacy Networks in International Politics.* Ithaca, NY: Cornell University Press.

Kharas, H. 2010. The Emerging Middle Class in Developing Countries, OECD Development Working Papers, January. http://www.oecd.org.

Laroche, J., and A. Bohas. 2008. *Canal+ et les majors américaines. Une vision désenchantée du cinéma-monde.* Paris: L'Harmattan.

Lee, N., and K. Madej. 2012. *Disney Stories: Getting to Digital.* New York: Springer.

Lefebvre H. 1958. *Critique de la vie quotidienne.* Paris: Arche.

Lehu, J.-M. 2007. *Branded Entertainment: Product Placement and Brand Strategy in the Entertainment Business.* London: Kogan Page.

Lieberman, M.B., and D.B. Montgomery. 1998. First-Mover (Dis)Advantages: Retrospective and Link with the Resource-Based View. *Strategic Management Journal* 19(12): 1111–1125.

Liebes, T., and E. Katz. 1990. *The Export of Meaning: Cross-Cultural Readings of Dallas.* New York: Oxford University Press.

Lipovetsky, G., and J. Serroy. 2013. *L'Esthétisation du Monde. Vivre à l'âge du capitalisme artiste.* Paris: Gallimard.

Loeffler, B., and B.T. Church. 2015. *The Experience: The 5 Principles of Disney Service and Relationship Excellence.* Hoboken, NJ: Wiley.

Los Angeles County Economic Development Corporation. 2015. Otis Report on the Creative Economy of California, April. http://www.otis.edu.

Löwy, M. 2004. Le concept d'affinité élective chez Max Weber. *Archives des sciences sociales des religions* 127(July–September): 93–103.

Löwy, M., and H. Wismann. 2004. Max Weber, la religion et la construction du social. *Archives de sciences sociales des religions* 127(July–September): 5–7.

Lukes, S. 2005/1974. *Power: A Radical View.* London: Palgrave.

March, J.G., and J.P. Olsen. 1989. *Rediscovering Institutions.* New York: Free Press.

———. 2005. Elaborating the "New Institutionalism". Working Paper No. 15, 4, Arena Center for European Studies, University of Oslo.

McChesney, R.W. 2015. *Rich Media, Poor Democracy. Communication Politics in Dubious Times.* New York: New Press.

McLuhan, M. 1964. *Understanding Media. The Extensions of Man.* London: Routledge & Kegan Paul.

Meehan, E., M. Philips, and J. Wasko, eds. 2006. *Dazzled by Disney? The Global Disney Audiences Project.* Leicester: Leicester University Press..

Meyer, C., and A. Schwager. 2007. Understanding Customer Experience. *Harvard Business Review* (February), 116–28.

Michalet, C.-A. 1987. *Le Drôle de drame du cinéma mondial: Une industrie culturelle menacée.* Paris: Découverte/FEN.

Miles, L., A. Borchert, and A.E. Ramanathan. 2014. *Why Some Merging Companies Become Synergy Overachievers.* Bain & Company, available at: www.bain.com.

Miller, T., N. Govil, J. McMurrin, R. Maxwell, and T. Wang. 2005. *Global Hollywood 2.* London: British Film Institute.

Molina Y. Vedia, S. 1998. Disney en México: observaciones sobre la integración de objetos de la cultura global en la vida cotidiana. *Revista Mexicana de Ciencias Politicas y Sociales* 171(January–March): 97–126.

Montebello, F. 2003. Les deux peuples du cinéma: usages populaires du cinéma et images du public populaire. *Mouvements* 27/28(May–August): 113–119.

Moul, C., ed. 2005. *A Concise Handbook of Movie Industry Economics.* Cambridge: Cambridge University Press.

MPA. 2008. Anti-Piracy Fact Sheet. Asia-Pacific Region. http://mpaa.org.

———. 2014. The Economic Contribution of the Motion Picture & Television Industry to the United States. http://mpaa.org.

———. 2015. 2014 Theatrical Market Statistics. http://www.mpaa.org.

Musso, P., and P. Durand, eds. 2005. Special Issue: Gramsci, les médias et la culture. *Quaderni* 57(Spring): 51–115.

Muzellec, L., T. Lynn, and M. Lambkin. 2012. Branding in Fictional and Virtual Environments: Introducing a New Conceptual Domain and Research Agenda. *European Journal of Marketing* 46(6): 811–826.

Nye, J. 2004. *Soft Power. The Means to Success in World Politics.* New York: Public Affairs.

O'Guinn, T., and R. Belk. 1989. Heaven on Earth: Consumption at Heritage Village, USA. *The Journal of Consumer Research* 16(2): 227–238.

O'Shaughnessy, J., and N.J. O'Shaughnessy. 2003. *The Marketing Power of Emotion*. New York: Oxford University Press.

Onuf, N. 1989. *World of Our Making: Rules and Rule in Social Theory and International Relations*. Columbia: University of South Carolina Press.

Ostman, R. 1996. Disney and Its Conservative Critics: Images Versus Realities. *Journal of Popular Film & Television* 2(24): 82–89.

Panofsky, E. 1966/1934. Style and Medium in the Motion Pictures. In *Film: An Anthology*, ed. D. Talbot, 15–32. Berkeley, CA: University of California Press.

Papazian, G., and J.M. Sommers. 2013. *Game on, Hollywood! Essays on the Intersection of Video Games and Cinema*. Jefferson, NC: McFarland.

Paris, T. ed. 2002. *Special Issue: Quelle diversité face à Hollywood ?, Cinémaction*, (March).

Pascal, B. 1958/1670. *Pascal's Pensées*. New York: E. P. Dutton.

Pasquier, D. 2005. *Cultures lycéennes. La tyrannie de la majorité*. Paris: Éditions Autrement.

Percy, L. 2014. *Strategic Integrated Marketing Communications*. Abingdon: Routledge.

Pine, J., and J. Gilmore. 1999. *The Experience Economy: Work Is Theater & Every Business a Stage*. Boston, MA: Harvard Business School Press.

Porter, M. 1998. *The Competitive Advantage of Nations*. Basingstoke: Macmillan.

PricewaterhouseCoopers. 2015. Global Entertainment and Media Outlook 2015–2019. http://www.pwc.com.

Punathambekar, A. 2013. *From Bombay to Bollywood: The Making of a Global Media Industry*. New York: New York University Press.

Quigley, E.S., ed. 2006. *International Motion Picture Almanac*. New York: Quigley Pub Co.

Rawson, A., E. Duncan, and C. Jones. 2013. The Truth About Customer Experience. *Harvard Business Review* (September), 90–114.

Rayport, J., C.-I. Knoop, and C. Reavis. 1998. Disney's 'The Lion King (A): The $2 Billion Movie. *Harvard Business School Cases*, Brighton, MA: Harvard Business Publishing.

Raz, A. 2000. Domesticating Disney. *Journal of Popular Culture* 33(4): 77–99.

Reading, A., and R. Jenkins. 2015. Transportation to a World of Fantasy: Consumer Experiences of Fictional Brands Becoming Real. *Journal of Promotional Communications* 3(1): 154–173.

Risse-Kappen, T. 1994. Ideas Do Not Float Freely: Transnational Coalitions, Domestic Structures and the End of the Cold War. *International Organization* 48(2): 185–214.

———. ed. 1995. *Bringing Transnational Relations Back in: Non-State Actors, Domestic Structures and International Institutions*. Cambridge: Cambridge University Press.

Ritzer, G. 1993. *The McDonaldization of Society: An Investigation into the Changing Character of Contemporary Social Life*. Newbury: Pine Forge Press.

Robinette, S., C. Brand, and V. Lenz. 2001. *Emotion Marketing: The Hallmark Way of Winning Customers for Life*. New York: McGraw-Hill.

Robinson, W. 2004. *A Theory of Global Capitalism: Production, Class and State in a Transnational World*. Baltimore, MD: Johns Hopkins University Press.

Rose, F. 2011. *The Art of Immersion: How the Digital Generation is Remaking Hollywood, Madison Avenue and the Way We Tell Stories*. New York: Norton.

Rosenau, J.N. 1990. *Turbulence in World Politics: A Theory of Change and Continuity*. Princeton, NJ: Princeton University Press.

Ross, A. 2006. Coming in from the Cold: Constructivism and Emotions. *European Journal of International Relations* 12(2): 197–222.

Sassen, S. 2003. Globalization or Denationalization. *Review of International Political Economy* 10(1): 1–22.

Schatz, T., ed. 2004. *Hollywood. Critical Concepts in Media and Cultural Studies*. 4 vols. London: Routledge.

Schmitt, B. 2010. Experience Marketing: Concepts, Frameworks and Consumer Insights. *Foundations and Trends in Marketing* 5(2): 55–112.

Scholte, J.A. 2005. *Globalization: A Critical Introduction*. Basinstoke: Palgrave Macmillan.

Schumpeter, J. 1939. *Business Cycles. With Theoretical, Historical and Statistical Analysis of the Capitalist Process*. New York: McGraw-Hill Books.

———. 2003/1943. *Capitalism, Socialism and Democracy*. London: Routledge.

Scott, A. 2004. Hollywood and the World: The Geography of Motion-Picture Distribution and Marketing. *Review of International Political Economy* 11(1): 38.

———. 2005. *On Hollywood: The Place, the Industry*. Princeton, NJ: Princeton University Press.

Singh, J.P., ed. 2010. *International Cultural Policies and Power*. Basingstoke and New York: Palgrave Macmillan.

Siwek, S. 2014. Copyright Industries in the U.S. Economy: The 2013 Report. http://www.iipa.com.

Skelton, T., and T. Allen, eds. 1999. *Culture and Global Change*. London: Routledge.

Sklair, L. 2001. *The Transnational Capitalist Class*. Oxford: Blackwell.

———. 2002. *Globalization: Capitalism and Its Alternatives*. Oxford: Blackwell.

Smart, B. 1999. *Resisting McDonaldization*. London: Sage.

Smith, A. 1990. Towards a Global Culture? *Theory, Culture and Society* 7(2): 171–191.

Smith, A. 1998a. 'Espace public européen': une vision (trop) aérienne. *Critique internationale* 2(Winter): 169–180.

Smith, D. 1998b. *Disney A to Z. The Updated Official Encyclopedia*. 2nd ed. New York: Hyperion.

Smoodin, E., ed. 1994. *Disney Discourse: Producing the Magic Kingdom.* New York: Routledge.

Sperb, J. 2012. *Disney's Most Notorious Film: Race, Convergence, and the Hidden Histories of Song of the South.* Austin: University of Texas Press.

Squire, J.E., ed. 2004. *The Movie Business Book.* New York: Fireside.

Staiger, J. 2005. *Media Research Studies.* New York: New York University Press.

Stewart, J. 2005. *Disney War.* New York: Simon & Schuster.

Stokes, M., and R. Maltby. 2005. *Hollywood Abroad: Audiences and Cultural Exchange.* London: BFI Publishing.

Strange, S. 1994. *States and Markets.* London: Pinter.

Strange, S., and J. Stopford. 1991. *Rival States, Rival Firms: Competition for World Market Shares.* Cambridge: Cambridge University Press.

Sum, N. L. and B. Jessop 2013. *Towards a Cultural Political Economy. Putting Culture in Its Place in Political Economy.* Cheltenham: E. Elgar.

Susanin, T.S. 2011. *Walt Before Mickey: Disney's Early Years, 1919–1928.* Jackson: University Press of Mississippi.

Sussman, G., and J.A. Lent, eds. 1998. *Global Productions: Labor in the Making of the Information Society.* Cresskill, NJ: Hampton Press.

Sztompka, P. 1999. *Trust: A Sociological Theory.* Cambridge: Cambridge University Press.

Taylor, M. 2014. *Film and Television Production: Overview of Motion Picture Industry and State Tax Credits.* Legislative Analyst's Office, April 30. http://www.lao.ca.gov.

Telotte, J.P. 2004. *Disney TV.* Detroit, MI: Wayne State University Press.

———. 2008. *The Mouse Machine. Disney and Technology.* Urbana: University of Illinois Press.

The Walt Disney Company. 2006. *2005 Fourth Quarter Report.* Burbank, CA: Walt Disney Company.

———. 2014. *2013 Factbook.* http://www.thewaltdisneycompany.com.

———. 1975–2015. 1974–2014 *Annual Report.* Burbank, CA: Walt Disney Company.

The Walt Disney Company Press Release. 2006. The Walt Disney Studios Moves to Increase Its Disney Branded Output Strategy, July 18. http://www.thewaltdisneycompany.com.

Theme Entertainment Association/AECOM. 2015. 2014 Theme Index & Museum Index: The Global Attractions Attendance Report. http://www.aecom.com.

Thiroux, S. 2003. Étude des processus identificatoires chez les enfants et les adolescents âgés de trois à seize ans et demi dans le cadre du visionnage de longs métrages d'animation de Walt Disney. Ph.D. supervised by Pascale Planche.

Towbin, M.A., S.A. Haddock, T.S. Zimmerman, L.K. Lund, and L.R. Tanner. 2004. Images of Gender, Race, Age, and Sexual Orientation in Disney Feature-Length Animated Films. *Journal of Feminist Family Therapy* 15(4): 19–44.

Tracy, J. 1999. Whistle While You Work: The Disney Company and the Global Division of Labor. *Journal of Communication Inquiry* 23(4): 374–389.

Tripathi S., and A. Rimmer. 2012. Profitable Growth Strategies for the Global Emerging Middle. Learning from the 'Next 4 Billion' Markets, PricewaterhouseCoopers. http://www.pwc.com.

Ulff-Moller, J. 2001. *Hollywood's Film Wars with France: Film-Trade Diplomacy and the Emergence of the French Film Quota Policy*. Rochester, NY: University of Rochester Press.

Utsler, M. 1989. Owning a Private Piece of the Public Disney Rock: Consumer Response and the Main Street Electrical Parade Light Bulb. *Journal of American Culture* 22(2): 19–23.

Van Der Pilj, K. 1998. *Transnational Classes and International Relations*. London: Routledge.

Veblen, T. 1979. *Théorie de la classe de loisir*. Paris: Gallimard.

Vogel, H. 2014. *Entertainment Industry Economics. A Guide for Financial Analysis*. New York: Cambridge University Press.

Wallerstein, I. 1974. *The Modern World-System: Capitalist, Agriculture and the Origins of the European World-Economy in the Sixteenth Century*. New York: Academic Press.

———. 1999. *The End of the World as We Know It: Social Science for the Twenty-First Century*. Minneapolis: University of Minnesota Press.

Walters, J., and Y. Kuo. 2015. *A Tale of Two Chinese Consumers*. Boston Consulting Group, available at www.bcg.com.cn.

Wang, S. 2003. *Framing Piracy: Globalization and Film Distribution in Greater China*. London: Rowman & Littlefield.

Warde, A. 2015. The Sociology of Consumption: Its Recent Development. *Annual Review of Sociology* 41(April): 117–134.

Wasko, J. 2001. *Understanding Disney: The Manufacture of Fantasy*. Cambridge: Blackwell.

———. 2003. *How Hollywood Works*. London: Sage.

Wasko, J., and I. Hagen, eds. 1999. *Consuming Audiences? Production and Reception in Media Research*. Hampton, VA: Cresskill.

Wasko, J., M. Phillips, and C. Purdie. 1993. Hollywood Meets Madison Avenue: The Commercialization of US Films. *Media, Culture and Society* 15(2): 271–293.

Wasser, F. 1995. Is Hollywood America? The Trans-nationalization of the American Film Industry. *Critical Studies in Mass Communication* 12(4): 423–437.

Watts, S. 1997. *The Magic Kingdom: Walt Disney and the American Way of Life*. Boston, MA: Houghton Mifflin.

Weber M. 1967/1905. *L'Éthique protestante et l'esprit du capitalisme*. Paris: Plon.

Weber, M. 1995. *Économie et société*. Paris: Plon/Pocket.

Weinbaum, B. 1997. Disney-Mediated Images Emerging in Cross-Cultural Expression on Isla Mujeres, Mexico. *Journal of American & Comparative Cultures* 20(2): 19–29.

Wendt, A. 1987. The Agent–Structure Problem in International Relations Theory. *International Organization* 41(3): 335–370.

———. 1999. *Social Theory of International Politics*. Cambridge: Cambridge University Press.

Williams, R. 1961. *The Long Revolution*. London: Chatto and Windus.

Wolf, M. 1999. *The Entertainment Economy: How Mega-Media Forces Are Transforming Our Lives*. New York: Times Books/Random House.

Wyatt, J. 1994. *High Concept. Movies and Marketing in Hollywood*. Austin: University of Texas Press.

Yale C. K. 2010. *Runaway Film Production: A Critical History of Hollywood's Outsourcing Discourse*, Ph.D, University of Illinois.

Zukin, S., and P. DiMaggio. 1990. *Structures of Capital. The Social Organization of the Economy*. 2nd ed. Cambridge: Cambridge University Press.

Index

A. Bohas, *The Political Economy of Disney*, International Political Economy Series, DOI 10.1057/978-1-137-56238-8